New Corporate Cultures
That Motivate

ADOLF HAASEN AND GORDON F. SHEA

Westport, Connecticut
London

Library of Congress Cataloging-in-Publication Data

Haasen, Adolf.
 New corporate cultures that motivate/Adolf Haasen and Gordon F. Shea.
  p. cm.
 Includes bibliographical references and index.
 ISBN 1-56720-642-5 (alk. paper)
  1. Corporate culture—Case studies. 2. Employee motivation—Case studies. I. Shea,
 Gordon F., 1925– II. Title.
 HD58.7.H3 2003
  658.3'14—dc21   2003045765

British Library Cataloguing in Publication Data is available.

Library of Congress Catalog Card Number: 2003045765
ISBN: 1-56720-642-5

First published in 2003

Praeger Publishers, 88 Post Road West, Westport, CT 06881
An imprint of Greenwood Publishing Group, Inc.
www.praeger.com

Printed in the United States of America

The paper used in this book complies with the
Permanent Paper Standard issued by the National
Information Standards Organization (Z39.48–1984).

10 9 8 7 6 5 4 3 2 1

Copyright Acknowledgments

The author and publisher gratefully acknowledge permission to use the following material:

Excerpts from "How to Avoid Enronism" by James Lucas. In *MWorld*, 1 (spring 2002). New
York: AMA Publications.

Contents

Illustrations

Preface

In the course of this extraordinary year two reflections have kept coming at me. The first is that the positive assumptions we make about people—that they are responsible, caring, creative, and want to make a difference—are turning out to be just as accurate about the majority of people in Pakistan, Brazil, or any other of the 22 countries we are in as they are about the majority of people in the United States. . . . To me the universal applicability of our assumptions is the most exciting discovery yet to come out of our ever-expanding global experience.

The second reflection is a bit more paradoxical. As we have freed up people to make more decisions, they have sought more advice and become more consultative. Said another way, the more AES people feel responsible for company decisions, the less likely they are to go off and do something completely on their own. So eliminating layers of approval has turned out to create more input and advice than if we had followed the typical hierarchical process.

Roger W. Sant, chairman of the board, AES Corporation
(from the 1999 Annual Report)

To many of us, the first of these two observations may seem obvious and the second somewhat timid, especially to Americans. Yet nothing could be further from the truth.

If the first of Roger Sant's conclusions is true, that American people (and by extension others abroad) are "responsible, caring, creative, and want to make a difference," why has it taken consultative management over 200 years to penetrate more than a few corporate, government, or other workplaces? And for his second reflection, Americans still hold the dominant model of the strong solitary decision maker as leader in their minds.

Organizational as well as many other types of cultures contain elite systems, assumptions, and patterned behaviors that tend to be accepted and practiced by most members without much thought or reflection. People hold that *that's just the way things are and ought to be.* At their core most cultures have evolved, often over a long period of time, from efforts to understand, interpret, and explain (to some degree at least) the group's experience, challenges, and creative accomplishments as best it can. The process produces a cosmology, a generally accepted pattern of habits and behaviors and often a set of dos and don'ts that serve most of its members reasonably well. Since all of these (and more) factors evolve over time, we have a myriad of distinctive cultures and subcultures worldwide.

The power of Roger Sant's first observation is that it enables AES to leapfrog over cultural differences and reach the core needs of all people: the need to be treated as mature responsible adults; to be able to use their creative and other special abilities and talents at work; to enjoy a warm and caring environment with others and to make a significant positive difference through what they are doing. As these needs are met, new elements will be added to each culture to strengthen, enrich, and make it more versatile—much as democracy has been grafted to many previously hierarchical cultures and societies.

Roger Sant's second point is more subtle and may offer a greater challenge to Western society than it does to others—though it is taking hold in them.

The mental model prevalent in much of the world today is that of the leader/executive who may consult with others but who makes all key decisions, sometimes without consultation. The assumption is that he or she knows best the situation and because of his or her position and power is compelled to make the important decisions. Therefore, to seek out too much advice will muddy the waters, as will engaging in much consultation. This is the model of the lone hero—the true leader. Roger Sant's notion of consultative behavior may seem weak and indecisive by comparison.

Historically, the layers of approval in the old hierarchical structure conveyed a mistrust of lower-level decision makers because they were believed to lack the greater judgment, the expertise, and the "big picture" attributed to people up the *chain of command.* Each level was checking on the perceptions of the level just below it. Little was made of the innate intelligence, ideas, and abilities of those at the working level.

Today at AES and at a growing number of other organizations people realize that the complexity of the problems to be solved, the talents and experience of the people available to help, and the knowledge within and without the group has created a new, more participative, and multifaceted dynamic that is far more powerful than any individual, no matter his or her position.

In a nutshell, the case histories of the seven organizations that we have analyzed and described relate this new type of culture, which is much more akin to today's work and business environment. It's a reality that should not be overlooked.

Gordon F. Shea

Introduction: A Few Thoughts about Organizational Culture and Motivation

In recent years, much has been written about corporate or organizational cultures. We have become keenly aware of how cultures influence behavior and performance of employees. They embody and explain "how things get done around here." In a nutshell, people and their relationships are the essence of cultures. They represent the "social architecture" of companies and lead to the shared assumptions of their employees.

It has been said, there are no "right" or "wrong" cultures. We may find companies with a rather structured environment and an overarching hierarchy where the culture is based on tight discipline and well-defined relationships. On the other end of the spectrum, we encounter firms with team-based and empowered cultures. Often, the founders or certain charismatic leaders have created their company's culture, as examples like Wal-Mart, Nordstrom, GE, or IBM show.

We firmly believe, however, that there are "right" cultures in terms of their impact on people's motivation and productive energy. That's what this book is all about. The case histories that we report on and that cover close to 100,000 employees give a lot of credence to our concepts. We are truly convinced that the examples of these unique cultures will offer you, our reader, a different perception of your own workplace or the one you are just applying to and will prompt you to ask some tough questions. Is it or will it be fun to work there? Are this company's values and principles consistent with your own? These are examples of the questions you may want to ask.

We have traveled around the country and as far as Merida in Yucatan, Mexico, to speak to inspired employees—"leaders" in their particular surroundings—in power plant operations, at the assembly line, or in the consulting office. These were uplifting experiences, with people telling us about the ideas and principles guiding them in a new workplace. In many instances in this book we let people's own words speak for themselves. Their message is very powerful: The unique culture of their organization stimulates them and leads to creative ideas and productive energy that seems to have virtually no limits.

At the same time, we considered it important to speak to the executives of these organizations—founders, CEOs, commandants, or other high-level leaders—to learn about their ideas and intentions in supporting, nurturing, or even pioneering the work cultures we were visiting and studying. The essence of these interviews is encapsulated in the "Executive Perspective" sections of each chapter; the dates of the interviews are cited in the chapter notes.

The organizations and workplaces we visited tell their own stories about how the people go about their business and what affects their feelings and motivation. There are a few common attributes, however, that highlight our concepts for today's new work environment. They are as follows:

- A new kind of human relationship is the essence of healthy and motivating cultures. People have their ideals. They look for meaning in their lives with work playing an important role in it. Instead of being treated as mindless laborers, people expect to be considered mature and responsible adults, capable of thinking, being creative, and being trusted.

- Top-down power structures and the corporate ladder have lost significance. The consequence is a "no-boss business" with the employees' entrepreneurial attitudes and participation replacing the former hierarchies. Decision making is being decentralized, which implies broader access to information for everyone. All these can be difficult changes to deal with because "we are too insecure to let go of command-and-control" (James Lucas in *The Passionate Organization*).

- We mentioned a different kind of human relationship before. In many of the organizations that we visited, we saw an unusual degree of interaction and communication, of a family or team spirit that helps generate motivational energy. People truly care for each other and share the joy of challenge and success.

- People look for learning opportunities "that stretch and amaze us" (Lucas). The acquisition of new skills broadens people's horizons and helps them to more easily adapt to new challenges and ever-increasing changes in today's business climate. By the same token, learning leads to personal growth and to higher professional competence, both healthy motivational experiences.

As a counterpoint to these healthy cultures, we have also analyzed several recently failing cultures—Enron among them—to identify some of the factors that contributed to their failures. At the same time, some of the organizations studied by us held up surprisingly well under recent duress. As we will show, some of the failing cultures are already on their way back, based on the memories and remnants of former strength.

Most of the authors who have written about corporate culture appear rather optimistic on the possibilities of changing and adapting a company's culture to new realities. They provide step-by-step recipes for culture change in a top-down approach under the leadership of senior management. We strongly disagree with this line of reasoning.

A new or enhanced organizational culture must be "organic" in nature—simple, basic, and close to human values. It isn't a program drawn up by staff experts or consultants. It has to resemble a living organism—a living whole. The senior executives may prepare the soil, plant the seeds, and provide nourishment, but the culture will only grow with the help of the employees, as we demonstrate in our case studies. We maintain that people inherently yearn to be free, responsible, and joyful.

Let us step back for a moment and look at the history and evolution of organizational cultures. At this stage of our introductory segment, it may be appropriate to offer some thoughts about organizational cultures and how they were structured in the past.

EVOLUTION AND HISTORY OF ORGANIZATIONAL CULTURE

All living creatures have an inborn instinct to survive. In humans, standing as we are at the top of the food chain, this process is extremely complex but potentially magnificent.

Founded on the deep unconscious and subconscious factors that each of us must deal with because we are human, we learn to adapt as best we can to our environment. And as we grow and become aware of it, we adapt to the nature of the culture that often invisibly surrounds us. But none of these things are inevitable or fixed.

What this book offers is a deeper and more insightful look at some of the innovations that are being used to create new, more dynamic and inclusive organizational cultures that enable and encourage employees at all levels to pool their energy, knowledge, know-how, talents, abilities, and creativity in ways that build exceptional levels of motivation and achievement.

Virtually everyone is motivated and nearly all of the time. However, individuals have to be almost on a life-support system, where all of their needs are met without effort, to be "unmotivated," even if it is only to get their backs scratched. People may not be motivated to do what you want them to do, and they may even be motivated to *not* do what you want them to do.

Motivation is an inner force that guides most of our actions—conscious or unconscious. Many of these motivational urges are hard wired into our brain and can only be denied with great effort. We eat when we are hungry (and sometimes when we are not) and will, in time, actively search for food, if none is readily available. You can't deny that a hungry person is motivated. However, if that urge is not satisfied in a reasonable time, the lack of food will debilitate the body so that the energy flow needed to keep up the pursuit will atrophy and as the energy level lessens, the person so denied will become passive and, if that condition persists long enough, will become inert and eventually dead. At that point that person is truly not motivated.

There is a lot of nonsense written and spoken about motives and motivation. It is time to get it straight if we are to truly harmonize individual motivation and organizational goals. While we'll reexamine some of the principles of motivational theory later in this introduction, let's focus for a brief moment on one very important aspect of it.

There is a delusional notion rampant in our society (especially in the assumed most-advanced segment of our global society) that you and I can motivate someone else. A more lucid assessment of reality would be that all we can offer is incentives, enticements, or rewards; threats, penalties, or punishment; or a similar external stimulus: The motivation to gain the good things, or avoid the bad, springs from within the person being so offered, as they perceive the proposition and as they believe they can achieve what they desire. That process of acting to gain or avoid is incredibly complex, yet such comprehension can offer great improvements to our society and its members if we can get it right.

During most of the human saga on this earth—which led to today's kaleidoscope of motivational options—change and development of people advanced at an evolutionary pace, that is, very slowly. Untold eons passed before the cumulative genetic changes in the human mind and body (and perhaps even spirit) brought us workably close to today's "human nature."

At that point human society, as it began to develop, advanced much more rapidly, and yet at what could then be called a glacial pace—still quite slowly. Generations would pass before anyone noticed much of a change from one generation to another.

Today we are moving along at what seems to be an incredible pace relative to our past and we are likely to keep our foot on the accelerator to keep testing the limits (if any) of our future. Yet we still have many people who are motivated by the expectations, aspirations, and opportunities of the Ice Age. And there are others who are determined (i.e., motivated) to keep them there.

So where does that leave us today?

First, we must grasp the truly complex motivational nature of the people we are dealing with and our own nature and potential.

Second, we need to explore the organizational environments we must create to manage this pace of change and build the cultures that support them, so that we can help employees to choose to be motivated to function effectively in the most creative, thoughtful, and productive society imaginable.

So what are we faced with?

TRADITIONAL ORGANIZATIONAL CULTURES

In most of the world, for most of the time since most of the people gave up hunting and gathering and began to settle down into communities and establish some type of civilization, at times resources—especially food— have been scarce. Typically some folks were stronger, swifter, and craftier than others were so they figured out ways that their children would fare better than the kids of others would if and when hard times arrived— presto, instant hierarchy. They found ways to pass their relative inherent power in such structures onto the chosen few, as the more powerful developed such devices as the hereditary monarchical system.

George Washington and his band of dissidents toppled a good deal of that system in the United States and slowly over the next two centuries elements of this heresy called democracy spread to some other parts of the world. The process embodies an inherent human desire for freedom and opportunity and is still continuing.

At its core, a culture grows out of the search by people to find out what works best for them in a particular environment and situation they find themselves in, with all of its problems and opportunities. Therefore, its members attempt to identify, define, explain, and communicate to others in their family or group guiding principles, assumptions, attitudes, beliefs, behaviors, and practices that they presume to be of value to their own and future generations. A culture also embodies the experience, skills, and creative talents that make life more satisfying, rewarding, and successful for at least those members who can exert some influence on their situation.

A given culture has a spectrum of possible outcomes. It can be alert, responsive, and adaptive on one end of the scale or out of touch, outdated, and rigid at the other end. Because of the flow of force upon them, organizational cultures unwilling to adapt or change toy with extinction. Today, each of us (or at least most of us in a free society) belongs to a multitude of cultures, including our national, regional, employment, ethnic, economic, religious, and even a possibly distinctive family culture or the emerging global culture—each one changing and altering the others.

Exhibit 1 illustrates the two most authoritative and exploitive systems (on the left side of the exhibit) under which most people lived out their lives throughout most of history and in most places in the world, especially in sedentary societies. There was virtually no check on the power holders, short of revolution, and their behavior could range from tyranny in its worst form to benevolence and anything in between, depending largely on the temperament and upbringing of a particular power holder.

Usually in these two models, workers tended to be passive, obedient, and even docile so that these behaviors became habitual and created a low self-image, even to the point of actually believing that the power holders were somewhat better than they were. Workers usually contributed only what was required—most often their physical strength or dexterity. They were also powerfully motivated to obey authority, avoid risk, and accept work standards kept low by their social collusion.

Overall, both of the authoritative systems produced low results or output, but because they dominated whole societies, these low production standards were generally as good as anyone got—so it was just assumed that those results were all that was possible.

However, in a practical sense, many aspects of these ancient structures remain in some organizations so that position power still leads to the perks and control of resources by a few. Hence instead of ruling by a modified form of royal edict, the top brass in some organizations continues to function through a system of rewards and punishments. The rewards may range from the benefit of employment itself (bestowed and continued for good behavior as management defines it) to special incentives and benefits where performance (usually of an individual) goes above and beyond some management-developed norm.

But as the two ancient focused systems of power and authority started to produce more wealth, new models started to become more common and new principles started to emerge. The more successful a society becomes, the faster it tends to outdate itself—particularly in democracies where people slowly gain power to exercise their voting franchise.

For instance, technological advances in the nineteenth century created a need for people with at least some education—the ability to read, write, and do sums. Once people learned to read, they bought books that expanded their horizons and encouraged them to set higher goals for their children. In the newer industrial societies, this induced people to become more active in the political process, leading to child labor laws, compulsory education for the young, new limits on the power holders, and so on.

By the early years of the twentieth century, the custodial culture had become common in government and in a few notably successful companies, and it either replaced or modified the benevolent authoritative model in many cases. As people became better educated, the technology more complex, and the ancient focus on property rights more widely shared, we saw a general shift from exploitive authoritative to the more enlightened managerial supervisory model shown in the far right column of Exhibit I.1.

Exhibit I.1.
Four Historically Dominant Models of Organizational Cultures

Model	Exploitive Authoritative	Benevolent Authoritative	Custodial	Managerial Supervisory
1. Foundation of the model	Arbitrary position power	Everyone knows one's place and position	Power to tax or tithe, or great market success	Power from position in hierarchy
2. Based on	Heredity or control of resources and capital	Heredity or control of resources and capital	Economic resources	Authority of rank or position
3. Managerial focus	Command and control	Paternalistic command and control	Setting work rules and regulations	Control through hierarchy
4. Managerial assumption	Employees limited and need to be directed	Chances and favors for deferential subservience	Limited autonomy for routine tasks	Autonomy within limits of hierarchy
5. Employee motivation	Obedience, no initiative unless self-oriented	Low profile, subservience	Focused on long-term security	Power and career goals within the hierarchy
6. Level of employee needs met	Survival and subsistence	Marginal, but usually adequate	Maintenance with some social needs	Recognition based on performance
7. Psychological consequences	Enduring one's work life	Dependence on boss's goodwill	Dependence on entity membership	Occasional frustrations with hierarchy
8. Morale measure	Compliance, don't make waves	Acceptance and submission	Moderate satisfaction with work	Conformity and hope for ascension

This culture worked reasonably well, especially as the twentieth century developed, and certainly better than earlier systems in that it was more focused on the needs and motivations of the individual. It also became more widespread and allowed for a multiplication of opportunities. However, like any successful human system in a democracy, it gradually outdated itself.

Simply put, as the economic pie grew more people wanted a piece and of course as large a piece as they could get. Also, much of the growth in the economy was due to self-motivated entrepreneurs backed up by a wide range of creative people. A host of other factors such as more complex technology, higher educational levels, and greater communications capacity and skills enabled more people to squeeze into the broadening realm of prosperity. This meant that more and more people were motivated by factors other than just adequate food, clothing, and shelter, that is, Abraham Maslow's physiological (or body) needs and the safety and security of the custodial model.

While many people still remained at the basic physiological needs level, others were demanding and getting improved safety and security such as fringe benefits (i.e., insurance, social security, unemployment benefits, etc.) and other stabilizing factors (most often). This brought a much larger segment of society in the advanced countries of the world to a greater level of security, involvement, and good feelings.

However, one of the most significant aspects of Maslow's concept of the "Hierarchy of Needs" (see Exhibit I.2) and its general impact on people's motivation is the upward arrow to the left of his pyramid. The basic message is that as the lower-level needs get reasonably well satisfied we tend to move toward higher-level needs, though those needs are not as imperative or pressing as the lower-level ones.

We have briefly looked at the older cultural models for three reasons:

First, as an organizational culture becomes more successful economically it also tends to evolve socially and the employees tend to develop psychologically—they are more aware of and demanding of their higher-level needs and wants such as a sense of belonging, acceptance, and recognition for their contribution to the group and the organization.

Second, as the educational and performance levels rise, freedom and opportunity seem more available to more people who "want in" for themselves and for their children. These factors produce a new incentive dynamic in virtually every aspect of people's lives. For example, as information becomes more available (through technology) people become more mobile, change their personal environment more rapidly, and gain in discretionary income choices as more options become attainable.

Third, as new ideas in management and more widespread wealth generation and availability appear, people become more self-directed and their cultures change more rapidly and expand to include more people in the society's talent pool.

Exhibit I.2.
The "Hierarchy of Needs"

The "Hierarchy of Needs"
Abraham H. Maslow

Maslow's book, *Motivation and Personality* (New York: Harper & Row, 1954), and the concept of a "humanistic psychology" that he created must both be seen in their historic context. Maslow proposed a comprehensive life philosophy to counter Sigmund Freud's psychoanalysis as well as the behaviorist school of psychology, with its stimulus-and-response approach to motivating others. Maslow believed in the potential of humans to exercise choice, to grow, and to arrive at a point of self-actualization. Creativity, responsibility, and self-actualization were concepts of no consequence to either behaviorism or psychoanalysis. Maslow considered this a significant shortcoming.

The central piece of Maslow's theory is a pyramid of needs:

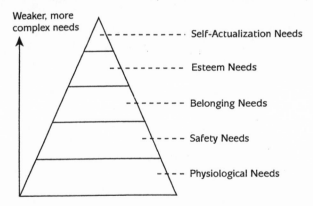

Maslow established the principle that needs generally must be fulfilled in sequence, starting from the physiological needs. According to his "prepotency principle," satisfying a lower-order need would enable a person to focus on the next higher need. Maslow's main focus, however, was on self-actualization. The drive for self-actualization might well advance even if there were a deficiency in a lower-order need.

If we look closely at Exhibit 1 we can see steps that create a more congenial organizational culture for the slave, serf, or employee but also see improvements in attitude, aspiration, and willingness to benefit the employer as we move to the right of the chart.

Examining the managerial assumptions about the employee and their consequent focus in the relationship, we go from command and control to paternalism and from there to managerial bureaucracy and hierarchy. Concurrently, we see marginal improvements in personal freedom and opportunity on the job. Looking at the lot of the employee, we move from virtually complete powerlessness and obedience to some sense of self and some hope for the future, at least in retirement.

In the realm of employee motivation we move from compulsory submission and no visible initiative—a kind of "yes boss" humility—to a possible dream of sharing a bit of authority and a sense of a career. If you work hard and faithfully, you *might* get some recognition for it (possibly in time a gold watch). But also there generally is the iron fist in the velvet glove that leads to conformity and caution and often to subtle office politics.

We also need to recognize that as new models gain ascendancy, the old ones seldom totally disappear. We still occasionally uncover covert virtual slave shops exploiting illegal immigrants in the United States as well as American firms exporting work or buying from foreign firms where conditions are no better.

Thus new models and more personally satisfying motivational cultures develop more rapidly. Therefore, we are seeing the newer cultures emerging, as in Exhibit I.3. Though some power holders still have a deep affection for their power and perks, and will fight to continue them, it is increasingly clear that the historically dominant organizational cultures of the past (as detailed in Exhibit I.1) are increasingly becoming obsolete, though still common in many of the developed countries of the world.

As our society becomes technologically more complex and our population better educated and free to choose their future, we are increasingly experimenting with or choosing the emerging models displayed in Exhibit 3. So what do these newer evolving models offer us?

NEWER ORGANIZATIONAL CULTURES

Participative leadership as an organizational cultural innovation began to seriously rival earlier models since the middle of the twentieth century as research-based new knowledge from the social, behavioral, and communications sciences began to emerge from academia, innovative organizations, and the media.

At an ever-quickening pace we began to realize that individuals and groups had far more to offer employers than previously realized or acknowledged. Training of supervisors, managers, and executives became increasingly common and more broadly based on findings from the

Exhibit I.3.
Four Currently Evolving Models of Organizational Cultures

Model	Participative Leadership	Collegial	Self-management	Community of Leaders
1. Foundation of the model	Self-confident leadership	Employees as equals	Diversity of inputs from partners	Competent and diverse partnerships
2. Based on	Employees as valuable contributors	Professional competence in one's field	Flexibility, multiple skills, task sharing	Sharing of information and responsibilities
3. Managerial focus	Developing employees	Coordination of tasks	Leadership based on best ideas	Providing mentoring and expertise
4. Managerial assumption	Manager's role is to support individuals	Autonomy based on professional competence	Manager's role to get support and resources	Serving and supporting partners
5. Employee motivation	Mutual trust and cooperation	Self-discipline	Develop self and become part of team	Highest possible self-actualization
6. Level of employee needs met	Recognition and self-esteem are possible	Pride in professional competence	Being valued for personal contributions	Consistent professional and personal values
7. Psychological consequences	Sense of opportunity and personal power	Membership in high-performing team	Enthusiasm for personal growth and development	Sense of full use of personal potential
8. Morale measure	Willingness to mature and explore options	Striving for ever-higher levels of competence	Sense of family and mutual trust	Abundant joy and fulfillment

human sciences. Those were then synthesized into practical tools that were then widely taught and used.

Out of this grew some real organizational changes such as participative management, better-educated employees, an increase in mutual trust and cooperation between management and employees, and a new sense of self-confidence and self-trust shared by more and more employees. If you examine each of the factors in that participative leadership model, you see for the first time employee motivation centered on mutual trust and cooperation.

During the twentieth century the collegial model as an organizational culture emerged from its rather exclusive origins in the classic professions (law, theology, and medicine) to become a catalyst for more inclusive, democratic and complex processes in many organizations and work groups. For example, in a hospital operating room, as medicine became much more high tech and complicated, the lone surgeon with a nurse assistant gradually became a complex team of people including those monitoring the instruments, the anesthesiologist, and lab technicians.

Out of necessity we went to complex teams where a high level of professionalism was demanded from people in several disciplines. Individual self-discipline became the primary motivational imperative for all members of the team and required professional pride in each team participant. The morale measure became the willingness to strive for ever-higher levels of personal competence. This meant seeing all members of the team as equals but different. It stressed willing coordination of activities and perpetual learning of new skills and techniques, including some interpersonal ones.

This of course brings us to a more democratic, inclusive, and mature model for people throughout the organization to share a common culture largely devoid of rank and privilege. In the organizations we have studied and reported on in the following pages, we have found that employees indoctrinated into these newer cultures are

- able to leapfrog from much earlier cultures to these,
- finding the jump very exciting and rewarding, and
- able to contribute much more effectively and significantly to the organization's overall success.

We have generally found a substantial openness; willingness to share feelings, ideas, and information; and actual joy (that is, fun) in doing so. We also have to recognize that many organizations hold to earlier models. Many managers are pessimistic about the possible results that could be expected from self-managed teams in their organization. In a way, they are right—in the sense that people conditioned to a command-and-control environment would tend to be ill equipped or prepared to take on personal responsibility for results. Yet when people from those earlier types of environments experience a newer one, there is often a period of disbelief followed by enthusiastic conversion.

We have found that most persons moving from a hierarchical culture to one where members contribute diverse inputs from their own background adapt rapidly and well to the fact that they are now dealing with well-rounded, able colleagues and that leadership passes from person to person depending on who has the best idea or information at a given time in solving a problem or developing a new product or service. This is because they soon realize that anything they know or contribute will be treated with respect.

Soon such people's level of motivation becomes centered in themselves and they want to develop more fully. Thus their self-confidence and their sense of self-worth grows as they develop a sense of unity with the group and appreciate the value of each other person.

When we enter the realm of the newer organizational cultures that developed fully during and since the last half of the twentieth century, we generally find far greater diversity in their composition as the case examples we provide attest. However, the four models are illustrative of these newer cultures.

In the participative leadership model we tend to find self-confident leaders who are well trained, often have effective coaches and mentors, and are themselves valued participants in the more open and encouraging cultural environment. They start viewing their employees as potential valuable contributors to their idea and information pool. As we move to the right, their associates are viewed and treated as equals; a source of input from *partners,* and eventually they see their diverse relationships as a series of equal partnerships. These relationships are based in the collegial model as professional equals, each doing their jobs with élan. In the realm of self-management they are appreciated for their flexibility and willingness to share tasks. In the community of leaders model there tends to be a free flow of information to where it is needed and best acted upon.

When it comes to the managerial focus and the assumptions about people on which it is based, we will encounter some interesting observations. In the participative leadership model we find a focus on developing each person's knowledge, skills, and abilities (KSAs) through support and training (and possibly some mentoring). In the collegial model there tends to be considerable autonomy based on each person's professional competence and judgment. Coordination is often achieved in a team environment. However, in the self-management model leadership often passes from person to person depending on who has the best idea or the key piece of information. The manager's role is shifted to focus on the support of team members and getting the resources the team needs. While almost any employee can lead the group from time to time, it may become difficult to condition old-line personnel to believe in, let alone adapt to, such an environment.

However, it is when we explore these models from an employee perspective that we really experience their enormous cultural impact. Here we get beyond employee manipulation and to where managers become virtually unnecessary. Impossible? Just watch and see.

When we look across the changes in employee motivation, it goes from mutual trust and cooperation, a pretty good relationship, to self-discipline, to an effort to develop oneself and become part of the employee self-managing team, to the highest form of self-actualization in a continuing effort to become all you can be. And as we discover more about the diverse potential of human beings, the possibilities grow.

As we review the employee needs met in the different models, we get a revolutionary change in organizational relationships. Recognition and self-esteem can be greatly influenced by one's supervisor and the organization. However, pride in one's professional competence is a self-generated feeling based on self-achievement. Being valued for personal contributions in a self-managed environment tends to come from one's peers and teammates. Finally, the individual seeks consistency of his or her own personal and professional values and will demand such from an organization before accepting employment with it.

The psychological consequences for employees range from a sense of opportunity and personal power through the satisfaction of membership on a high-performance team, to enthusiasm for their personal growth and development, to a personal sense of the full use of their personal potential.

The general measure of organizational morale reaches a peak across the columns from left to right. In the participative leadership model, we get a willingness to mature in social interactions on the job. Moving to the right, we see an active lifelong striving for ever-higher levels of competence. Based on a sense of family in the workplace, mutual trust and a dedication to each other seem strong. Finally, what we have witnessed in the organizations we have studied is abundant joy and fulfillment based on a sense of mutual achievement.

The case studies we offer here have demonstrated that the businesses' success based on creation of a quality organizational culture provides them with a powerful competitive advantage.

ORGANIZATIONAL CULTURE'S IMPACT ON PEOPLE

The term *culture* as we use it to describe the customs and environment of corporations and organizations is taken from sociology and represents a set of distinguishing practices, principles, and beliefs that have developed over time within a particular community. Strong cultures are a powerful influence throughout an organization. The myths and legends that propelled American institutions like GE, IBM, Procter & Gamble and others are remembered almost everywhere. How can we understand culture, and what does it look like? Let's start with an example that shows its leverage on people.

Not far from a major industrial center in the Northeastern United States, a small division of a major paper company manufactured quality corrugated boxes for packaging. Its equipment had seen better days and breakdowns were frequent. Supervisors for production and maintenance would squabble over priorities and customers were upset with missed deadlines and unkept promises. The division was losing money and, as a result, the general manager of the division was finally fired.

His replacement had applied for this particular job from an executive staff assignment at headquarters. For him it was a lateral move at best, but he was anxious to escape the bureaucratic environment of the corporate administration. He longed to return to the small division where, at one time in his career, he had been happy and successful.

As he started his new job, people at the division were surprised to see him tour the plant and ask for their input about what needed to be changed to make the facility productive and profitable. Their suggestions were taken seriously and implemented wherever possible. He eliminated supervisory positions and let people work in self-managed teams. He brought equipment operators and maintenance together, let them find ways to make small repairs during shifts, and with this new procedure avoided major breakdowns. Manufacturing people started talking to customers to understand their needs and keep the deadlines.

In summary, the division's way of operating changed completely. The new general manager held periodic informational meetings to keep his workforce updated on the progress and let them participate in further improvements. People all over the plant would take financial courses to better understand the interrelations of the business. In a short period of time, the division reversed its losses and became quite productive and profitable. It turned into a true model of what a self-managed and motivated workforce is able to accomplish and the general manager started being invited to business conferences to share the success story with other companies.

At headquarters, however, executives were not happy. They favored a tight hierarchy and top-down practices. The general manager's participative approach seemed to threaten the established rules and, in addition, the executives were jealous of his favorable publicity. They did not wait long to replace him with someone they could trust. Gone were the days of asking for people's input. The old supervisory structure returned. People were disappointed and lost their energetic approach. Some of them left. With the changes introduced in the past, however, the division continued to be profitable for some time.

Sound familiar? You bet! It happens every day in corporate America and proves the powerful impact that an organization's culture has on its people.

What, then, are some of the elements that determine the nature of culture?

THE DETERMINANTS OF ORGANIZATIONAL CULTURE

John P. Kotter, in his pioneering 1992 book *Corporate Culture and Performance*, differentiates between visible and invisible characteristics of culture. The visible elements are behavior patterns and common ways of acting to be followed by members of a community. Certain well-publicized and accepted objectives, goals, mission, and vision may support the visible part of a culture.

The invisible elements have developed over time and are more deep-seated and difficult to change. They include shared assumptions, convictions, and values like integrity, mutual respect, trust, and fairness. Often these elements bear the hallmark of the founder of the corporation or of certain heroes or role models who captured the imagination of their coworkers. Almost as the result of "social learning," these elements became solidly embedded in the organization's culture.

J. R. Collins and J. I. Porras, in their 1994 book *Built to Last: Successful Habits of Visionary Companies*, talk about the importance of aligning the "big picture" of an organization's culture with the day-to-day "little things." "People want to believe in their company's vision," they explain, "but will be ever watchful for tiny inconsistencies." The personal behavior of senior management—"walking the talk"—is crucial for the process of creating and maintaining a strong culture. Any favoritism or greater tolerance toward employees who are closer to management will destroy that trust. Similarly, distant locations or diverse business groups may lead to varying subcultures. While it is common to adapt the cultural focus to specific local or business needs, subcultures tend to share the dominant belief systems of the principal organization.

Kotter firmly believes in the role of an organization's leadership "to win over the hearts and minds" of its people. Mentioning the hearts points to the strong emotional component of culture that becomes ever more prevalent in today's organizations. James R. Lucas, in his book *The Passionate Organization*, comes to similar conclusions. He talks about people's "zest for life"—their passion to make a difference and to give meaning to their lives—as a driving force for a successful culture.

As stated before, work has become more of an integral part of people's lives. Today many of us expect to live our personal values in the organizational culture with which we associate. The workplace becomes family; people share the emotions of challenge and success with each other. Celebrations are part of the rituals of today's cultures. People treat each other as human beings rather than as ruthless competitors for corporate advancement. Under the dispassionate and matter-of-fact veneer of the workplace glows the human spirit, providing the motivational glue that accords culture its purpose. In other words, today's cultures feed on the heart and help to unleash intrinsic motivation and boundless productive energy.

There is a rational component of culture as well—the minds mentioned by Kotter. E. H. Schein, in his masterful and comprehensive writings on *Organizational Culture and Leadership,* advocates a broader view of culture—to include strategies, processes, common concepts, identity, authority, and status—elements of a more rational connotation. The mind versus heart antinomy, however, may lead to an uncomfortable trade-off. In his new book *The Corporate Culture Survival Guide,* Schein tells us that "managers who have worked their way up in the organization usually learn that humanistic, environmental, spiritual, and other non-economic values have to be subordinated to the pragmatic problems of running the business and keeping it financially viable."

As we mentioned before, there is no "right" or "wrong" culture. However, in today's cultural environment, the subordination of the hearts to the minds will undoubtedly lead to emotional responses, which will affect people's motivation and productivity. This becomes particularly relevant in a "no-boss" environment where employees are expected to take the initiative and make decisions.

The key to success of the new corporate cultures is a fresh approach to energize people and unlock their strengths and productivity. It is based on intrinsic motivation—motivation that emerges from inside people. Generally, intrinsic motivation is the "outcome," the result of a work situation or a culture that people enjoy for several reasons. They have "ownership" and are in charge of their job. They enjoy learning opportunities that lead to new challenges. And last but not least, they are satisfied with their job, being part of a "fun" environment. We'll summarize some of these concepts in a later chapter.

This may be an opportune time to revisit some of the principles of motivation and to get a better understanding why "right" cultures—"right" from a motivational standpoint—will more strongly impact performance and productivity.

A LOOK AT MOTIVATIONAL THEORY

Motivation has long been the focus of extensive research in the field of psychology. Our motivational preferences will not only drive us to behave a certain way but will also define the vigor and intensity of that particular behavior. Since its beginnings psychology has attempted to study and explain the concept of motivation and we would therefore like to explore some of it. While certain of the precepts cited here may seem far removed from the underlying idea of our book, they offer important clues for understanding cultures and how the "right" ones have an extraordinary impact on the people associated with those organizations.

Let's start by looking at recent research that substantially changed the understanding of motivation.

BEING MOTIVATED BY "FUN"

In 1990, Mihaly Csikszentmihalyi, former chairman of the Department of Psychology at the University of Chicago, published *Flow: The Psychology of Optimal Experience.* The findings of his research revolutionized the understanding of motivation, with the term *flow,* or *optimal experience,* describing a period of intrinsically motivated behavior. Our purpose here is not to teach Csikszentmihalyi but to help us understand how people become really motivated.

In his research, Csikszentmihalyi often detected a particular kind of experience in which people's performance seemed to be effortless. They wanted to continue forever in their task and learn additional skills to master more demanding challenges. The fun and enjoyment of an activity, the sense of control generated by being able to handle a particular challenge, and the growth of self from a specific achievement—all these were typical *flow* experiences.

Even before, other studies had shown that people's ability to control or self-direct an activity would lead to intrinsically motivated behavior. However, the concept of *flow* added a new dimension to intrinsic motivation. The "enjoyment" of a particular challenge and the fun at certain activities gets people emotionally "hooked."

Let's look at a few examples: Playing a tough game of tennis that stretches our ability leaves us exhausted but happy. Reading a book that reveals things in a new light or having a conversation that leads us to express ideas we didn't know we had brings us intellectual excitement. Similarly, closing a contested business deal, or finishing a piece of work well done, gives us a lot of satisfaction. None of these experiences may be particularly pleasurable at the time they are taking place, but afterward we think back on them, say, "that was really fun," and wish they would happen again. We know we have learned and our selves have grown.

Following these concepts, there are three major elements that bring forth this exceptional motivation: being in control of an activity, increasing our skills to keep mastering ever-more-difficult challenges, and the fun and enjoyment that all this causes. All this brings about *flow*. The *flow* experience is uplifting because it makes our life more rich, intense, and meaningful. The key to *flow* experiences is in adding to our skills and in the growth of self. Csikszentmihalyi's research has provided the foundation for powerful new motivational approaches.

SOURCES OF MOTIVATION

Let us step back for a moment and ask the question, What is motivation? What really energizes people at work? What lets them take ownership of their jobs? We mentioned "intrinsic" motivation before, which comes from inside people and is self-generated. What about "extrinsic" approaches? Can we motivate others to perform at superior levels?

Exhibit I.4 shows the changing concepts of motivation as they have developed since the middle of the last century. The motivational factors

Exhibit I.4.
Our Changing Concepts of Motivation

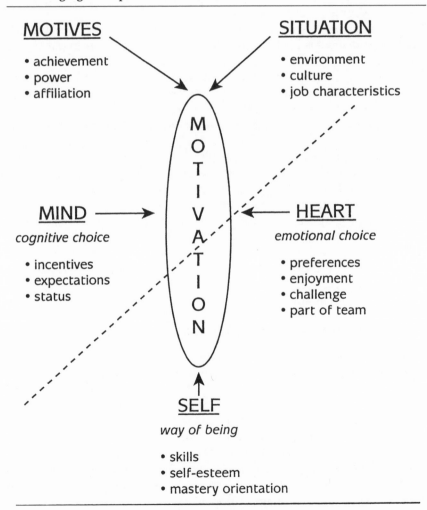

above the diagonal line are mostly extrinsic in nature, while the sources of motivation below the diagonal line reflect the more recent understanding of the intrinsic factors.

The leading motivational theories of the 1950s and 1960s focused on human needs. Motives—the origin of the word *motivation*—were seen as prompting people to adopt certain behaviors in order to satisfy specific needs. Based on this understanding, industry developed sophisticated programs to appeal to people's needs for achievement and power, for recognition and social advancement. Managers were trained in how to evaluate, handle, and "motivate" their subordinates. Indeed, "motivational talent"—knowing how to get others to work harder—became a desirable quality for upcoming managers. Looked at another way, motivation was turned into manipulation.

Need motivation was strongly influenced by the work of Abraham Maslow and Frederick Herzberg, influential authorities in motivational psychology during those years. To this day, Maslow's ideas on people orientation, with their focus on human values and the need for meaning and purpose for one's work life, as well as Herzberg's concepts on job attitudes, have not lost their impact. At the top of Maslow's list of motives are the need to enjoy self-respect and the respect of others and the need to grow our personal potential to the extent possible. Similarly, Herzberg has listed among his most important "positive job satisfiers" the need for recognition and for achievement. While both Maslow and Herzberg conceived an external focus for these important needs, they continue as motivational factors in the subsequent intrinsic and self-motivating approaches.

In summary, approaches and programs based on needs motivation gained wide acceptance in business through the 1980s. Although these theories seemed to work, they didn't get to the "heart" of the matter—the deeper emotional and mental phenomena that drive outstanding achievements in both our personal lives and our work lives. Csikszentmihalyi and *flow* fundamentally changed the understanding of motivation.

THE REAL POWER OF INTRINSIC MOTIVATION

Let's face it: We cannot motivate anyone in a definite and lasting way by traditional external means. We can offer incentives and rewards to get people to do what *we* want, but such results tend to be short term. People's motivation focuses on *their* needs and wants rather than on ours. There are also significant dangers and shortcomings to external approaches. Motivation can easily turn into "manipulation." Relying on the power of our position, we lean on those whom we have hired to help us, dangle money, offer a pat on the back, or voice an implied threat. And when none of this works, we may try to evaluate the worker's personality to see which of these and other clever stratagems appeal to his or her "way of being"—all this just to get someone to do what we want! This is clearly not ethical and corrupts the hope of building a relationship based on honesty, respect, and mutual trust.

The implications are manifold: As we have learned, intrinsic motivation at its strongest comes about as the "outcome," the effect of a work environment and a culture that people enjoy, that feeds their inner person— their spirit, their mind, their soul. We talked about that "inner power" that enables us to excel in what we do.

In the past, job security was what people hoped to get out of work. It led to being a loyal employee. Similar loyalty was expected from the employer. As we know, that's virtually all gone. Instead, people have moved to choose their place of work in line with their own values and aspirations. They look for meaning to their lives and expect work to play an important role in it. People look for consistency of values that apply to their work life and their personal life.

Emotional stimulation unleashes almost unlimited energy for getting things done. Those emotions emanate from an environment that allows people to be "human." They go with a workplace that inspires trust and mutual respect, that gives people autonomy and control over their job, that allows them to grow both professionally and personally. Many of us had the experience of being confronted with a serious challenge at work and just barely being able to cope with it. What an exhilarating and deeply motivating experience! We think back on those challenges and say, "that really was fun" and wish they would happen again.

The pages that follow describe organizations and their cultures that provide this kind of emotional stimulation. Their culture gives rise to unusual intrinsic motivation of the people working there. Our observations will illustrate some important conclusions as to "right" cultures, which we'll try to distill into certain recommendations for our readers. We hope this will lead to some improvements in how we structure our work environments.

PART I

The Power of Culture

The three case studies we offer to demonstrate the powerful impact that new corporate cultures have on the people could not be more dissimilar: We'll introduce you to a small Texas plumbing and air-conditioning contractor, TDIndustries, which has been ranked consistently by *Fortune* magazine among the best places to work in the country. Next you'll get a surprising account of the culture of a large military service organization, the U.S. Coast Guard, and an employee initiative that brings considerable change to the way the government operates. Third, you'll learn about the truly unique culture of a global power company, AES Corporation.

What do these organizations have in common? The case studies tell a fascinating story about structuring environments in a way to allow people to use their innate talents and have the fun of achievement in their job; about listening to the workforce and giving them appropriate recognition for their accomplishments; and about close relations between the executive management of these organizations and their employees.

As you will see, the different cultures of these three organizations, each in its own way, become powerful motivators to their people. At the same time, they fulfill the desire of their people for meaning in their lives, with work playing an important part in it.

CHAPTER 1

TDIndustries: Practicing Servant-Leadership at a Plumbing and Air-Conditioning Contractor

TDIndustries is one of the leading contractors for air-conditioning and plumbing in the nation, with $205 million in revenue and close to 1,400 employees in 2000. Since 1999, *Fortune* magazine has ranked TD among the best employers in its list of "Great Places to Work," based on survey results in the areas of communications, fairness, respect, pride, and team spirit. TD owes much of this success to its culture, which is firmly rooted in a little-known management philosophy called "Servant-Leadership."

The concept of Servant-Leadership goes back to the teachings of Robert K. Greenleaf, a former AT&T executive, who in 1970 published a thoughtful essay titled "The Servant as Leader." It is based on the notion that leaders are to serve those who work for them. We'll describe later in this chapter how it relates to TDIndustries and its employees.

Jack Lowe Sr., the father of the company's present CEO, Jack Lowe Jr., founded TDIndustries in 1946. In the middle of the 1950s, Lowe Sr. took ill with tuberculosis and was confined to his home for almost one year. It was a time of introspection and learning for him and got him interested in questions of social justice and equality in community and workplace. While previously Lowe Sr. had instituted stock ownership and profit sharing for TDIndustries's employees, he now embraced the concept of Servant-Leadership and started promoting and discussing Greenleaf's ideas with his people.

In several ways, TDIndustries employees became partners in the business (at their own suggestion, employees are called "partners" today). Lowe Sr. introduced a vision of management founded in consensus and open communications. At the same time, employee ownership through an employee stock ownership plan (ESOP) was expanded to a level where, as of today, TD employees hold 100% of the voting rights of the company. Since he took over as CEO, Lowe Jr. has continued and expanded his father's vision of participatory management. Once or twice a month, he holds breakfast meetings with about 20 employees to discuss their questions and concerns. The biweekly "Friday Forum" provides information on the course of TD's business or introduces interesting speakers to all who wish to attend. And once a quarter, a "Super-Business Meeting," which is always well attended, gives a more detailed overview of the business and addresses questions of safety or customer feedback.

Lowe Jr. plans to expand TD's business and take it into neighboring states like Arizona, Georgia, Colorado, or the Carolinas. As he sees it, there is some assurance of success by sending "experienced and indoctrinated TD folks along," people who are able to spread the gospel of the TD culture and Servant-Leadership.

SERVANT-LEADERSHIP: THE ESSENCE OF TD'S CULTURE

In Exhibit 1.1, we have reprinted TDIndustries's Vision, Basic Values, and Principles of Leadership, which are contained in a small brochure distributed to all employees. The text explains, "if our organization is to live up to its Basic Values and Mission, a key ingredient will be the *Leadership* provided by a large number of us." In our discussions with a cross section of TD partners, we probed for essential elements of the TD culture, epitomized by the tenets of Servant-Leadership.

Mutual respect, fairness, and equality were high on people's lists. "Everyone is equal here and everybody is treated with respect," affirmed Kurt Dodge, one of TD's project superintendents, with 14 years of service. And Rudy Camarillo points to openness and honesty in dealing with his managers. "You get straight answers," says Rudy, who has a Mexican background and is also a project superintendent. He likes TD's helpful diversity programs. "Lots of classes are taught in Spanish," he continues, "and language courses are available in Spanish and English."

Tim McNew, project manager for TD, reminisced about joining the company five years ago, directly out of college. "The reason I came to work here was that I wanted to work for a company that was growing, have a cool job, and make some money," recounted Tim. "I had heard stories about Servant-Leadership and thought that's the touchy-feely stuff for the production guys . . . But when I got into it, it didn't take me long to figure out that the key to my success was these guys' success . . . [It became] the measure for my own work how well they succeeded. So, my mission is to make a lot of great people succeed!"

Exhibit 1.1.
Vision, Basic Values, and Principles of Leadership for TDIndustries

VISION STATEMENT OF TDINDUSTRIES

"We are committed to providing outstanding Career Opportunities by exceeding our Customers' Expectations through Continuous Aggressive Improvement."

Our organization is committed to the accomplishment of this vision over the long term. We do not believe in seizing short-term benefits to the detriment of our long-term vision. We believe in continuous, intense "people-development" efforts, including substantial training budgets. We believe in investing in tools, equipment, and facilities that enable us to better accomplish our vision.

BASIC VALUES OF TDINDUSTRIES

At TDIndustries, we try to follow these Basic Values in all our relationships with customers, with suppliers, within our communities, and among ourselves:

1. Concern for and Belief in Individual Human Beings

   The basic character of our group is, above all, a concern for individual human beings. We believe that the individual has dignity and importance, that people are basically honest, and that each person wants to do a good job. We believe that no has ever really found the limits of human ability. If we draw our strength from the uniqueness of each individual, together we can become greater than the sum of our members. TDIndustries is best thought of as a group of individuals—not as an impersonal "company." We, as a group, own it and do its work.

2. Valuing Individual Differences

   We will be an organization in which the full range of individual differences exist and are valued among all of our stakeholders.

3. Honesty

4. Building Trusting Relationships

   We believe people react positively when trust and confidence are placed in them and when the best is expected of them. We try to reflect this belief in all our relationships.

5. Fairness

   Fairness includes equal treatment and equal opportunity for everyone.

6. Responsible Behavior

   We have high expectations of each other. We expect people to act responsibly and to work for group goals. We expect them to be dependable and to work hard.

7. High Standards of Business Ethics

Exhibit 1.1.
(Continued)

LEADERSHIP—AS DEFINED BY TDINDUSTRIES

In his essay "The Servant as Leader," Robert Greenleaf successfully expressed our views of how people can and should work together to grow our company. If our organization is to live up to its Basic Values and Mission, a key ingredient will be the *Leadership* provided by a very large number of us:

- Simply and plainly defined, Leaders are people who have followers. They have earned recognition and respect.
- Leaders are first a servant of those they lead. They are a teacher, a source of information and knowledge, and a standard setter, more than a giver of directions and a disciplinarian.
- Leaders see things through the eyes of their followers. They put themselves in others' shoes and help them make their dreams come true.
- Leaders do not say, "Get going." Instead, they say, "Let's go!" and lead the way. They do not walk behind with a whip; they are out in front with a banner.
- Leaders assume that their followers are working with them. They consider others partners in the work and see to it that they share in the rewards. They glorify the team spirit.
- Leaders are people builders. They help those around them to grow because the leader realizes that the more strong people an organization has, the stronger it will be.
- Leaders do not hold people down, they lift them up. They reach out their hand to help their followers to scale the peaks.
- Leaders have faith in people. They believe in them. They have found that others rise to their high expectations.
- Leaders use their heart as well as their head. After they have looked at the facts with their head, they let their hearts take a look, too.
- Leaders keep their eyes on high goals. They are self-starters. They create plans and set them in motion. They are persons of thought and persons of action—both dreamers and doers.
- Leaders are faced with many hard decisions, including balancing fairness to an individual with fairness to the group. This sometimes requires "weeding out" those in the group who, over a period of time, do not measure up to the group needs of dependability, productivity, and safety.
- Leaders have a sense of humor. They are not stuffed shirts. They can laugh at themselves. They have a humble spirit.
- Leaders can be led. They are not interested in having their own way but in finding the best way. They have an open mind.

We were told that Servant-Leadership is really about working for one's people, supporting and helping them. "There are a lot of servant-leaders in this company," agrees Erick Johnson, also a project superintendent with 12 years of service. Erick's manager supports him a lot. "You strive to do that same thing, which is the definition of a servant-leader."

"THE SERVANT AS LEADER"

It may be well to stop for a moment and to reflect on the meaning of Servant-Leadership, as it permeates TDIndustries's culture. In placing service and support ahead of giving directions, in making sure that leadership's first priority is to serve other people's needs, the concept of Servant-Leadership, as described in Greenleaf's essay, seems almost paradoxical. However, TDIndustries is a living example of how this approach can work in practice. TD's rich culture is embodied by a caring team spirit and a sense of community; by ethical, trusting, and responsible behaviors; and by the belief in people's ability to grow.

The ideal of the servant-leader has become a very real and practical credo for the company. There is much respect in management for TD's "partners" but, more importantly, partners respect management. "I like working for somebody who works," is a telling remark of Jesse Rodriguez, shop supervisor, who came to work for TD in 1990 after 20 years with a union. Managers are respected for giving guidance and being mentors to their people. In this they become role models for the organization.

Along similar lines, Servant-Leadership prompts an attitude of "giving back" to the community, of helping the poor and elderly. TD technicians volunteer on a regular basis for an industry initiative called "Heat the Town," repairing and replacing heating equipment for their less-fortunate neighbors within Dallas County. "So many of our people are involved in community work," confirms Laura Price, project manager with 17 years at TD.

TDINDUSTRIES—A LEARNING ORGANIZATION

Learning is a definite priority at TD—the company promotes the idea of lifetime learning for its partners. People are expected to take 32 hours per year of some type of education, half of that on their personal time. "It's by choice; you don't want to stagnate," says Tony Ford, field service technician with six years of service. "Once I get my education done, nobody can take it away from me." It's a good thought in today's conditions of declining job security.

At TDIndustries, there is a sincere effort to "build partners" by helping to advance their careers. Christina Bell came to TD almost three years ago and coordinates all training efforts. "We are still building demand for training," says Christina. Most of the training is done in-house, with trainers provided from the company ranks, including Lowe Jr., who teaches Total Quality Management to new partners.

As an example, there is a "production career path" outlining the curriculum suggested for learning a specific trade. Along similar lines and to provide for more flexibility, cross training between trades is recommended. However, course offerings do not stop there. They include basic education in Spanish, English, and even in literacy. At the other end of the spectrum, TDIndustries provides a leadership curriculum, to be taken over a period of four years. The author and consultant Ann McGee-Cooper teaches Advanced Servant-Leadership, while Steve Covey presents his "Seven Habits of Successful Managers." In order to strengthen and individualize career path development, TD considers introducing individual development plans (IDPs) for its people.

THE OAK ROOM COUNCIL

The Oak Room is a particular section of the TDIndustries lobby, with hundred of framed portraits of TD employees on the walls. Each partner who has been with the company for five years is honored with his or her photograph in the collection. At this moment, almost 400 portraits are displayed in the Oak Room.

However, there is more to the Oak Room than just portraits—it reminds people of an important instance in TD's history. In the late 1980s, when oil prices collapsed and the Dallas economy came to a standstill, construction projects quickly dried up. To counter the downturn, TD started to aggressively bid on out-of-state projects. While the company was able to win substantial contracts, the lack of experience with this type of business and significant cost overruns led to huge losses. By the end of 1989, TD had lost about 40% of its net worth.

At that point, Lowe Jr. called a meeting of the Oak Room Council, which included all employees who had their portrait hanging on the Oak Room's walls. TDIndustries's dire straits were discussed at length. To save the company, the Oak Room Council members agreed to the termination of their overfunded pension plan, which would return $1 million to TD's coffers. In addition, they decided to contribute $1.25 million, out of their retirement funds, in exchange for company stock. "It was a black year," said Sylvia Stephens, who has 20 years of service. "I voted yes, that was the easy part. The hard part was [to turn the company around]."

Looking back, this was a difficult moment for Lowe Jr. and his senior management team, but it turned into an amazing vote of confidence by TD's partners. The Oak Room Council continues to meet every other year to discuss major policy changes or decisions for TDIndustries's future. The council is still integrated by everyone whose portrait is up on the Oak Room walls.

Even before 1989, TDIndustries's ESOP was a major shareholder, controlling about 75% of the voting stock for many years. Today the employees own 100%. In other words, the partners—at least in theory—would have the power to replace Lowe Jr. as CEO and vote for a different board of directors. TDIndustries is totally owned by the ESOP—its shares are not publicly traded. However, the TD stock is valued by an outside appraiser on a regular basis and can be freely traded between employees. Traditionally, TDIndustries always stood ready to repurchase shares offered by partners, although back in 1989, the company did not have the funds for stock purchases for a while.

THE FUTURE OF TDINDUSTRIES'S CULTURE

In our conversations with partners, we asked whether or not the company's culture is bound to change, considering Lowe Jr.'s plans for significant out-of-state expansion and the concurrent arrival of new and different people. Partners felt that it would be important for the future to set examples for new employees and, in particular, help those farther away.

McNew summed it up: "With growth, everything is changing. But as long as you have good people, centered around a few core values, which in our case are Servant-Leadership, valuing diversity, and [embracing] honesty, it doesn't matter if you are 1,000 or 10,000 people—you will be the same company you were before." Stephens adds a note of caution: "[You have to] make sure that our people, our managers, are servant-leaders. And if they are not, they have to be held accountable. We talked about [Servant-Leadership] for so many years. It's as basic as it gets."

Do the partners participate in the important strategic decisions that are going to shape the company's future? Price answers: "[Again,] it goes back to Servant-Leadership. You trust your partners that they are doing their job. There is the strategic planning committee [integrated by senior executives] and you trust upper management to do their job." Adds Stephens: "It does not come down as tablets from the Mount. The people around Jack who help in developing the vision for the future are trusted and there is input from all over [the company]."

These are strong statements and the group around the table exudes confidence that TDIndustries will continue to be a "Great Place to Work" for its partners, where the sky is the limit. It's "we": In the words of Dodge, "we need to get it done, we'll have to figure out a solution and make it happen."

The Executive Perspective: Jack Lowe Jr.— Listening to TD's Partners

"What we have around here is a sense of community, of caring for each other. Someone's spouse or mother dies. You attend the funeral and two-thirds of our people are there. And nobody organizes it. We just go. It's beyond team, it's community!"

This is how Lowe Jr. describes TDIndustries's culture. He became CEO in 1980 when his father, Lowe Sr., the company's founder, died of a heart attack at age 67. Lowe Jr. very much embodies this culture: down to earth, straightforward, and a good listener. At the same time he's totally unassuming: He works out of an 8 ft. by 11 ft. cubicle, right in the middle of TDIndustries's general office.

"But there is something we added during the last 10 years," he continues. "It's performance excellence. We got a lot better in what we do. And people really like being good at what they do. We try to learn and grow and improve—that's what our Vision Statement says."

As discussed in this chapter, back in 1989, TDIndustries was in deep trouble. Talking about the memorable meeting of the Oak Room Council, Lowe Jr. recalled: "It was a significant emotional event. I was worried about the whole situation. Talking to my partners about it was hard [enough]. But [I worried more about] the dilemma we were in: The bank was broke, the debt holders wanted their money, the bonding company cut us off, many of my executives were panicking, and we were about to go out of business."

It was a harrowing experience for Lowe Jr. and he did what he could to save the company and, more importantly, people's investment. And still he had to lay off almost half of the employees, without being able to buy back any of their stock. "It bonded us together," he says. That's when the learning curve for performance excellence started.

"Effective leadership is not a simple matter of managing events and people," states the Robert K. Greenleaf Center for Servant-Leadership in one of its newsletters. "The leaders need skills like listening, collaboration, teamwork, and reflection." For several years, Lowe Jr. has been chairman of the board of trustees of the Greenleaf Center and helps spread the ideas on Servant-Leadership through participation in workshops and annual conferences.

The Greenleaf Center's mission is "to support those who, through the practice of Servant-Leadership, seek to create organizations in which individual stakeholders become healthier, wiser, freer, and more autonomous; and in so doing, build a better, more humane society which welcomes the full diversity of the human family." Servant-Leadership is about people's freedom and autonomy, about recognizing other people's unique and individual talents, and about a caring work environment.

Along these lines, Lowe Jr. has helped to establish a set of values at TDIndustries that everyone can agree with and support. "They were not written up by a consultant or by the executive group," he explains. "They came from these breakfast meetings that I had with the people all the time. [These values] have been evolving and may change from time to time. They are about trust and trusting relationships, about valuing people and about straightforwardness and honesty—that's really what we value."

Everyone is a "partner" at TDIndustries. "That came out of these conversations [as well]. At first, it was real hard to use, but a few years later everybody was using it. And they do in fact own the company. But my belief is that psychic ownership is ten times more powerful than economic ownership. [When they say] 'This is my company,' they are not talking about shares of stock."

How does Lowe Jr. envision keeping Servant-Leadership fresh and maintaining TDIndustries's culture? In effect, he has several excellent ideas. One important area is communications: "We are stepping up communications on our expectations [for Servant-Leadership]. If you don't feel like you can live up to this, you should probably find yourself another place to work." Another focus is learning and attaining excellence: "We have changed our whole curriculum of education. We are adding to it, it's different now." And finally, it's involving TDIndustries's partners even more: "It's important to have the people affected by a decision involved in making that very decision. I hope we do a pretty good job in listening."

Under Lowe Jr.'s persistent stewardship, there is little doubt that TDIndustries will continue to be one of America's "Great Places to Work." And with the concerted effort at leadership development and succession planning, there is little doubt that it will continue well after he's retired. (The interview with Jack Lowe Jr. took place on July 14, 1999.)

CHAPTER 2

U.S. Coast Guard: Culture Shift in Government

The U.S. Coast Guard established a new performance management system for its civilian personnel in the late 1990s, which is now in full operation. This new system of appraising both its Appropriated and Non-Appropriated Fund (NAF) civilian employees uses the acronym EARS for Excellence, Achievement, and Recognition System. It applies to the approximately 6,000 General Schedule (GS/GM) and Wage Grade (WG) civilian employees covered by these pay systems and the approximately 1,500 NAF employees whose salaries are paid from the Coast Guard business lines (that is, its exchanges, service clubs, etc.) located at Coast Guard facilities. Evaluated a year later, survey respondents were cautiously optimistic, giving EARS a neutral rating of 3.3 (out of 5) in overall satisfaction, which suggests they are taking a "wait and see" attitude but are willing to "give it a chance to achieve the intended goals." The experts who conducted the survey see this overall satisfaction rating as positive, given that major system changes, in their experience, generally produce much lower satisfaction ratings and far less receptivity in the first year.

When an organization changes its system of measuring a person's performance, which can affect his or her pay, you are talking about a potential "red alert" change. The most interesting phenomenon about the process being examined here is how the agency went about successfully dealing with possible employee reservation, resistance, and apathy.

BACKGROUND

Important as the new system is, the greatest impact on the Coast Guard culture may yet be on *how* the project was carried out. The typical line and staff "expert culture" response to such an important human resources need, in the past, would have been to convene a group of highly trained and experienced "personnelists," with perhaps some similarly trained consultants. They would have interviewed the organization's executives as to their needs and wishes and then retreated into isolation in their "ivory tower" to design a "perfectly rational" system. Often in such cases when their product "hits the street," many, if not most, employees and first-line supervisors would see it as another management fad and imposition and treat it with indifferent compliance, annoyance, or resistance.

However, the Coast Guard's experience in this case disproves the notion that people *naturally* resist change. People resist change that is too sudden, too intense, or likely to last too long, that is, too stressful. They particularly resist change that seems to have little or no perceived relationship or benefit to themselves. By contrast the Coast Guard designed a decision-making strategy that increasingly will serve as a successful model for achieving change in other government agencies at the local, state, and federal levels. From its earliest planning efforts, Coast Guard personnel strove to minimize anxiety, maximize openness, and build user understanding and support every step of the way.

An organization as large as the U.S. Coast Guard (between 35,000 and 40,000 active duty military and civilian personnel) with varied missions, a vast geographic spread, a civilian and military workforce mix, and an often-intense relationship with the public, the transportation industry, and other federal departments and agencies cannot be characterized by any limited category of organizational culture. In a very real sense, the Coast Guard has many traditions, practices, beliefs and commitments. Yet the Service continues to adapt its culture to encompass its ever-changing missions while achieving high levels of personal motivation and performance.

Changes in national policies governing personnel management, the national call for results-based performance, and the Department of Transportation's emphasis on recognizing and rewarding results, promoting more effective communication and performance feedback, and linking individual performance to organizational outcomes were the key factors prompting the Coast Guard to overhaul its civilian performance management system. To quote a Coast Guard source, "Over the years, many Coast Guard employees and supervisors have expressed dissatisfaction with the [then] current appraisal system. The [then] current program does little to foster communication between supervisors and employees, and does not hold supervisors accountable for effectively managing performance." The EARS system was created to overcome these deficiencies.

The Coast Guard approach was based on a well-executed study of organizational human resources "best practices," customer input, and teamwork. Admiral James M. Loy, the Coast Guard commandant (1998–2002) whose leadership opened the door for a program like EARS when he headed the then Office of Personnel and Training, has stressed that "Preparation Equals Performance." In that phrase, he embodied his belief that the Service had to reorient its performance management systems to be "Semper Paratus, Always Ready."

DEFINING THE PROBLEM AND DEVELOPING AN ANSWER

The key players who authorized and guided this effort created four teams:

- a design team
- an events-planning team
- a marketing and implementation team
- a rewards and recognition team

EARS emphasizes enhanced two-way communication between supervisors/managers and their employees; establishes accountability and joint ownership of performance goals and outcomes; provides meaningful recognition and rewards; and fosters a learning environment that develops and motivates employees.

The process used to develop the new policy was unique and, as Nancy Raum, the former office chief and proactive leader and major promoter of EARS, described it, "a new way of doing business" for the Coast Guard. A customer-based design team was used to lay the groundwork for EARS, led by Bonnie Garin, a 30-year veteran with the federal government and over 8 years with the Coast Guard (Bonnie has since moved on to NASA).

Bonnie and the division chief, Norma Bullock, conceived of the plan to make a difference and invite nontechnical customers to join the team, rather than develop EARS with only personnel experts. Bonnie was willing to listen and her basic question was: "What kind of policy would you as customers design, given all opportunities?" She was looking for different strategic options, not for the technical details of the design. "We had an excellent consultant," Bonnie told us, "who helped us to stay open minded and move away from our prior closed way of thinking."

One of Garin's customers on the team, Sheryl Smalls, an administrative assistant at the Finance Center in Chesapeake, Virginia, with more than 11 years with the Coast Guard, said: "It was very interesting to participate and develop a fairer [civilian performance management] system for the Coast Guard. I was excited to be part of the Design Team." And Lynn Heirakuji, who has worked with different government agencies, transferred to the Department of Housing and Urban Development, and has since returned to the Coast Guard as chief of the Workforce Relations Division, added: "I have never seen such a customer outreach effort in government. Not only was the design done with the help of customers but also the implementation. From beginning to end it was a broad-based effort."

"The Coast Guard was not accustomed to doing that," comments Garin. "New systems were expected to be handed down by edict. And EARS created a lot of fear, both at the supervisory and employee levels. Flexibility always brings about fear. But we undertook marketing at every step of the way, and our major advantage was that it was a customer-designed program."

In a similar fashion, the buy-in from the top echelon of the Coast Guard was crucial to the success of the project. Beverly Johnson, who had almost 25 years with the Coast Guard and, at the time, was chief of the NAF Personnel Division, gave some primary reasons: "Not only was the buy-in important for conceptual questions, but we also needed funding to pay for travel to off-site meetings, to hire a consultant, and to invite focus groups for better customer input."

At the overall leadership level, a guidance team of 12 organizational leaders was established to steer the EARS effort. It included a flag officer, a then chief financial officer—a Senior Executive Service (SES) member—and several mostly civilian high-level managers. Garin was pleased with the guidance team: "They were our champions at the top who helped market the program to the commandant and his leadership team."

DESIGNING THE NEW SYSTEM

EARS was truly designed with a customer-focus orientation. Of the 10 design team members, 4 were "personnelists" who provided insight and experience for understanding the goals and needs of the system. The other 6 members were future customers. All represented a microcosm of the Coast Guard organization: They included employees, supervisors, and managers; people from the field and from headquarters; and employees from different occupations, grades, and pay plans. "They started out as individualistic thinkers," recalls Garin, "but a team spirit evolved with more feedback from the field." And Smalls makes an important point: "My coworkers wanted a system where they would have some input. It's their career; it's important to them."

After the initial meetings of the design team, it became clear that more customer input was needed to add to the framework of ideas. "We were insecure about only 10 people designing such an important new system," explains Garin. Focus groups seemed to be the best way to discuss the proposals with a broader audience.

Therefore, a total of seven focus groups, one at the Washington, D.C., headquarters and six at Coast Guard field locations, were brought together to capture the input of over 300 civilian and military employees and supervisors. The groups represented a cross section of occupations, grade levels, pay plans, and work experiences and participated in four-hour sessions to discuss and help improve the design. To have both civilian and military employees and supervisors around the table was a significant success factor. It allowed the different components of the Coast Guard family to compare their needs and to model the new system to the reality of their workplace and workday.

"The design team rarely voted on certain proposals. They would rather try to convince each other," Garin made clear. "It was important that we determine the best and most balanced system for the people. And we felt we should be able to reach consensus on critical features." Part of the success of the design team was in the ability to leave sensitive issues in the legal or technical areas to the specialists. In addition, after approval of the concept and framework of the new system, implementation was to be handed over to a different team with experts looking at all the ramifications. But, at that point, the design was firm and no further change was to be expected.

Common themes emerged from customer feedback:

- *Appraisals*—There was agreement that the previous system was too time consuming and bureaucratic and that supervisors were not held accountable for managing it effectively. There was also an expressed need for a simplified, flexible, and fair system that makes supervisors responsible for effective performance management.

- *Setting goals*—Customers felt that goals provide clarity and direction, improve operations, encourage employee buy-in, and should be linked to the job and customer needs.

- *Communication and feedback*—It was stressed that feedback on performance should be job specific, continuous, timely, and documented. Effective communication between supervisor and employee was often identified as a critical factor of improved performance management.

- *Employee development*—Surveyed employees expressed concern that training and employee developmental programs were inadequately funded and there should be more emphasis on Individual Development Plans (IDPs). They identified a strong need for:
  - cross training
  - job-specific training
  - updating skills
  - mentoring
  - career growth opportunities (not necessarily linked to an employee's current position)

Division Chief Norma Bullock, who has program responsibility for civilian performance management with more than 37 years of federal service (nearly 19 with the Coast Guard), described several ways to get the team members involved to accept the proposed changes: "In the design process, the Coast Guard also used information-age communications techniques beforehand that go beyond simple teamwork, such as 'seeking consensus,' and 'Storming and Norming,' to condition participants for building successful group processes and getting them at least to the point where team members could sincerely say, 'I can live with this,' and then move forward in their deliberations." Mutually setting ground rules in advance also helped enhance team cohesion and sharpened the focus on the tasks and overall goals of EARS.

EVENTS PLANNING

A critical but seldom heralded effort—how to get the workforce oriented toward EARS and obtain its buy-in—was quietly worked out by an events planning team, which was responsible for planning the EARS orientation blitz. This meant coming up with a training approach suitable for civilian and military supervisors and employees at sites throughout the Coast Guard—from the large units to a few scattered people in local offices. The team reflected the many diverse characteristics within the workforce itself, including geographic dispersion. Team members sought to determine, from a customer's perspective, what would be needed to familiarize them with the new system.

MARKETING AND IMPLEMENTATION

Marketing EARS began virtually at its inception, though selling the new system may not have been a conscious effort at that early point. As with other military services, many officers and enlisted and civilian personnel of the Coast Guard have been molded to operate in a command-and-control cultural environment. The hallmark of that environment often tends to be secrecy, which generates spurious rumors, distrust, and misinformation. This tends to seriously compromise acceptance of any change. However, the use of decision-making teams and the intentional seeking out of advice, information, and ideas from other than direct-reporting personnel and supervisors represented a great change in organizational openness.

Employee inclusion was a key component of the EARS marketing plan. Throughout the process, leaders, managers, supervisors, and employees were kept informed of developments and results, as well as invited to submit questions about the evolving system as change was occurring. This was accomplished through a monthly newsletter, where, for example, employee questions were answered openly, key events publicized, benchmarks noted, training sessions announced, and project developments and participant concerns addressed.

The *EARS Newsletter* was published in hard copy but was also made available on the Coast Guard Civilian Personnel Home Page, which is available desk to desk for a great majority of civilian and military personnel. Each announcement listed a point of contact, by phone or E-mail, and where to forward new questions about EARS.

The use of customer-based focus groups to bring together diverse groups of managers, supervisors, and employees representing a variety of occupations, grade levels, pay plans, and work experiences at each location probably produced ambivalence at first but later resulted in a very positive reaction. Going out to include in the study people such as a union steward and a union member on the design team and employees in focus groups who might be inclined toward adversarial confrontation represented a significant cultural change and sent a clear message that this time something was different.

A surprising summary of the EARS process comes again from Bullock: "The centerpiece of the EARS design is communication. The goal is more frequent dialogue between supervisors and employees. And the supervisors need better communication skills—that's a missing ingredient that needs to be built. It's a difficult task in an organization more accustomed to hierarchy and command and control." The details of the EARS approach to create and embed this new system in the organization can be considered a model for bringing about cultural evolution and change in other key areas of the Coast Guard operations, demonstrating an economical and efficient way to alter organizational paradigms and adapt to shifting organizational needs.

Training in the use of the new system was initially provided to employees and supervisors at the Coast Guard sites visited during the design phase. These began in 1998 and continued throughout the Coast Guard for supervisors and employees. By the end of the training phase, over 3,000 people were trained extensively in how to use the new system effectively. As supervisors develop their skills and confront the new communication challenges presented by EARS, they will begin laying a foundation for a more powerful, adaptable, and inclusive place to work.

All in all, the EARS process was unique and, because of its success, may become a model for other agencies. Heirakuji confirms this: "I have had to explain the process a lot. But [every agency's] culture has to be willing to adopt a similar process. It has to be consistent with its [own] critical values."

As somewhat of a surprise, the process of developing EARS brought forth a new partnership between management and two key Coast Guard unions. Gary Harris, a 25-year veteran of the Coast Guard and then steward for one of the five labor unions at the Coast Guard Yard in Baltimore, Maryland, felt it was an excellent experience to have participated on the design team. "The union has to play a different role today," he says. "We have to get away from the old days of threats."

REWARDS AND RECOGNITION

The participants surveyed pointed out that cash awards have lost much of their intended significance due to the low dollar amounts. They asked to be given a choice between cash awards, time off, or learning opportunities as optional forms of recognition. They also noted that nonmonetary recognition is meaningful and should be used more often. A "toolbox" of alternative awards was developed for supervisory use.

The fact that the design team was awarded the Commandant's Superior Achievement Award (Bronze Medal)—the highest civilian award in the Coast Guard (presented to the team personally by the commandant)—for their work showed high-level support of the project. This marked the first time such recognition had been accorded an entire team rather than an individual and sent a message of strong support for the Service's more democratic approach to developing and implementing new policies and procedures.

An unexpected consequence of this effort was that a delegation of government officials from the newly independent nation of Slovenia (formerly part of the Yugoslav Republic) visited Coast Guard Headquarters and asked to be briefed on the EARS system. Although the Coast Guard is helping Slovenia to develop their own coastal service, this particular session emphasized the need these Eastern European nations have for building a new and more motivating culture in their governmental organizations.

In summary, EARS is bound to significantly advance a shift in the Coast Guard's culture. A system that is recognized as less cumbersome, fairer, and more directly related to achieving the organization's mission—so that each person can more clearly perceive the value of his or her contributions—is certain to improve the personal motivation and the morale of most employees. The bottom line is greater productivity and better service delivery.

In most government agencies, the twentieth century saw a gradual shift—as with society—from punishment to rewards. This century may see a shift from rewards to intrinsic motivation!

Exhibit 2.1.
Key Features of the New Appraisal Program

Previous Program	*New Program*
5 rating levels	3 rating levels
Critical job elements (CJEs)	Core competencies (CCs)
Not predetermined, weighted	Predetermined, not weighted
Not all critical	All critical
Narrative summary for each CJE	One overall narrative summary
Employees may provide comments concerning the rating	Employees are encouraged to list accomplishments on appraisal form
One feedback session	Two feedback sessions
Covers GS, GM, WG	Covers GS, GM, WG
2–3 approval levels	2 approval levels
Linked to awards	Linked to awards

Items listed below the dotted line did not change from the previous system.

Exhibit 2.2.
Core Competencies

The former performance management system was based on using critical job elements (CJEs), which were specific and individually tailored to each job. EARS uses core competencies (CCs) that link individual performance with organizational goals. There are a total of nine CCs and employees are rated on a minimum of four (with no maximum number of CCs).

Nine Core Competencies in the New System

- Applied Job Knowledge & Skills (mandatory for all)
- Supervisory Leadership (mandatory for supervisors)
- Customer Service
- Communication
- Teamwork
- Quality of Work
- Timeliness & Quantity of Work
- Funds Management
- Safety

Exhibit 2.2.
(Continued)

Each CC has generic performance standards that provide specific examples of performance at the "Meets" level. Employee performance is measured against these generic standards.

All CCs for a given position are critical and equally weighted, meaning that failure to meet any one will result in an overall rating of "Fails to meet." In addition, the streamlined process means that supervisors provide an *overall* narrative summary rather than a narrative summary for each CJE, as previously called for.

Exhibit 2.3.
A Short History of the U.S. Coast Guard

At its birth, the United States was essentially a coastal nation. This new republic's first Congress established a protective tariff to produce operating income for its use. Alexander Hamilton, the first secretary of the treasury, requested 10 cutters "properly manned and armed" to enforce the tariff. On August 4, 1790, Congress authorized acquisition of these vessels for a service that came to be named the Revenue Cutter Service.

Hamilton insisted that officers of these vessels be given military rank. During hostilities with France from 1798–1800 and the War of 1812 with England, these cutters were operated with the navy. In 1831 the secretary of the treasury, recognizing the cutters' ability to perform rescue work, ordered them to cruise during the winter months to look out for vessels in distress. During the 1800s cutters began to enforce navigation laws and those against piracy, wrecking and plundering ships, and, eventually, the slave trade.

The origins of the Lifesaving Service date from 1844, and by 1854 there were 137 Lifeboat stations along the coast. In 1878 Congress created the United States Lifesaving Service, which worked closely with the then Revenue Cutter Service. The United States Coast Guard was established by an act of Congress on January 30, 1915. In 1939 the Bureau of Lighthouses, also an early American agency, was transferred from the Department of Commerce to the U.S. Coast Guard.

During all U.S. wars since the founding of the nation, the Coast Guard in one form or another has assumed a military role and has also been a key player in the interdiction of contraband in such periods as prohibition and the war on drugs. In 1967, the Coast Guard was transferred to the U.S. Department of Transportation.

Exhibit 2.4.
The Coast Guard's Missions

Today, the Coast Guard's missions fall into 13 categories: Aids to Navigation, Boating Safety, Defense Operations, Environmental Response, Homeland Security, Ice Operations, Maritime Law Enforcement, Marine Inspection, Marine Licensing, Marine Science, Port Safety and Security, Search and Rescue, and Waterways Management.

The Coast Guard's Homeland Security mission has become more prominent following the terrorists' acts of September 11, 2001.

In peacetime the Coast Guard operates under the Department of Transportation. In times of war, or when the president so directs, it is under the Department of the Navy.

The Executive Perspective: Admiral (ADM) James M. Loy— Leading Cultural Change

Considering that the U.S. Coast Guard is part of the country's five military services, its commandant, ADM James M. Loy, would seem to have quite an unusual background. "I spent half of my career at sea driving ships," he told us. "But when not at sea, I was in the personnel business—as an assignment officer, in policy development, teaching at the Coast Guard Academy, and finally as chief of the Office of Personnel. It was part of my upbringing before I made flag."

We talked about the EARS process and how it came about. "At the time, it was fortunate that several change dynamics occurred simultaneously," explained ADM Loy. One of those dynamics he was referring to was the quality management flurry of the early 1990s that had taken hold strongly in the Coast Guard. "[One of its principles]," continued ADM Loy, "was listening as carefully as possible to our customers."

Secondly, during 1995 and 1996, the Coast Guard conducted a workforce cultural audit. It was a controversial project at the time, but "I pushed very hard for the value of what we would learn from that experience and I got the support to do it," said ADM Loy. The result of the audit was that three fundamental areas of the Coast Guard work environment required improvement, namely

- communication in both directions—top-down and bottom-up,
- diversity management, and
- career development.

"This was a very intensive eight to nine months' effort," continued ADM Loy. "As we listened to our workforce, these three things jumped out."

Thirdly, at that same time, the federal government had begun to promote results-based performance and several congressional mandates were focused towards rewarding agencies pursuing these goals. "It was a license to do something creative," reflected ADM Loy. "It was an opportune time for EARS: Listening to our workforce about performance, evaluating performance and the recognition that was an appropriate part of it. The fact that we comprised [sic] the study team from the troops as well as from the top was absolutely the right thing."

When asked whether careers in government differ from those in private industry and about loyalty and workplace uncertainty that affect today's corporate culture, ADM Loy replied: "It's the same generation of people— X, Y, or whatever label you want to give it. We have gathered into government service our share of that generation. It really comes down to whether or not the owner of the operation—government or private—is consciously concerned about the work environment, mission, goals, and objectives and markets those to the employees. You have the same responsibility in government as in the private sector, to the degree that you are able to create a work environment that honors diversity, lets its mission and operation be first-class, and allows every member of that workforce to reach his or her potential."

Shortly after ADM Loy started his "watch" in May 1998 as Commandant of the United States Coast Guard, he issued the *Commandant's Direction*, which was mailed to the home of every single Coast Guard person. It outlined his plans, goals, and objectives for the Coast Guard to be accomplished during his tenure. By choosing this method of distribution, ADM Loy addressed one of the concerns expressed in the workforce cultural audit—communications. "I was trying to listen to what I had been told by the workforce. It was an effort to tell everybody . . . and give them feedback."

Among the Coast Guard's longer-term programs is "Workforce 2015," which is a Coast Guard initiative to promote greater diversity throughout its ranks. "We need to help the majorities in our workforce understand the two fundamental principles of why we should be focusing on this as an organization," reflected ADM Loy. The first he calls the "simple moral foundation" of the diversity effort. The second is the dependence of the Coast Guard's performance on the attainment of a diverse, representative workforce requiring a concerted organizational outreach to recruit and retain minorities.

One of the central tenets of the 1998 *Commandant's Direction* was teamwork. ADM Loy wrote: "We understand that teamwork is essential to success both inside and outside our service." As we talked to him, this focus became even more pointed. "Small team dynamics is a great strength of this organization because that's the way we do business." With this, ADM Loy referred not only to the Coast Guard's operational teamwork but went much beyond. "It's the notion of how we breed team play with other agencies, among the other services, and with the international missions that we are required to accomplish." Another example is the regional emergency response teams who operate successfully under the leadership of the Coast Guard captain of the port. They are amazingly successful. Why? "Teamwork is an absolutely essential parameter of what we do for a living," was ADM Loy's response.

Returning to the EARS process, ADM Loy again warmed up to the topic: "As a classic team to bring together that effort, I wanted those people who would be most impacted by the product they were building." As we know, in the end he awarded the Commandant's Superior Achievement Award (Bronze Medal) to the design team. His explanation was telling: "To have allowed them to work so hard to build something we are very proud of, and then fail to recognize them, would have been against the principles we had asked them to develop."

ADM Loy ended his tenure as Coast Guard commandant in May 2002, but there is little doubt that his legacy will last, not only in starting to prepare the organization for the challenges of future decades but as a model for other government agencies and services. Admiral Loy now heads the Transportation Security Administration in the newly created Department of Homeland Security. (The interview with Admiral Loy took place on July 30, 2001.)

CHAPTER 3

Having Fun at Work?—AES Corporation

"AES desires that people employed by the company and those people with whom the company interacts have fun in their work. AES's goal has been to create and maintain an environment in which each person can flourish in the use of his or her gifts and skills and thereby enjoy the time spent at AES." This factual and rather dry statement from the company's annual 10-K report to the Securities and Exchange Commission (SEC) casts a powerful spotlight on one of the principles and values of its culture.

Explains Chairman Roger Sant: "The word 'fun' can be misleading. We are not talking about having parties all the time. That's not why AES is fun. It's fun because the people who work here are fully engaged. They have total responsibility for decisions. They are accountable for results."

As we got to know AES Corporation and its people, it became clear that "fun" is not about Friday beer busts or employee appreciation parties. Letting people have fun at work really means recognizing them as human beings with all their dreams and aspirations. AES tries to fulfill the most basic needs of their people: to be treated as mature and responsible adults; to be able to use their creative abilities and talents; and to have the opportunity to fully live out their own personal values.

A 1998 *Forbes* article on the company rightfully asked the question of whether "AES was a business or a religion." It is awesome how the principle of "having fun at work," combined with three other core values of fairness, integrity, and social responsibility, has set in motion a world of excitement, motivation, and joy, with people trying to make a difference.

Hard to believe? Let's take a closer look at the company and its history since it was founded in 1981.

AES'S JOURNEY TO SUCCESS

Back in the 1970s, Roger Sant and Dennis Bakke met in Washington, D.C., and jointly headed energy conservation efforts in the Ford administration during the days of the energy crisis. Soon they convinced themselves that a better way to solve energy shortages would be to produce energy more efficiently and in a competitive environment. In 1981, they took the initiative to found AES Corporation as a private power company.

Starting with those years, there began an ever-increasing trend away from government-owned and -regulated market structures. Both in the United States and abroad power plants started being privatized. AES became very successful in establishing itself as a nongovernment energy producer, participating in the bidding on deregulated facilities. As of today, AES has grown into the world's largest independent power company, with nearly 200 plants spread around the globe.

AES Corporation went public in 1991, after 10 years of being in business. At that time, the company had just under a dozen generating plants, all of them in the United States. Business exploded thereafter, with AES expanding into Central and South America and into the countries of the former Soviet Union, as well as into Europe, Pakistan, and China.

AES sees its mission as "Serving the World's Needs for Electricity." This ties into one of AES's principles—social responsibility. The company pledges to be involved in projects that provide certain social benefits: lower energy costs, safe and reliable power generation, or a cleaner environment. But AES may aim yet higher: In Pakistan the company has helped build schools in the plant's neighborhood, where the adult literacy rate is below 40%!

The AES values of fairness—treating fairly its people, customers, suppliers, stockholders, communities, and government authorities—and of integrity—acting consistently and truthfully and honoring commitments made—are unequivocal, although not always easy to follow in AES's global setting. More difficult to interpret is fun, in particular in third world countries where AES's presence is significant. Having the freedom to act and to make decisions goes counter to the tradition of the all-powerful "patron" in Latin America. In similar fashion, employees from the countries of the former Soviet Union look at changes in the inherited power and hierarchy structures with considerable distrust. In many of the developing countries of the world, the concepts of learning, of personal growth, and of ever-increasing challenges strengthening one's abilities is totally new and unaccustomed. Making mistakes is not considered part of a healthy learning process, but may lead to losing one's job.

Part of the "fun" for AES people is the fact that leaders give advice rather than make decisions. Again, that's not easy to uphold in AES's global presence. In the 1997 AES Annual Report, Roger Sant and Dennis Bakke emphasize, "Probably the biggest single problem in both new and existing AES enterprises is overcoming the natural desire of our leaders to make decisions and control others." Giving up conventional "management" goes against the established traditions of both industrial Europe and developing Latin America. However, it's crucial to making AES a "fun" workplace.

Fairness, integrity, fun, and *social responsibility*—what a compelling foundation of shared principles! "We are building this company," stresses Dennis Bakke, "on the assumption that every person, no matter what his or her culture, color, faith, nationality, or gender, is capable of thinking and making decisions; is responsible and accountable for results; is fallible, unique, and wants to be part of a cause that makes a difference in the world." Visiting certain of the AES facilities, speaking to the people, and witnessing how these values guide their professional and personal lives was for both of us a truly exhilarating experience that we would like to share with our readers over the next few pages.

AES THAMES IN EASTERN CONNECTICUT

It's a pretty spot on the banks of the Thames River, about five miles north of New London, Connecticut. While those names sound very global and European, it's a typical New England neighborhood. In the New London area was a major submarine base, which provided a good labor pool, as the shipbuilding industry was in decline.

The AES Thames plant was built in 1988 as a "greenfield" facility. AES Corporation was still small and privately held at that time. AES Thames was the third power plant AES had built and was very successful from the outset. But, more importantly, the plant became somewhat of a legend within the corporation because it turned into a model for the AES values in action. The people hired for the facility, in time, became true ambassadors for the AES principles and in particular for fun.

George Gurnee, who leads the materials handling team and joined AES Thames during the construction phase, reminisces: "At first, I didn't know what to think [about fun]. But now 'fun' to the majority of the people here means being involved, feeling accomplished, enjoying coming to work and the people you work with, and having a sense of fulfillment." Joe Oddo, a maintenance technician who came to AES from submarine builder Electric Boat in 1992, adds: "[Coming here] opened up my ability to do what I wanted to do. It makes it a more 'fun' place to work."

AES Thames helped spread the company's values deep into the AES organization—in a very literal sense: Over the years after 1988, many of the original AES Thames workers moved to other AES facilities to explore opportunities for personal growth and the experience of a new challenge. As a matter of fact, of the first 24 people hired when AES Thames opened at the end of 1988, today two are vice presidents and group managers, eight are plant managers, and seven are team leaders, mostly at other locations. It's a point of pride for AES Thames that its people have moved to AES plants around the world!

In this way, AES Thames also represents the global character of the company. We felt it was a rather revolutionary concept to have people transferred abroad instead of across the street, but Bob Gardner, a senior maintenance technician, disagreed: "At AES you are not transferred [by the company]. You have the opportunity to take on a different responsibility and to learn something new. It's your choice." Adds Bob Price, plant manager of AES Thames: "AES Thames has alumni all over the world. Being a growing global company provides many leadership opportunities."

The Thames facility got a firsthand experience of the closeness and camaraderie of the AES organization prior to a plant power outage in 1999, when it posted on the company E-mail a request for volunteers to help supervise the work of contractors in this first major overhaul of the facility. "We had a great time," commented Don Chagnon, who is a plant operator. "Many different folks from other plants came to help. It was a good learning experience for all of us." Similar volunteer opportunities for everyone are quite common throughout the AES organization. Again, it's each individual's choice, but the decision will have to consider the needs of one's team!

Bob Price found a good analogy to summarize AES's practices: "AES is good at letting you drive down the road by yourself, but pointing out to you the ditches left and right. You don't worry about optimum efficiency for every single decision and every step of the operation. Even the guys that have been here longer have learned to step back and let the new person experience the fun of decision making. You keep them out of trouble, you don't let them get hurt, but you don't take the fun away!"

AES CAYUGA IN UPSTATE NEW YORK

The second AES facility we visited—in a beautiful setting right on the shore of Lake Cayuga, one of the "finger lakes"—told us the AES story from a different angle. AES Cayuga was acquired from New York State Electric & Gas (NYSEG), a public utility, in May 1999. When we visited at the end of 2000, it was still in transition from its NYSEG past toward the AES culture. From NYSEG times the plant was unionized, which added to the problems as many of the older employees were deeply rooted in the union. While the operation certainly needs more time to adapt to the AES culture, it was interesting to listen to people's comments as they started appreciating the new AES values.

AES Cayuga employs 87 people. In operations, 30 of them work in three 8-hour shifts, while in other areas AES has started to offer 12-hour shifts, which many people like. Ron Jackson started with NYSEG in 1990 as a "laborer" who mostly did the menial jobs, like dumping the garbage cans. He continues in operations: "AES doesn't really like the term 'laborer.' They want people to take it upon themselves: If something needs painting, go ahead and do it. On the other hand, people don't want to step back. They started in operations at the bottom job and worked hard to make it to the top as control operator. For them, to do certain jobs means stepping back."

This comment illustrates some of the problems of the adaptation process. However, "AES is doing a good job trying to get people exposed," says Jerry Goodenough, who is team leader in the control room. "Darryl went to Thames, Marty went to Hawaii. Once you get out and see how AES really works, it answers a lot of questions." Interjects Marty Hilliard, who also joined NYSEG as a laborer in 1990: "Here, team leaders dress nicely and walk around. They don't get in the stuff. In Hawaii, the team leader for operations was working inside of a boiler, pulling boards off, covered with dirt." "Under the old NYSEG mindset," adds Ron Jackson, "[that would mean] he is doing my job and taking away my overtime. Now it's different: You pitch in to get the job done."

Dan Hill, a 22-year veteran of NYSEG and a supervisor at Cayuga for the last 15 years, made a very telling remark on the difference in the decision-making process before and after the AES acquisition: "In the old days, the core group of supervisors would get together, come up with your policies, procedures, or plans, and force it down the throats of the plant people. That didn't work all that well. Now you have a committee, a team that comes up with an idea how to fix a problem. It takes a lot longer, but it's a nice process. Once you take off with a decision, you have much more support. It's their idea."

Darryl Schirrmacher, an electrician with 16 years with NYSEG and the union steward for the plant, addressed some of the difficulties of the transition: "The union has been trying to be a strong part of this. It has principles and values of its own and I can't see why they cannot be blended together. The problem is that some people want to hold really tight to the structured union contract and that's where the conflict arises." Jerry Goodenough adds: "The AES concept is businesses to be run individually and the individuals in the business to be businesspeople. As far as the union goes, there are good chances for a marriage with the union contract. The problem is just the mindset. Things will have to be worked out."

In general, there was enthusiastic support for AES values and culture. Bob Morey, a power plant technician with 14 years at the Cayuga plant, talked about fun: "At first, I didn't know what it meant. What I understand now and what I experienced is that 'fun' is the chance to make your decisions. Now *you* get to select the contractors and vendors you want. And there is nobody above you pointing and saying 'you are going to do it this way'." And Jeff Kopp, a 20-year NYSEG veteran who started as janitor and is now the leader for environmental issues, jumps in: "So far, I have enjoyed the AES experience. For me 'fun' is being allowed to grow yourself and to be creative, whereas before you were held in one spot."

Herb Beckwith, who started with NYSEG 27 years ago as a laborer and worked his way up to supervisor, was happy with the AES culture because he had practiced it before. "As shift supervisor I had my own crew and had a lot of faith in them. When we had a problem with a piece of equipment, I would get them together and ask what we ought to do. And I stood by the decision the crew came up with but was criticized by NYSEG for running a crew like this. [I just thought] the person close to the equipment should know better what to do. When you get into AES, that's the culture, that's what they want you to do. To me it works so much better!"

These comments by the participants in our round table discussions show the difficulties of moving from the environment of a unionized public utility to the AES culture of personal involvement and people orientation. "It is always the same in these transitions," cautions Mark Adams, AES Cayuga's new plant manager who transferred from AES's Shady Point facility in Oklahoma. "Some people are strong, step out, and become the natural leaders. Others are not as strong but have great ownership in the work they do. And some will just go along and be followers."

We talked about management at AES, which is more like leadership, devoid of direct influence and power. "AES doesn't have the old-style 'dictatorship' management," says Adams. "Our leadership style is more of being a resource, giving advice, helping people to see the pros and cons. But they have to go and make that decision. It requires a lot of education. We have courses going on for people to understand the budget process and the financial pro forma that drives the plant. It helps people to get involved and make good business decisions."

Adams has been with AES eight years and the company has changed enormously during that time. Much of AES's new capacity is located in faraway places like Pakistan, India, China, and Kazakhstan. How does he feel about this development? His response is unequivocal and positive: "If you truly believe in what AES is about from a cultural viewpoint, it's good because we have been able to go into other countries, not only to supply electricity but to provide jobs and facilitate a different way of living in terms of a work environment. People who lived under old dictatorships now have the freedom to make their own decisions and run their plants. [Investing in the international arena] has brought in a whole enrichment of our culture, which otherwise we would have never had."

This strong endorsement of AES's international expansion mirrored our discussions with the people we interviewed. AES's facilities abroad were seen as an opening to new challenges and also as a stabilizing influence on the business. Adams agreed: "The longer we own this plant, the more people will step out and take advantage of the opportunities. We are fortunate that a lot of people got into the international world and really took it on as a challenge. There were always people volunteering to go teach the AES culture and help AES businesses to grow."

There was much similarity in our impressions of AES Thames and of its "alumni organization" around the world. Being global seemed to be an important trait of the AES character. It made us curious to travel abroad and observe AES's culture and values in a non-U.S. setting.

AES MERIDA III IN MEXICO

AES Merida III is a greenfield facility, built right on the outskirts of the historic colonial town Merida, the capital of Mexico's Yucatan province. The Mexican government started the process of energy deregulation in 1997 when AES in a public tender won the right to build the plant. However, at this point all of Merida III's electricity goes to the Federal Energy Commission (FEC). Still, deregulation seems to be an important political issue, as former Mexican president Ernesto Zedillo made it a point to attend the inauguration of the facility in early June 2000.

AES Merida III has a work crew of 36 people, mostly Mexicans with a few AES expatriates from Hawaii and Argentina mixed in to help the start-up. Plant manager Ruben Soroeta has eight years of experience with AES. He is an Argentinean who had worked in the San Nicolas, Argentina, plant prior to its acquisition by AES, then transferred to the UK (AES Medway) as a participant in an experiment to live the AES values in a place different from Argentina. From there he moved to the Dominican Republic and now heads the new Mexican venture. "It's part of the AES culture to be open to accept new challenges," says Soroeta. "One important feature of this culture is that it gives you freedom—freedom to work and to assume responsibilities."

Many of the people hired by AES Merida III came directly from a university. Working for the plant became their first serious job. Others had experience in private industry and a few even held jobs with the FEC. Experience or not—they all were surprised with the degree of autonomy they started enjoying at AES.

Graciela Loya de la Cruz joined AES Merida III during the construction phase in 1998. A chemical engineer by training, she is in charge of the permit area. She still marvels about her ability to make decisions. "Even in private industry," she says, "there are limitations of authority. You can't make the decisions you would like, because somebody else is there to control them." Miguel Rocha Barranon, who has six months with AES Merida III and worked before in maintenance of a mining firm, adds: "It took some effort to adapt to the new system where I am the one who makes the decision. But it's motivating because one has to get ready for it." Still, autonomy takes time to be introduced: In Mexico's "patron" work culture "the problem with assuming responsibility is 'if something bad happens, I lose my job'," explains Soroeta. "As it is not easy to find jobs, people are afraid."

People enjoy the new culture and appreciate the company's values. "It's difficult to believe that you can establish these principles in Mexico," marvels Miguel Rocha. But Lorenzo Noh Tun, who joined AES Merida III during the construction phase in early 1999 and worked before as a mechanic with a large Mexican firm, ventures much beyond: "[The AES] values have become part of our lives. We not only live them at work but try to apply them at home to our family and friends."

We mentioned earlier that some AES expatriates came to Merida to help in the start-up and to explain the company's values. Robert Shampoe, who joined AES in 1990 after a long career in the navy, transferred from Hawaii, where he worked in operations. "He joined us to help organize the plant prior to start-up," says Soroeta. "He came for the fun of it. He is very talented in teaching people and is well respected by the group." Andres Edgardo Arbizu worked at the San Nicolas plant in Argentina, which was acquired by AES in 1993. At AES Merida III he leads the control room, but mostly he walks through the facility to talk to people and teach the AES culture. "The values of AES are just human values," he says. "Getting up every day and enjoying to come to work is a great achievement brought about by the people around you and by the opportunities provided by the company to use the human potential of its people."

We questioned the perception of AES as a foreign corporation and the career opportunities of local employees within this environment. Raul Matla Cessa, who joined AES Merida III as a maintenance technician, had prior experience with foreigners in a nuclear research center. "It was sad to see that many foreigners look down on Mexicans and don't think they have the intellectual capacity [to do research]," he explains. "At AES it's different. There is no distinction between different nationalities." And Soroeta adds: "In an organization without hierarchy and without many executive levels, you just cannot presume that a person, because of having one nationality or another or one origin or another, would be better or worse in performing certain tasks."

Carlos Estrada Gamboa, Pedro Hernandez Solis, and Victor Perez Concha joined AES Merida III after resigning from the FEC. For Carlos, it was an easy move. At the FEC he had gotten a job because his father worked there. In spite of an engineering degree from a university, the FEC hired him as a mechanics helper, at the very bottom of the pyramid. Jobs in Mexico are difficult to come by! At AES, Carlos was hired as a shift operator. Pedro, who is now in charge of AES Merida III's warehouse, had a similar job with the FEC. "It was different," he says. "At the FEC, I had five or six levels of hierarchy above me. When I started here, I coordinated with the plant leaders the initial inventory needs, negotiated with the suppliers, set up the warehouse, internal controls, planning, and buying." For Victor, the move to AES Merida III was a difficult step because he had an established career and had worked nine years with the FEC. He explains: "[I finally decided] I wanted a different challenge in private industry, with the possibility to advance and learn more. There may also be an opportunity to move on."

Opportunities for advancement and possible transfers to other countries were echoed by almost all participants in our discussions. Lucio Bastarrachea Chan, who joined AES Merida III as a field operator after some work experience with the Mexican TV station Televisa, has his reasons: "At Televisa, there was nothing, no career development, no values, no communications. Here at AES, one has the opportunity to learn and to move forward, even move to a different country."

Many of the comments and thoughts reminded us of our visits to AES Thames and AES Cayuga. "People at AES don't like to stay in one place," reflects Graciela Loya. "They want the opportunity to move. It strikes me that if I were to go to India, for example, [I would do it] not so much to work in a different plant—it may be identical to the one here—but to see how to make decisions under more constraining circumstances. Over there, you don't have the same conditions of life, and you would learn a lot and appreciate many things that you take for granted in your home country."

AES Merida III may be a new facility and a recent addition to the AES family, but as many of the observations attest to, AES values have taken a firm hold already. "One of the major obstacles to make people believe in them is the work culture in which they grew up," says Soroeta. Taking one or the other of his people along to AES's quarterly management meetings may be a great opportunity "for people to see the fact that what one is preaching really happens there."

TRYING TO SUMMARIZE . . .

As we reflect on our visits to the different AES facilities and on some of the exceptional features of this extraordinary work culture, we would like to refer to Chairman Roger Sant's comment from the AES 1999 Annual Report: "The positive assumptions we make about people—that they are responsible, caring, creative, and want to make a difference—are turning out to be just as accurate about the majority of people in Pakistan, Brazil, or any of the 22 countries we are in, as they are about the majority of people in the United States." It's an amazing statement, substantiated by our findings at AES Merida III. People everywhere like to be treated as responsible adults, to be involved, to be creative, to decide their own destiny, and to have a sense of fulfillment. And AES's global presence "has brought in a whole enrichment of our culture, which otherwise we would have never had."

The AES principles allow people to use values they were brought up with; in other words, there is much consistency between their professional and personal lives. "The AES values have become part of our lives. We not only live them at work but try to apply them at home to our family and friends." Having people take responsibility and make decisions really lets them become owners of the corporation. Alongside, AES has perfected the "fine art of giving advice" (see Exhibit 3.1), leading to a thorough analysis of all major decisions but leaving the responsibility where it belongs. It's not easy to let go: "The biggest single problem in both new and existing AES enterprises is overcoming the natural desire of our leaders to make decisions and control others." Soroeta's comment illustrates the dilemma: "When I have to render an account of my work, obviously I am responsible for what I didn't decide."

Management is an important skill, vital to company success, and we cannot abdicate responsibility for using that skill. However, it should be a skill built on business expertise and on the ability to lead by giving advice and building trust. Managers need to become role models, teachers, and mentors. As far as AES is concerned, we need not worry. Back in 1997, in response to a question on the annual survey of employees, over 98% of the people stated that they would accept work at AES again if they had the opportunity to do it over. No wonder—AES is a "fun" place to work!

Exhibit 3.1.
The Fine Art of Giving Advice

The company's advice process is at the very heart of the AES culture. Senior Vice President Ken Woodcock describes it as "the glue that holds the whole system together." Several important aspects of the AES culture are being supported by the advice process—with amazing results:

"FUN"

In line with the company's goal to create a fun workplace for its people, the advice process allows a great number of individuals to make important decisions and become real businesspeople instead of being used as a "pair of hands." Assuming business responsibilities and being accountable certainly makes working for any enterprise fun.

Exhibit 3.1.
(Continued)

ALLOWING NEW TALENT TO COME FORTH AND GROW

AES has an ever-increasing need for new business leaders who can serve as incubators for future growth and support the rate of expansion that the company has experienced in the past. The advice process can be compared to the case study systems of major universities, steadily preparing people for new and more difficult challenges.

MAKING BETTER DECISIONS AND SHARING INFORMATION

Without question the advice process leads to a thorough review of major decisions and allows for the input of all people who are familiar with particular problems. At the same time, it provides for important linkage of all sectors of the organization, as everyone will be informed about the thoughts and intentions of the individual about to make a decision. However, the ultimate say belongs to the person closest to the problem and will come as no surprise to the rest of the organization.

LEARNING AND PERSONAL GROWTH

Obviously, this is the most important benefit of the AES advice process. As people ask for input from peers, colleagues, and leaders throughout the organization, they learn from the experience of others and gain a full understanding of all aspects and ramifications of a particular issue. Sometimes there is even conflicting advice. What better incentive to walk through the thought process again and learn some more! And this is real-life decision making—we mentioned before the simulated case studies of major business schools that teach students to think through their decisions. At AES, the advice process produces a deeper understanding of a problem and serves as a great learning experience. It leads to personal growth and helps develop unusual leadership talent.

POSTSCRIPT

During 2001, AES went through an unusual and difficult experience, seeing a reduction in earnings as the result of the combined effect of currency devaluations in Latin America, soft electricity prices in the United Kingdom and the United States, and the cancellation of an acquisition attempt of a plant in the Mohave Desert, all hitting at the same time. Concurrently, in the post-Enron era global capital markets tightened and left AES scrambling for funds. The stock price fell from its high in the $70s to a low of around $2. Those have been difficult times and have taught AES a bitter lesson.

AES responded by restructuring at the executive level, expanding the executive office by inviting four new chief operating officers (COOs) from the cadre of executive vice presidents to share the CEO's burden of responsibilities. From this group of veteran AES executives, Paul Hanrahan replaced Dennis Bakke as CEO on June 18, 2002. Hanrahan, once an officer on a fast-attack submarine, knows how to handle pressure. "In a submarine, you learn to operate in very difficult circumstances, and everyone has to pull together to achieve remarkable things," said the new CEO in a June 24, 2002, interview with the *Washington Post*. Hanrahan is expected to bring more financial discipline and control to the company's operations and to reduce AES's staggering $21 billion debt to more reasonable levels.

Because of limited liquidity, capital spending has been reduced or delayed, costs were cut in the business around the world, and AES moved to reduce its exposure in certain markets and exit others, which should contribute to undue risk. The goal is to reduce AES's Latin American exposure and the competitive supply businesses. At the same time, AES expects substantial savings from centralizing certain functions like purchasing and procurement. While the responsibilities of the new COOs will focus on certain geographic areas, their broad experience will allow them to simultaneously deal with issues like asset review, cost savings, and overall benchmarking.

While Hanrahan plans to strengthen the central functions at AES and increase the size of the Arlington office by about 80 people, he reaffirmed the basic tenets of the AES culture. "We'll have more centralized support, but the general decentralized nature of the company will not change," Hanrahan said during the same *Washington Post* interview. With the stormy waters surrounding it, AES has indeed strengthened its culture. To preserve cash, the leadership has broadly offered reductions in cash salaries in exchange for future options, a sign of the confidence and trust in the company's future.

Will AES continue to perform? Will it continue to reach out globally? Will it continue its vision to serve the world and try to live its shared values? "Definitely," argues Ken Woodcock. "You have seen us at a time of incredible growth. Then you saw us in a period of change. It will be fun to look at us a few years from now!"

The Executive Perspective: Dennis W. Bakke— A Journey Teaching Purpose and Values

On June 18, 2002, Dennis Bakke resigned as CEO of AES Corporation, making way for his longtime colleague Paul Hanrahan, one of the company's veteran executives, to steer AES through recent turbulent waters "with more discipline, accountability, control, [and] efficiency," in Bakke's own words. When we interviewed Dennis Bakke in August 2001, those financial difficulties were hardly on the horizon. With the agreement of the new AES leadership, we have decided to keep a significant part of the interview with Dennis Bakke, as it helps to explain the AES culture and how it developed.

For more than 20 years, Dennis W. Bakke, cofounder of AES Corporation, was the driving force behind the AES culture. He is serious and passionate about it. People enjoy hearing him teach it. "Where it comes from for me," explains Bakke, "is trying to figure out a way to live out my faith in a fully integrated way." Bakke is deeply religious and integration for him means living consistently "inside and out," as an individual as well as the cofounder of a multinational corporation.

In terms of its purpose and values, the AES culture developed early on, within the first three to four years after the firm's beginning. "Maybe its purpose is the most radical thing about our company," comments Bakke. "It comes right out of [the book of] Genesis. The purpose of human beings on this earth—and in this a company can be considered a collection of individuals—is to take care of the resources of this world and manage them. Doing this we serve others and, at the same time, take care of ourselves." As to the values, AES initially started out with a larger number, but soon narrowed them down to today's four: fairness, integrity, fun, and social responsibility. "We just took them from our personal experience," continues Bakke. "From then on it has been a journey: Our understanding of what they mean and how they work has expanded."

"Take social responsibility as an example. It is trying to be the best in what we are called to do—supplying electricity in a safe, clean, reliable way. Obviously, not all problems of the world are solved by providing electricity. So we do some other things along the way [like building schools, planting trees, and supporting local programs]. In this people [in other companies] tend to get mixed up. They think their daily work is "dirty" and, therefore, they feel the need for a social responsibility like building homes for Habitat for Humanity. At AES, I wanted our business to be our primary social responsibility!"

Over the years, Bakke has been out teaching and interpreting the company's purpose and values. "I spent about 50% of my time writing, interpreting, and teaching," he says. We talked about today's trends in the work environment, about people looking for a workplace with values and principles consistent with their own. "There is another trend that gets in the way," comments Bakke. "People want to merge their business life into their personal life; they want to telecommute; they want to be able to be the same person in business as in their personal life—which is fine; we like that, too. But what we ask for is a little harder than that. It has to be a two-way street. When people cheat on their income taxes or on their spouses, when they do things that are inconsistent with our values—that's not acceptable to us. What we mean by integrity has to go both ways. The trend of 'privacy in my own life' or of 'no one can touch my personal life' does not fit well with our shared values. It has to carry over."

Bakke realizes that this may not be for everyone. "There is a lot of self-selection going on," he says. "But people who choose to stay know a lot about the principles and values we talk about. If they don't like that kind of stuff, especially those who want leadership roles and want to become bosses, they go to one of our competitors."

Maybe the most important of the AES values—albeit the most difficult to understand and interpret—is fun, a term first used by Sant in a workplace situation. "It was a genius word for us because no one understood it in the context of work," marveled Bakke. "It meant we had to explain and talk about it every time. When you don't have to talk about it because everybody says 'I know what it means,' then you are dead. Fun affects our organizational structure; there is a lot of linkage to our organization. We had to structure our organization in a way that people would be able to use their gifts and skills to make decisions and take actions. That creates a fun workplace and affects everybody's daily life."

"Our interpretation is what makes our values unique," continues Bakke. "[For us], fairness is not having a level playing field and treating everybody the same. At AES, everyone is treated appropriately, as an individual, which makes him or her unique and, therefore, we hope, everyone is treated differently."

We asked Bakke about his personal role in all this and about the concept of leadership at AES. "Leadership is different at AES," explains Bakke. "The main thing that leaders generally do is to make business decisions and, for the most part, we have taken that away. It's a certain problem because decision making on business issues is what leaders usually get paid for and it's what they learned in business school. It's what no other corporation in America will do: To have a fun place to work takes a most difficult thing; that is, having all leaders give up most of their power to decide, because for the individual [worker] to make a decision and to take action is the single most important factor for a fun workplace. So what do we substitute for it? The main responsibility of our leaders—and my own—is to be the keeper, interpreter, and decision maker on our principles and values. Does that lead to anarchy? No—I am a great believer in authority. And our leaders have authority, in a narrower but most important way. Leaders' responsibilities at AES revolve around the all-important shared values and in choosing the people [who] will make the business decisions."

As we have witnessed during our visits to the AES facilities at Thames, Cayuga, and Merida, this system is sometimes hard on the leaders and plant managers, but it provides the foundation for AES's great culture. Leaders are the chief advisors, they keep score on the actions and decisions of their people and remember and celebrate the good and the bad ones. "Keeping score or being accountable is part of the fun," continues Bakke. "The leaders make sure that it happens."

How does one find talented people and steer their careers in order to have them educated and experienced for the next challenge? "We started off with the idea of starting a central company university," responds Bakke, "but then realized that it was at odds [with our principles] and we abandoned it. [Instead] I think we have created one of the best learning institutions in the history of the world at AES. People learn faster, grow faster, become leaders faster than we could have imagined. This came about by accident: Trying to have fun, giving up power and decentralizing decision making, combined with the advice process, gives people about the best education they can get. It's magical: When people become decision makers and do things they never dreamed of doing—they get educated and they become leaders!"

In a 1999 interview with the *Harvard Business Review*, Bakke had stated: "I sometimes worry that AES will be run by someone who does not feel as strongly about our central tenets as I do." So we question how the unique AES culture could be kept alive. "The top person matters a lot," responds Bakke, "but it will take a strong leader to push change toward a more conventional environment because people have had the freedom to live this way [for a long time]. The culture will not stay unless people care, but there is a huge number of people all through the company that bought into it in a major way and will not let it change."

The AES culture is an amazing accomplishment that its people cherish. It has been a long journey to get to where it is today. We sincerely hope that the AES leadership will be able to keep it going.

CHAPTER 4

A Closer Look at Culture

As we look back on the first three case studies, we seem to deal with different cultural models, even as we find a lot of similarities in people's responses. How do we make sense out of comparing a small Texas plumbing and air conditioning contractor with a large military service organization, and both again with a global power company? However, as we stated in the introduction, people are the essence of culture and that is where we can perceive certain similarities among the three companies. So, as we start analyzing these cultures, two questions come to mind:

1. How exceptional or unusual are these three organizations? In other words, is their culture unique and unattainable to the regular company around the corner from us, or is what we read about part of a growing trend in today's corporate world?

2. When we discussed culture's impact on people, we determined that "culture" represented a set of distinguishing practices, principles, and beliefs that characterized a particular community of people. Which ones can we identify at TDIndustries, the Coast Guard, and AES Corporation?

Dealing with the first question, we find that one of the unique aspects of the three organizations is the genuine concern that the top executives have for the people who work for them. Can this be a model for other organizations? By all means! It may well be the secret of these three institutions' success. Let's look for some proof of that.

Back in 1989, when TDIndustries was in big economic trouble, Jack Lowe Jr. was not only trying to save the company, he was equally concerned about people's investment of their life savings in TDIndustries.

There was some give and take between Lowe and the employees and "it bonded us together." Ten years later, *FORTUNE* ranked the same company one of America's "Great Places to Work."

At the U.S. Coast Guard, we heard Admiral James M. Loy describe the EARS process: "Listening to our workforce about performance, evaluating performance, and the recognition that was an appropriate part of it. The fact that we [constituted] the study team from the troops as well as from the top was absolutely the right thing." It is surprising to see participative management in the military, but it probably explains why there is a lot of trust today in the Coast Guard's role in Homeland Security, after the September 11 terrorist attacks.

Finally, Dennis Bakke, cofounder of AES Corporation, told us about fun, the company's most important value: "We had to structure our organization in a way that people would be able to use their gifts and skills. That creates a fun workplace and affects everybody's daily life." What better testimony for the company's achievement than Andres Edgardo Arbizu at AES Merida III saying, "Getting up every day and enjoying to come to work is a great achievement brought about by the people around you and by the opportunities provided by the company to use the human potential of its people."

What is so unusual about participative and inclusive management? Often, the problem is that managers like to be in control and to make decisions. That's what they learned in business school and that's what they feel they get paid for. It is very difficult to give it up. And let's not have any illusions: To this day, the world order of large corporations and organizations—the military is no exception here—is characterized by hierarchy and pyramidal power structures. While in the public domain we all believe in our right to choose our leaders, democracy still has to penetrate the workplace.

If there is one growing trend to be observed with today's work population, it is the desire for meaning in one's life, with work playing an important part in it. It is interesting that back in 1982, Tom Peters in his business classic *In Search of Excellence* already pointed to the importance of it: "We desperately need meaning in our lives and will sacrifice a great deal to institutions that will provide meaning for us. We simultaneously need independence, to feel as though we are in charge of our destinies, and to have the ability to stick out." Peters goes on to state that excellent companies seem to provide meaningful jobs rather than only focus on financial targets. They are successful as well in creating environments where people can grow and develop self-esteem to become true participants in the business.

What gives meaning to our job and our work life? People expect to be treated as mature adults and they would like to have the opportunity to be responsible, creative, and trustworthy. That's what happens in organizations like TDIndustries, the U.S. Coast Guard, and AES Corporation and makes them so successful. As we hear it from Admiral Loy: "You have the same responsibility in government as in the private sector, to the degree that you are able to create a work environment that . . . allows every member of the workforce to reach his or her potential."

Today's organizations will have to emulate these cultures because people have already begun to make choices regarding their jobs and their work life. They look for a consistency of values both in the personal and professional area. At the same time, the job has to leave them certain freedom and flexibility to pursue their personal dreams and ambitions.

Moving on to the second question, can we identify a set of distinguishing practices that characterizes the culture of the three organizations? Again, let's make some practical observations.

Looking at TDIndustries, we are surprised by the frequent use of "we": It's an indication of a close partnership between TD's leadership and employees. It fits in with this culture that CEO Jack Lowe Jr. works out of a small cubicle, right in the middle of TD's general office. There is further evidence of this partnership in the company's definition of leadership "provided by a large number of us" as a key ingredient of its culture. Leadership is not reserved for the executive ranks.

TDIndustries has adopted a particular kind of leadership, Robert Greenleaf's "Servant-Leadership," which envisions the leader serving his or her followers. It is the leader's responsibility to help people succeed in their jobs. In this way, leaders become role models and mentors, expected to give support to the organization.

There is a third element of significance to TDIndustries's culture. The company is committed to "building partners," providing them with the possibility of learning and advancing their careers. The spectrum of learning opportunities is extensive: It ranges from different curricula for specific trades to language education, as well as to courses in leadership and Servant-Leadership. Learning is an important priority within TD's culture.

Moving on to the Coast Guard, an obvious consideration is the fact that the Coast Guard is part of the military services, which by tradition and definition are command-and-control organizations. However, the EARS process was somewhat of an unusual initiative and a new beginning, which has caught our attention. It is the first time where people's performance is to be managed in partnership with their supervisors. As Sheryl Smalls said so well: "It's their career. It's important to them." From now on, for the many civilian employees covered by the EARS system, there will be true ownership of their goals and honest recognition of their achievements.

More significantly, the *process* as to how EARS was handled by the different teams was new and exciting. No more "handing down by edict": The EARS system was developed with broad participation of civilian and military employees and supervisors, through the design team and subsequent focus groups. It was "modeled to the reality of the workday." This new and unique process has aroused the curiosity of numerous other government agencies and may usher in a whole new era of employee participation in government.

Finally, we observe AES Corporation advancing the principle of fun. It translates into people making all the decisions concerning their job, being trusted as responsible adults, and being able to use their creative abilities and talents. With *fun, fairness, integrity,* and *social responsibility,* the AES culture espouses strong values that "are just human values," as AES Merida III leader Andres Edgardo Arbizu points out. They make it easy for the people who work for AES to experience complete consistency of their personal and professional lives, embracing similar values in both.

The role of management at AES is totally unconventional. The company has turned the system of giving advice into a fine art that supports the organization in the decision-making process and strengthens the review of all ramifications of major decisions. It's never easy because leaders "have a natural desire to make decisions and control others." But in our visits to several AES plants, we have been able to see leaders who have become excellent role models and mentors for their organizations.

A third pillar of the AES culture is learning, here embodied by ever-increasing challenges that advance people's abilities and lead to personal growth. With the company's large assembly of facilities around the globe, people looking for personal growth have many opportunities to move on, be it just for the fun of spreading the AES values to a group of newcomers in a different region or some faraway country or for the possibility of advancement and learning more. We want to underscore, however, that these are not mandated transfers or contractual obligations of a cadre of expatriates being sent to the next assignment. It is clearly people's choice to move on and enjoy the fun at another facility. Some of the AES people just stay where they are and prefer to be followers. Others are great in what they do and see opportunities to advance but rarely venture on. And again others have strong personalities, step out in front, and become leaders of the AES world.

How can we summarize the distinguishing practices, principles, and beliefs that describe the culture of these three companies?

BEING TRUSTED AND VALUED; IN SHORT, FUN

A basic notion of trust is the assumption that people are generally dependable and responsible, even though pressures, fear, anger, grief, poor upbringing, bad judgment, and emotional rigidity may cause some individuals to be self-defeating. Trust means seeing others as legitimate and their needs as valid. At the same time, negative behavior should be confronted and, if necessary, stopped effectively.

Trust implies belief in the whole person. People shouldn't be expected to leave their feelings at home and appear at the workplace as fragments of their selves. Trusting, supportive, and concerned relationships are the key to efficient environments producing long-term results. In contrast, autocratic methods only create an illusion of success.

As people become more self-managed, confident, and able, they are increasingly trustworthy and more willing to extend thoughtful trust to others. This overall rise in the trust level creates a climate where great advances in all aspects of our society are possible.

Organizational as well as personal success depends on effective interactions among people. Therefore, the building of trust is critical to high-performance organizations and the people working for them.

Let's look at a different aspect of trust. One of the recent management buzzwords is *empowerment*. A few years ago, *Harvard Business Review* (HBR) published an interview with AES's Chairman Roger Sant and former CEO Dennis Bakke under the title "Organizing for Empowerment." We think HBR missed the target trying to describe an important element of the AES culture. Empowerment by its very definition is a top-down approach. To empower someone means to delegate certain power to that person, while the ultimate authority—the "strings"—stay with the original holder. Empowerment can be rescinded at any time. We submit that this is not a fair basis for trust and is certainly no fun! What we observe at AES, in the Coast Guard approach (in spite of the guidance team), and at TD is a different relationship. These organizations trust their employees because they are considered responsible and known to manage their personal affairs quite responsibly. The three organizations have made positive assumptions about their people and on that basis entrusted them with the conduct of their business or of a certain process. No strings attached! There may be advice, guidance, or leadership of a servant variety, but there is no delegation of power with the original holder looking over people's shoulders.

This is where the real fun comes in: There is no boss taking the praise when things go well. Being fully in charge gives people a true sense of fulfillment and a great feeling of accomplishment when their decisions have a positive outcome and lead to the next challenge. At AES, it works to the extent that even long-term coworkers step back and let their newly joined colleagues experience the fun.

TRUE PARTNERSHIP AND THE SPECIAL ROLE OF MANAGEMENT

True partnership means that employees must be able to make job-related decisions, to dictate the speed at which they are operating, to modify procedures and make improvements, and to innovate and be creative.

To let this occur, the role of management, as we have traditionally known it, has to change. Managers have to renounce the authority of their office, which is based on the power of the organization chart. The future manager must become a source of experience and expertise, earning trust and respect as a role model for the organization. His or her task will be to coordinate and inform, to develop strategies for the future (building consensus on how to implement that strategy), and to be a coach and mentor for his or her people. Managers must learn not to interfere in the day-to-day activities in order to let people enjoy the fun of their autonomy.

As an organizational leader, it's difficult "to overcome the natural desire to make decisions and control others." Nonetheless, at TD, during the EARS process at the Coast Guard, and, more clearly, at AES, the role of management has changed. At TDIndustries, the leader has to "serve" and to be a resource for counsel and support. "I like working for someone who works," is a telling remark that illustrates Servant-Leadership. The leader is ultimately responsible for the success of his or her coworkers.

While the Coast Guard continues to largely be a command-and-control organization because of its military responsibilities, the EARS process represents a different structure, where managers have agreed to limit themselves to be of guidance and to help market the new system to their fellow managers and the commandant. It is certainly no coincidence that the Commandant at that time, Admiral James M. Loy, had a human resources background from his prior assignments with the Coast Guard.

Among the three organizations, AES Corporation has moved forward the most in devising a special role for management. The company has perfected its system of advice so it assures that all major decisions are analyzed to the extent necessary. However, each decision is eventually made by the person responsible for that particular segment of operations. The skill and expertise of the manager or leader is not lost. His or her opinion and advice carries weight. But he or she does not decide in order to leave the fun where it belongs. The AES system seems to be extremely effective, although in recent history there have been some missteps and problems. We are told, however, that the internal discussion about these matters has strengthened the cohesion among employees and leaders and the resolve to continue on the path. It's a path that is not always easy to follow. The words of Ruben Soroeta, plant manager of AES Merida III, resonate with us: "I am responsible for what I didn't decide." But Soroeta is an excellent role model and mentor for his plant team of 36 coworkers!

LEARNING AND PERSONAL GROWTH

In several ways, learning is a healthy motivational experience. First, the very process of learning is highly satisfying in itself. Each of us has had to deal with a situation where our skills were barely sufficient to handle a particular problem. Yet we managed to stay on top—an exhilarating and deeply motivating experience. The ability to meet ever more difficult challenges translates into personal growth. With time, people choose their level of challenge and develop their personal orientation.

Second, learning refreshes us mentally. It keeps us flexible and helps us to adjust to changes in our business and in the economic climate around us. Creating this "learning disposition" adds to our personal mastery and self-esteem.

Third, learning may help us to understand the broader context of our business and the interrelationship of its operations. We see our role in relation to our coworkers' contributions. We learn to appreciate what they do and become enthusiastic to support them. Again, this orientation clearly makes the organization more productive.

In all three organizations, there is considerable commitment to "build partners," as TD expresses it. It may be classroom learning, as we find at TD, where a formalized curriculum helps to develop people's careers. In the same manner, the Coast Guard is leaning toward individual development plans (IDPs) that offer learning opportunities for the employee's present position or, more importantly, for a career move outside of the person's present job.

At AES, opportunities for personal growth are entirely the employee's choice. On the one hand, people may request training in an unrelated job to foster a possible career move. On the other extreme, interested individuals may apply for open positions, posted on the AES internal E-mail, in one of their worldwide facilities. In between, there are temporary volunteering opportunities available at other plants in the United States or abroad that need help with a particular expertise or as the consequence of a major breakdown. As Mark Adams, AES Cayuga plant manger, puts it: "There are always people volunteering to go teach the AES culture and help AES businesses to grow."

Whatever the particular system, the general emphasis is on learning, to foster the coworker's career and his or her personal development. It is always exciting to expand one's skill horizon and flexibility, which can be an advantage in times of changing economic conditions.

A FEW FINAL THOUGHTS

Reflecting on culture and on the overall model offered by the first three case studies, we revert to an earlier observation that people and human relationships are the essence of culture. Human values form the staunch foundation of our lives and our society. It is, therefore, crucial that organizational cultures be guided by the same principles.

The gain is particularly evident at AES Corporation, where we were told that "[the AES] values have become part of our lives. We not only live them at work but try to apply them at home to our family and friends." The consistency of personal and professional values renders an organizational culture immensely motivational, as this has been the basic yearning of humanity.

The principle of social responsibility espoused by AES Corporation may provide another good example of this consistency of values. Obviously, the company's primary social responsibility is its business purpose, to supply electricity to people in a safe, clean, and responsible way. But it goes further: The company funded the building of schools in Pakistan to help eradicate illiteracy in its neighborhood. The plan was born among the local employees. With proper advice they approved the project and felt great about it! That's where personal and company values converge.

We remember a similar situation at the manufacturer of corrugated boxes mentioned in the introduction. The general manger at the time encouraged employees to help in a nearby soup kitchen—on company time! And one of the workers made this comment: "I have been on the other side of the counter and, believe me, it's different to wash the plates or to have to eat from them." Again, social responsibility is of deep concern to people and brings home the point that personal and company values are consistent.

The three "distinguishing practices" we pointed out—to be trusted and valued as an employee; true partnership, which assigns a special role to management; and learning as a way to advance people's careers—are integral ingredients of human relationships within the three organizations. There may be others—broad information patterns, as an example, that help support the climate of trust prevalent there—but they are of a different category. The three traits we mentioned are certainly indicative of the new corporate cultures we are describing.

A FEW GOOD IDEAS TO BE ADOPTED

For the benefit of our readers, we want to highlight here some attributes that make the cultures of the three organizations truly exemplary and inspiring.

Spreading the Culture

In large organizations, there is a natural tendency to have the development of subcultures of a regional, departmental, or even hierarchical nature. People band together in their little clans or fiefdoms and soon a "we vs. they" attitude develops, to the detriment of a common culture for the whole organization. AES has found ways to counter that trend and unify their culture. In several ways, they allow their people to freely interact and interchange within their organization:

- At their own free will and choice, people can apply for special assignments, to help troubleshooting, or in the start-up of a new facility. Implicitly, part of their task in those assignments is to teach and spread the AES values.

- Job openings are posted at the company's internal Web site and transfers are encouraged. Again, this contributes to closer ties between different areas of the organization. We may remember the pride of the AES Thames people, who sent so many ambassadors of the AES culture to other plants all over the world!

- As a special incentive, the AES plants allow certain of their employees to participate in project work, in ad hoc committees, or in the quarterly management meetings, which will provide for a broader vision and depth of experience. Similarly, participating in the Coast Guard design team left an indelible image of an important mission in people's minds.

Fostering Personal Growth

The motivational aspect of the learning opportunities that we have witnessed in the three organizations is beyond question. However, an additional benefit to their culture may be less visible. There is a message being sent by the three organizations that people's personal growth and professional development is a definite priority, above and beyond the missions, goals, and successes of these organizations. This sense of human worth, providing opportunities and meaning for people's work lives, will be reciprocated by the enormous commitment of the employees, establishing strong cultural bonds to the organization for which they work.

PART II

Cultures with a Passion

All of us have experienced passion. It's an emotional charge that jolts us. It gives us power and strength and it sharpens our focus on whatever it is we are doing. We use all the effort and force we can muster. We give it our very best. It makes us more open and honest in how we communicate. It reveals our basic beliefs and our true self when we are working with a passion!

A particular emotional attachment of people to their organization is frequently observed in a start-up situation or during an exciting growth period. In that sense, the two case studies offered in this segment, Mercedes-Benz of Alabama and Southwest Airlines, are fortunate examples of cultures with a passion. Other times, a crisis situation may lead to that emotional charge and fire up an already inclusive and participative culture. The danger here lies in dealing with and confronting reality: Honesty, truth, and openness are absolutely crucial. There must be a solid foundation of values, both at the organizational and individual level. The crisis at Arthur Anderson before its demise is a recent example in which the sudden rise of passion among its employees, who went on the street to demonstrate, was not supported by admissions of prior deceit by management.

It is amazing to observe how people's passion at work carries over into their private lives or flows from there into their work. Passionate people get involved in community work, take special care of children and family, and fight to get the job done, all at the same time.

CHAPTER 5

M-Class: The Making of a New Mercedes-Benz

INTRODUCTION

"M-Class leads Mercedes sales for the fourth consecutive month," reported the March 2000 issue of *The Inside Line*, a newsletter for the team members of the Alabama facility. And in August 2000, DaimlerChrysler management announced that it would spend $600 million to double the size and capacity of the Alabama plant to 160,000 vehicles a year. What a well-deserved tribute to the M-Class team on both sides of the Atlantic! And what a surprising outcome for the most unlikely automobile manufacturer to produce a new sport-utility vehicle in the United States: Mercedes-Benz, the premium brand, passenger-car unit of DaimlerChrysler.

As a measure of the unprecedented success of the M-Class project, the new car achieved a share of about 10% of total Mercedes-Benz revenues, beginning in 1999. Is there one important factor that contributed to this accomplishment? Most certainly, yes! It is the fact that the leadership of the project was able to create a melting pot of German and American work cultures, of management of different backgrounds and deliberately diverse experiences, and of traditional and advanced manufacturing techniques, all of which have made the M-Class successful beyond expectations.

Reprinted from *Organizational Dynamics*, Vol. 27, no. 4 (Spring) by Adolf Haasen. "M-Class: The Making of the New Daimler-Benz," pp. 74–78. Copyright 1999, with permission from Elsevier Science.

WHY DEVELOP A SPORT-UTILITY VEHICLE?

It was 1989, and the weak dollar had taken a heavy toll on the imported Mercedes-Benz vehicles. Then the upscale Lexus and Infiniti models were introduced at significant lower prices, which began to drive Mercedes-Benz out of the U.S. market. It showed the vulnerability of the company's concentration on the luxury segment of the passenger-car market. Mercedes-Benz was in danger of becoming the Rolls Royce of the twenty-first century.

Management wasted no time in inviting all senior members as well as some young "revolutionaries" to a brainstorming session on Mercedes's options for the future. The new strategies were to include new and different car models. Mercedes-Benz had to become more productive and learn to develop and manufacture cars using more advanced techniques and procedures. Another strategy sought greater globalization.

During 1991 and 1992, several ideas became the focus of feasibility studies. One of them dealt with developing a suitable successor to Mercedes's "G-Wagen," short for "Gelaendewagen," a low-volume sport-utility vehicle originally designed for military use. Andreas Renschler, a young management assistant who had joined Mercedes-Benz in 1988, was put in charge of the project.

Renschler brought together a team of people from development, production, marketing, and finance. Among its members was Dr. Gerhard Fritz, who had championed the effort of overhauling the G-Wagen since 1987 and became responsible for the process of creating the M-Class vehicle.

The group's goal was staggering: The G-Wagen had to be redesigned in order to aim at a larger market. This in turn would allow for a sales volume of 75,000 units at a market share of 10%. The new vehicle would need innovative new features to make it attractive to a broad group of buyers. And intensive cost targeting was necessary to make it price competitive.

In the absence of more suitable offices, the group took residence in an office trailer at an old railroad yard located next door to the Untertuerkheim facility. The space had been acquired by Mercedes-Benz for future expansion. The isolation helped create a unique culture that made a departure from Mercedes's past easier. To achieve the goals set the company would have to utilize more efficient manufacturing methods as highlighted by the 1990 Massachusetts Institute of Technology (MIT) study of the automotive industry.

Renschler's charismatic style shaped the group. The excitement of participating in a fundamental change of direction for Mercedes-Benz and the sense of mission to accomplish the goals of the project led to long hours in the office trailer. The result was a proposal to the Mercedes-Benz board to manufacture an innovative sport-utility vehicle in the United States, which the board approved by the end of 1992. Not surprisingly, Renschler was put in charge of its implementation.

THE M-CLASS FUNCTION GROUPS

Dr. Fritz sponsored the innovative concept of parallel "function groups" in order to speed up the development of the new vehicle. Teams of developers, designers, cost accountants, production planners, and marketers were given full responsibility to develop major M-Class segments, targeting its cost and selecting suppliers to help in the final development and production of subsystems. "People were able to make their own decisions," observed Fritz. "That generated the right motivation."

It was imperative to bring the people responsible for construction, testing, quality control, and maintenance together with the other team members in order to get everybody's viewpoint around the table. Fritz did this by holding weekly progress meetings with all 13 function groups. Communications were essential. At a later stage, suppliers were integrated in the development process, many times offering new innovative concepts for certain segments of the M-Class. At the end, teams negotiated supply contracts for the life cycle of the vehicle, some in total value as high as $1 billion.

For all participants, about 150 people in the function groups and 700–800 in all, this was an enormously rewarding experience. "These guys fought every day and were able to move things forward—they were totally motivated," acknowledges Fritz. Again, a unique culture developed. As Dr. Fritz was unable to find appropriate offices in the neighborhood of the Sindelfingen or Untertuerkheim plants, he ended up leasing an old shutdown crane factory conveniently located near Untertuerkheim. Here the different function groups set up camp, in close contact with each other and with Dr. Fritz, who remained accessible to all. The core team of the developers came from the G-Wagen operation at Steyr in Austria, where many U.S. automobile manufacturers were located as well. This gave them a broader perspective on the industry than they might otherwise have had.

The function group concept helped to accomplish several important goals:

First, the speed of the M-Class development based on the close and simultaneous efforts of the groups broke records. The project started in early 1993 and reached design freeze in February 1994. Prototypes were available by March 1995, barely two years after the start of the project.

Second, customer and market input drove the development to a degree unheard of with other Mercedes projects. Given the importance of the U.S. sport-utility market, the M-Class was tailored to the needs of the American customer in terms of a more comfortable ride, fuel economy, safety, and reliability.

Third, cost targeting became an early priority of the function groups. While maintaining important Mercedes quality features—a unique new engine, for example—the reliance on the experience of specialized outside suppliers and the extended use of subsystems simplified and reduced the cost of the assembly.

WHERE TO MANUFACTURE THE M-CLASS?

Based on the fast-expanding sport-utility market in the United States, the feasibility study had already recommended locating the M-Class facility there. The official announcement of an American factory for this project in April 1993, therefore, came as no surprise. However, the choice of Alabama for the plant site was unexpected, given the recent preference of the Carolinas and Tennessee for automotive facilities.

The site selection team included Linda Paulmeno (PR), Steve Cannon (marketing), Herb Gzik (engineering), and Renschler. Selection was based on operating cost analysis. "However," adds Cannon, "the employee base was a major decision factor as well." Paulmeno describes the commitment of the people they met in Alabama: "They wanted to be our partners. Alabama would rise and fall with Mercedes-Benz."

Other states were strong contenders. They all offered similar incentives. But in Alabama the people embraced and welcomed the Mercedes team. There was a level of identification and support that would help make the project successful. In essence, that decided the site selection.

Seven years later, Paulmeno is convinced that the team made the right decision: "There is such a strong sense of partnership that Alabama not only came through with their promises but exceeded our expectations."

TEAM ALABAMA: THE MAKING OF THE M-CLASS

"Opportunities galore, huge challenges, but a company that lets you do things," commented Bill Taylor on the M-Class project in September 1993. Taylor joined the M-Class team as VP operations and became CEO in early 1999. Taylor previously headed Toyota's start-up at its Cambridge facility in Canada. At the same time, Bob Birch was hired from Nissan as VP of purchasing and logistics. Emmett Meyer, VP of human resources and administration, came from Westinghouse. With the Mercedes-Benz people like Renschler, Dr. Fritz, and Dr. Gzik already on board, Mercedes-Benz U.S. International (MBUSI), as the new company was called, became a melting pot of different experiences. "The Alabama experience has been a learning adventure for all of Mercedes-Benz," reminisces Dr. Fritz, and the team members agree. While the workload was heavy, the excitement of the M-Class development, the opportunity for personal impact and unusual responsibility, and the enjoyment of seeing the Alabama organization grow more than compensated for their tribulations.

The configuration of the new facility ignited strong debate. The plant layout was an important prerequisite for the proposed manufacturing methodology. "Everybody comes with baggage," says Taylor. In the end, the final concept included everything, administration as well, under one roof to support both team and cost consciousness. The facility became the foundation of MBUSI's culture of teamwork and open communications.

"Once the general direction was clear, we started hiring people who had the experience," explains Meyer, referring to the next level of managers and department heads. But for the people to work on the line there was no automotive experience in Alabama. "We decided to hire just good people and train them in Germany," says Taylor. MBUSI looked for team players, workers with good education and certain technical and problem-solving skills. One hundred sixty of the new hires were sent to Sindelfingen for further training and became "multipliers" for the rest of the plant. In addition, Mercedes sent about 80 trainers from Germany for the start-up.

Wolfgang Roehm, who started with Mercedes in 1986, was one of the trainers responsible for the paint shop. "It was an exciting time, I wouldn't want to miss it" is his assessment. Training of the American team members started in Germany in 1996. There were no language barriers: "They didn't speak very good English and we spoke no German. So we got along absolutely fine," remembers Joe Greene, who leads a maintenance team today. "Actually, we broke them in." Wolfgang stayed as a technical specialist and helped introduce more automation in the paint shop. "Being on the M-Class team was a real challenge," he says. "I gained a lot of experience and have seen things done differently here from Germany."

The M-Class production system is based on a team approach, with a succession of stations staffed ideally with six people. Since start-up, cycle time has come down from 3.6 to 3.0 minutes. Team leaders work at least half of their time replacing absent team members. Otherwise, they are responsible for certain coordination functions and for the training of fellow team members. People are trained in the different positions of each station and rotate every two hours at break periods. "As long as the guys keep their job up to par, they can set their own rotation," explains Steve Locke, a group leader for two teams in the body shop. "It's ergonomically better." The rotation schedule includes the stations immediately before and after each station, where team members also train. This increases the flexibility of the workforce. It also creates customer orientation: Workers should understand the needs of the stations that send or receive their work.

Production runs two eight-hour shifts, starting 12 hours apart, using the intermediate time period for preventive maintenance. However, as demand for M-Class vehicles continues to be heavy, shifts may extend from the normal 8-hour schedule to 9 or 10 hours to make up for line stoppages and guarantee production of 170 or 180 cars per shift. The exception is Friday, when the 8-hour schedule will be maintained and the night shift starts two hours earlier to let people get home in time for the weekend. "That was a good decision," comments Locke, "and it was team member driven."

Training continues to be a concern, as it leads to increased flexibility and quality orientation. On-the-job training and job rotation are complemented by classroom instruction. "People have the opportunity to cross-train and learn new things," says Greene. Since 1999, MBUSI supports skill acquisition with a scheduled pay progression program.

By design, the production teams have control over the step-by-step procedures to maintain the highest possible level of quality and efficiency. As a matter of fact, during the first trial production when the processes for all stations were defined, teams literally wrote their own standard methods and procedures (SM&Ps). "It was a phenomenal learning curve," comments Taylor.

Even today, teams have the opportunity for improvements. They are discussed at weekly assembly line meetings, which are attended by development and engineering, or within the area team, which congregates representatives from all areas. "Still today, after five years of production," says Greene, "we find things that could have been done better. Changes are driven by production, and then maintenance and engineering sit down together to see how we can make it happen. And we'll try it out on weekends and find a new path."

All stations have cords for light signals—yellow to indicate a problem, red to stop the line. Taylor sees it as indicative for the ability of the organization to be successful. By asking for help, a station tries to maintain cycle time and to protect the integrity of the plant's production level.

People have worked hard to create a "one team" concept at MBUSI. There is a general "team wear" consisting of casual slacks and shirts embroidered with people's first names along with the three-pointed star that is the Mercedes-Benz logo. As this is quite different from practice in Germany, we asked Roehm how he felt about it. "I like it [wearing a T-shirt] and communications here are a lot better than in Germany. Office spaces are open. If you need to talk to someone, you just go and talk to that person." But the MBUSI culture is also different from traditional U.S. companies, as Locke confirms: "Where I came from was an old style production. In fact, I was a supervisor there, telling my people: 'I am the boss, you do what I say.' Here it's totally different. If we have a problem in the group, we sit down and discuss what needs to be done."

While the expansion of the plant has added many new people and has contributed somewhat to losing the "personal touch" of the early days, "teams still reflect the way the company used to be on a smaller level," affirms Greene. "A lot of our teams get a chance to do things together [outside of work]." And Austin Dare, who heads internal communications for MBUSI, adds: "As part of our culture, we try to integrate family members as well. They play a big role in the success of the company."

LESSONS TO BE LEARNED FROM THE
M-CLASS STORY

As we reflect on the odds of the M-Class development to succeed and on the substantial risk that Mercedes-Benz took at the time, some distinct factors, unprecedented in Mercedes-Benz history, stand out that drove the project to accomplish its goals.

First, Renschler and his teammates were given complete control of the M-Class project. This allowed them to combine modern concepts of car making like simultaneous development, market-driven design, and integration of suppliers in the development process with the concern for quality and workmanship inherent in the Mercedes-Benz culture. Using a "best of the best" approach, combining Mercedes-Benz experience with the new initiatives of U.S. and Japanese automobile manufacturers, the team had the opportunity to incorporate many advanced elements into the M-Class production process. The ability of the people to shape the destiny of the project was enormously motivating and created the culture that made the M-Class successful.

Second, the use of multiple and diverse teams was an important contributor to the success of the M-Class project. Much has been written on teams—on their organizational aspects of increasing efficiencies and making better use of resources, or on their social dimension of facilitating role differentiation and greater involvement of members. However, with the M-Class project, being part of the extraordinary effort to develop and build the new car created extreme emotional stimulation and powerful motivation for the teams. Renschler's charisma, the isolated sites away from the large Mercedes facilities, and barbecue weekends and family days helped develop a unique team culture. All of them—the function groups, the site selection squad, and Team Alabama, now 1,900 people strong—were indomitable in their efforts and proud of their success.

Thomas Harthun, who joined MBUSI in the days of groundbreaking and today is assistant production manager, sums it up: "DaimlerChrysler is a large company with lots of opportunities in the world. But in Sindelfingen with its 40,000 employees, your job in life may be to develop the left rear door lock for E-Class cars. In comparison, Alabama responsibilities are broader based, extending to the whole vehicle. And the density of information is much higher than in Germany. Everybody here gets information on the business."

BRINGING IT TO THE END

To conclude the M-Class story, we would like to introduce Carla Huntley, who worked her way up to group leader in the assembly, in charge of the #2 trim line. Carla's ascent is typical of the opportunities available in this culture of emotional drive.

Prior to joining MBUSI, Carla had worked with the University of Alabama and then as advertising manager of a smaller firm. In January 1996, she was hired for the human resources (HR) department. Her duties included helping develop policies and plans for production personnel. Soon she was involved with interviewing applicants for manufacturing.

At that moment, in April 1996, Carla decided to change course and apply for a production job. The selection process was in part based on some assembly abilities, unaccustomed skills for the average office person: "I actually had to install a wheel, complete with hubcap," remembers Carla.

Carla was selected to go to Germany for training. "The environment is so different" is her comment on those six weeks. "They have only a few women in the workforce over there." When she came back she was given the opportunity to participate in all aspects of the start-up, writing SM&Ps, developing tool lists, starting the actual work process, and providing feedback.

All this gave her enormous satisfaction. Carla made important suggestions in developing a rotation schedule for her team members to protect them from ergonomic strain. "I had worked the door line, the trim line, and trim #2," explains Carla. "With the experience in all three lines, I was able to help establish a rotation plan for the teams, matching the jobs to their skills."

"Looking back," we asked her, "was it the right decision to move from the university job to the one in HR and then on to the line?" Carla didn't hesitate for one second in her response: "Absolutely, no question."

Mercedes-Benz and DaimlerChrysler have created a culture of strong motivation to participate, one of open communications and close people relations. That culture was bound to make the M-Class project ultimately successful.

The Executive Perspective:
Andreas Renschler—
Think Globally and Act Locally

We first met Andreas Renschler at the new Mercedes-Benz M-Class facility in Tuscaloosa, Alabama. In 1992, Renschler was put in charge of the project to develop the M-Class sport-utility vehicle and manufacture it in the United States. This chapter tells the story of this successful venture, which marked the beginning of a new era at Mercedes-Benz.

In many ways, Renschler, who is in his early forties, represents a new breed of global multiskilled managers, vital to the success of the mega-merger of DaimlerChrysler. In early 1999 Renschler went to Auburn Hills on a unique mission, as head of Executive Management Development. Here he put certain ideas in motion that will have significant impact on the future of DaimlerChrysler. Much of this interview was dedicated to these ideas.

In late 1999, Renschler was promoted to CEO of Micro Compact Car smart GmbH, initially a joint venture between the Swiss economist and entrepreneur Kurt Hayek and Mercedes-Benz. When things went awry and losses started accumulating, Mercedes-Benz bought Mr. Hayek out. "As one of Mr. Schrempp's [CEO of DaimlerChrysler] favorite fix-it men," we read in the September 27, 1999, edition of the *Wall Street Journal*, "Mr. Renschler will be under pressure to put a tourniquet on smart's heavy losses."

THE DAIMLERCHRYSLER MERGER

Much has been written about the possible success or failure of the DaimlerChrysler merger. The initial scheme of a "merger of equals" has given way to increased involvement of the Daimler side, due to the enormous economic difficulties at Chrysler. We took the opportunity to question the future outlook for DaimlerChrysler. Renschler was adamant that the merger is bound to be successful: "There is such an enormous number of talented people at both Daimler and Chrysler," he asserts, based on his firsthand knowledge of the executive ranks. Chairman Schrempp, in an earlier comment, seconds this view: "I am learning that, ultimately, a company is people."

As to the right management philosophy for DaimlerChrysler, Renschler preaches what he practiced in Alabama: "Think globally and act locally." Sport-utility vehicles were seen as an important target market for pre-merger Daimler-Benz. It was a worldwide market, but the highest market share and most significant growth existed in the United States. This led to the decision to build a new factory in Alabama. From that point on, Renschler "acted locally," introducing motivational ideas, the "one team" approach, and T-Shirts that the MBUSI team members wear in typical local fashion. "T-shirts would not go well with German business culture," comments Renschler with a grin.

In similar ways, argues Renschler, the driver for DaimlerChrysler's success will not be any form of joint worldwide culture but the diversity of "brands" as part of a "global offering to mankind." The merger allows DaimlerChrysler to pool different know-how and varied components that may be of use to each other, with the benefit of larger production scales. This global enterprise, however, needs managers with firsthand work experience in these different brands, sites, and local organizations. And, following this concept, the nationality of the individual in charge should not matter at all. Americans in Auburn Hills need to be familiar with operations in Stuttgart and vice versa. Similarly, key DaimlerChrysler people in Japan or India require firsthand knowledge of what is going on in Germany or the United States. In other words, people will have to rotate their jobs on a systematic basis.

"[With this in mind,] it is important to be aware of available management talent at different locations and to have an instrument to identify up-and-coming people on a worldwide basis," stresses Renschler. To arrive at a system of uniform evaluation of key managers was Renschler's main assignment during his stay in Auburn Hills as senior VP for executive management development. After a lot of benchmarking with other global firms, Renschler initiated project LEAD (leadership evaluation and development), a global data bank for management talent around the world, based on an objective system of evaluation, devoid of personal intervention by superiors. "It's a giant step forward for all of us," comments Renschler. "In a global world your nationality cannot be a decisive element for your career's success." In parallel, Renschler pioneered a set of general guidelines on how to promote the exchange of key executives and on how to foster their knowledge of global operations. As an example, members of the second management level, directly reporting to the DaimlerChrysler Board of Management, are required to have a "2+2+2" experience: It means they should have or gain experience with two DaimlerChrysler divisions, two operating units, and two geographic regions. Obviously, this will take many years to accomplish. Nevertheless, LEAD will be crucial for the future success of the company and support the diversity of people, brands, and operations of the new global giant. Given the importance of this system, we provide more details in Exhibit 5.1.

Exhibit 5.1.
Leadership Evaluation and Development (LEAD)

The LEAD process is designed as an instrument to evaluate performance, identify management talent, and guide personal and professional development on a global basis. A joint team from Auburn Hills and Stuttgart worked hard on LEAD to assure its worldwide relevance. The process comprises five steps that build on each other: goal setting, performance appraisal, appraisal of potential, executive development conference, and feedback and development plans.

- *Goal setting*—At the beginning of each performance cycle, employee and supervisor jointly define six measurable goals, in line with the individual's professional aspirations and corporate objectives. While most of these goals will be work related, at least one of them will be reserved for development of human resources within the person's area of responsibility.
- *Performance appraisal*—While as a primary step the achievement of the agreed-upon goals is verified and rated, it is overlaid by an evaluation of the individual's leadership behaviors, which include:
  - thinking strategically and establishing direction
  - leading change
  - challenging people to top performance
  - sharing knowledge and experience
  - driving value creation

  The supervisor's evaluation will be validated by a review of the next level manager or of the individual's peers. This will create an objective inventory of the individual's strengths and weaknesses.
- *Appraisal of potential*—Above-average performance will determine this next step in the LEAD process. It means that the individual is able to take larger responsibilities and move to the next level of management. The formalized appraisal of potential is a crucial step in preparation for the executive development conference.

Exhibit 5.1.
(Continued)

- *Executive development conference (EDC)*—The EDC brings together the individual's supervisor, his peers and colleagues, and the next level manager. In this annual conference, which validates the appraisal of potential, succession planning and strategic leadership development are discussed. The EDC helps identify exceptional talent and guide their development needs.
- *Feedback and development plans*—Constructive feedback will gauge the individual's professional development, in line with personal expectations and corporate objectives. Both employee and supervisor are responsible for this process of career development, which is to be handled proactively.

In *summary*, the EDC clearly is the centerpiece of the LEAD process. In the U.S. corporate environment, it may seem to be an unusual step, as it may lead to critical and confrontational discussions among colleagues. By the same token, however, it is an excellent communicational tool, indispensable for today's global enterprises. Echoing Renschler's assessment, it will be quite important for DaimlerChrysler to gain a broad understanding and knowledge of available management talent at different locations throughout the world.

M-CLASS AND SMART: WHY DIFFERENT RESULTS?

With Renschler's direct involvement in these two new ventures, it was tempting to ask for his assessment. He responded with surprising candor: "[People's] best motivation cannot be kept alive without success. We need a positive outlook to the future in order to maintain our efforts and commitment." The M-Class development benefited a lot from close cooperation with experts in other Mercedes-Benz operating groups. There was broad exchange of ideas and findings, and peers from other divisions joined M-Class road trips. At smart, people were triggered differently. Mr. Hayek, who maintained "that cars ought to be sold like watches," did not appreciate close cooperation with his business partner. "But success was also elusive due to some bad luck," admits Renschler. "The conceptual affinity to the A-Class, with a similar 'sandwich platform,' led to delays. Then came problems with winter stability and with the 'Elk test,' which is totally unfair, misused, and outright crazy." With Hayek gone, Renschler's therapy for smart is based on close cooperation with other divisions, exploring whatever synergies are available.

Renschler is an excellent role model for the global executive needed for DaimlerChrysler's future: He is well versed and experienced in different divisions, many operations, and at least two geographic regions. English is the company's official language, but Americans need to learn German when they come to Stuttgart. Says Renschler: "Europeans have a better starting position [in our global corporation] because they grow up differently. However, it must be possible [in the future] to find young people in the United States with a similar background. College education is going into that direction."

While recent history at DaimlerChrysler seems to tell a different story, Renschler stands squarely behind what, back in September of 1999, Chairman Schrempp wrote in a "Dear Colleagues" letter to Chrysler employees: "You have every reason to be proud of DaimlerChrysler and enthusiastic about its future." (The interview with Andreas Renschler took place on March 3, 2000.)

CHAPTER 6

The Culture of "LUV": Southwest Airlines

In 1995, Southwest Airlines won an unprecedented fourth annual Triple Crown—being #1 among all major airlines in on-time arrivals, luggage handling, and customer satisfaction, as determined by the U.S. Department of Transportation. This unusual feat prompted Chairman Herb Kelleher to present his troops with a challenge: "If you earn a fifth annual Triple Crown, I'll paint the name of every person in this company on a Boeing 737." In 1996, the Southwest people did. And Herb Kelleher did. And now, "Triple Crown One" takes off from Dallas's Love Field, right after "Silver One," to celebrate Southwest's 25th anniversary in 1996, or after "Lone Star One," highlighting the airline's ties to its home state of Texas.

This little episode is revealing evidence of the culture at Southwest and the relations between the company and its over 34,000 employees. The family spirit of its people embraces customers and communities alike. Southwest Airlines as a company and as an example of good management practices has been written up often. Therefore, we do not want to burden our story with many details of Southwest's history and business. Our focus will be on the Southwest culture, which is rich and uniquely supported. Its employees are proud of that "Southwest spirit" and feel real ownership of the company. They are clearly the force behind the airline's success.

"YOU ARE NOW FREE TO MOVE ABOUT THE COUNTRY"

This statement on the cover of Southwest Airlines's 1998 Annual Report in many ways symbolizes the company's business philosophy. Legendary low fares now allow people to fly to destinations they had to drive to in the past. Flights between city pairs are direct and frequent to give customers a maximum of flexibility. And even connections are quick, because Southwest ground crews turn flights around in less than 20 minutes. And in line with the company's culture of "LUV," Southwest people are able to reach out to their customers and provide a service second to none.

It may be worthwhile to look at some statistical data, which shows the explosive growth since Southwest began operations in 1971.

Deregulation of air traffic in the United States occurred in 1978. As Exhibit 6.1 shows, up to that point in time, Southwest was a small local carrier, serving 10 cities in Texas. That picture changed significantly during the next four years, with Southwest expanding to neighboring states and to the West. Early on, California developed into an important bastion of business for the airline. Still today, California alone accounts for 22% of Southwest's capacity, with all Western states contributing almost half of the total. Until the end of the 1980s, Southwest expanded its service to eight new states, including the important hubs of Chicago-Midway, Nashville, and Detroit, while the size of the fleet and the number of employees started skyrocketing.

This expansion created a major inconvenience for Southwest: Because the airline is flying out of Dallas's Love Field, its headquarters location, the Wright Amendment would allow direct flights or "city pairs" only within Texas or to four of the neighboring states. Flights to other stations would require a stop somewhere in between. This represented a huge problem for Southwest's internal communications and for training new employees and introducing them to Southwest's family culture. People in California started complaining that interaction with their friends at headquarters was "just not like it was before." COO Colleen Barrett and her people decided that enough was enough. It was time to take headquarters and the Southwest spirit out to the field. In 1991, Southwest's "culture committee" was born. But we are getting ahead of ourselves.

Before we go on, let's look at Exhibit 6.2, which compares Southwest Airlines's operations and performance with that of three major U.S. airlines. Wall Street's financial analysts have always attributed Southwest's positive development to its short-haul no-frills service, quick gate turnaround, and low cost per available seat mile (ASM). But Exhibit 6.2 adds another perspective: Southwest's low-cost status is clearly manifested by the average fare amount of $75, which is one-half to one-third of the other airlines. The low expenses per ASM, however, are by no means the consequence of Southwest paying lower salaries or utilizing fewer people. The explanation is found in the last two lines of boxes of Exhibit 6.2: Southwest people turn planes around faster, which results in fewer employees per plane. Similarly, Southwest people handle more passengers. Both sets of

Exhibit 6.1.
Growth of Southwest Airlines Operations 1978–2001

Year	Size of Fleet at Year End	# of Employees at Year End	# of Stations at Year End	New Stations
1978	13	1,119	12	All in Texas
1982	37	2,913	21	Neighboring States (LA, OK, NM) & West (AZ, CA, KS, NV)
1985	70	5,271	26	AR, CO, IL, MO
1990	106	8,620	33	AL, IN, MI, TN
1994	199	16,816	45	ID, KY, MD, OH, OR, UT, WA
1998	280	25,844	53	NE & East (FL, NH, NY, RI)
2001	358	33,000	59	NE & East (CT, VA, NC, NY)

Exhibit 6.2.
Southwest Operations in Comparison with Other Airlines (1998)

	SWA	AA (*)	DL	UAL
Revenue (in MM$)	4,164	17,449	14,138	17,561
Net Income (in MM$)	433	1.050	1.001	821
Expenses per ASM (in cents)	7.3	9.3	8.9	9.2
Load Factor	66.1%	70.2%	72.2%	71.6%
Employees (at Year End)	25,844	92,000	70,846	91,000
Size of Fleet (at Year End)	280	648	569	577
Revenue Passengers (x000)	52,586	105,000	104,148	87,000
Average Fare	$75	$166	$136	$202
Employees per Plane	92	142	125	158
Revenue Passengers Per Employee	2,035	1,141	1,470	956

(*) AA data refers to Airline Group. Size of fleet excludes American Eagle operation.
Certain numbers are estimated.

data demonstrate higher productivity and, in spite of the low fares, render Southwest operations more profitable.

BONDING WITH PEERS: THE SOUTHWEST CULTURE COMMITTEE

Asked about the mission of the Culture Committee, Jane Compere, flight attendant for Southwest since 1992, had an intriguing response: "Setting an example for others to follow is a very big part of the Culture Committee's duties." In a nutshell, Culture Committee members try to convey an understanding of the history, spirit, and culture of Southwest to new hires and fellow employees of faraway stations. "We are working hard to keep the family spirit that we are so proud of," adds Joyce Rogge, Southwest's senior VP of marketing, who joined the airline in 1988 and was on the original Culture Committee. She is considered a "lifer," which means that she continues as part of the alumni segment of the active committee.

In 1991, when the Culture Committee was founded, it had about 30 members. Early on, a maximum two-year term was established to prevent burnout and duty overload, as committee duties go on top of people's job responsibilities. But from the beginning, employees rolling off the committee were "crying to stay on," explained Colleen Barrett, "because it meant a lot to their own rejuvenation." This is how the alumni organization was formed. Today, Southwest counts on about 100 to 120 Culture Committee members, which is the maximum effective and manageable number of participants. In addition, there is an alumni organization of about 150 to 175 people. And over the last two or three years, local committees have sprung up at most stations, some small and others, like in Houston, Detroit, or Chicago, with 60 or more members. This no doubt represents a huge effort to promote and maintain Southwest's ideals and values. Initiatives include fund-raisers for employee emergencies, community projects such as cleaning up a public park or adopting a piece of a highway, or just getting together for pizza or burritos and for some fun to celebrate small and large special accomplishments.

Being on the main Culture Committee involves meeting in Dallas three times a year with fellow committee members to discuss present and future activities. More importantly, however, people join teams, which concentrate on certain problem areas or support certain sectors of the airline. As examples, there may be teams dedicated to customer appreciation, to supporting Southwest's reservation agents, or to recognizing Southwest's maintenance operations.

"Hokey Days,"an event celebrated at multiple locations at different times of the year, represents such an initiative. The "hokey sweeper" is a symbol for cleaning, and the support of the Culture Committee is directed toward the crews who clean the planes, probably one of the least inspiring jobs all over the airline. All the more reason to show these fellow workers that "we care about what you do." People's eyes light up while talking about Hokey Days, which are great for taking time out for helping with the cleaning job and bonding with these and other fellow employees. Management up to the executive VPs participates as an expression of belonging and family spirit. It is a great opportunity to strengthen Southwest's culture throughout the country.

"Second Wind" was quite a different and more serious initiative of a Culture Committee team, dealing with stress and burnout on the job. The program has led to setting up "helping hands" and resource centers at many Southwest stations. Second Wind counsels employees on how to avoid getting into a negative work spiral and makes specific recommendations for exercise and proper nutrition, for opportunities to grow both professionally and spiritually, and for enjoying love, fun, and friendship. "The team is committed to providing information, resources and tools that can be used to enhance the health and emotional well-being of our employees," states Colleen Barrett's introductory letter. Where on earth did we hear before of such mindfulness of an employee's personal situation?

Culture Committee "alumni" are asked to pledge participation in at least three events each year. As a case in point, Hokey Days are a perfect opportunity for alumni to be involved. But there are other possibilities, as Jon Shubert, Southwest's manager of executive office communications, tells us. Jon joined Southwest in 1989, was invited to the Culture Committee in 1992, and has been part of the alumni organization since 1994. "It's fun to be active," says Jon, "and to do some of your own ideas." Jon decided to adopt some of the smaller and remote Southwest stations, like Lubbock, Texas, Boise, Idaho, and Portland, Oregon. He visits them once a quarter, attending events of the local committee or simply providing some fun and entertainment to the local folks. And people wonder what he is doing. After a recent visit to Birmingham, the station manager commented to a colleague: "Jon Shubert from the Executive Office was here. He visited with us, he threw bags, he checked in customers at the gate. And he fed us barbecue. But I am still not sure why he was here."

"WALK A MILE IN MY SHOES": SOUTHWEST'S UNIQUE CULTURE AND VALUES

"Walk a mile in my shoes" was an early Culture Committee initiative, introduced as a formal program in 1994. It was probably modeled after "Days in the field," a program from the early days of Southwest that held managers close to operations. The idea behind it was to have people get a different perspective about fellow workers' jobs and eliminate preconceived ideas about certain segments of the airline being more or less productive. While free travel passes provided some incentive to participate, the success of the program passed all expectations: About 12,000 of the 15,000 employees at the beginning of 1994 participated in "Walk a mile in my shoes."

Jane Compere still remembers today her first workday as a flight attendant on "Black Wednesday," the day before Thanksgiving, which is one of the hottest travel days of the year. Can you imagine her surprise when Chairman Herb Kelleher showed up at the galley to provision her plane? "They never ask us to do what they would not do themselves," comments Jane approvingly.

Shubert "walked his mile" in a more dramatic way, working with the aircraft cleaning crew, putting down new carpeting in the sticky heat of a summer night. "The cleaners are called aircraft appearance technicians," explains Jon, "and they work in the middle of the night when the aircraft is turned off . . . Let me tell you, I never sweated so much in my life and I never worked so hard . . . I got so much of an appreciation for what the aircraft cleaners do . . . " What an amazing way to get to know your fellow workers! And Liz Short, a secretary with seven years of service at Southwest, "walked her mile" in Los Angeles. One interesting feedback was, "I didn't have any idea that flight attendants had to pick up dirty diapers."

Supporting each other and reaching out to fellow workers very much characterizes the family culture at Southwest. One may see pilots picking up trash or gate agents helping load baggage in the rain. Depending on personal needs and convenience, people are allowed to "trade shifts" with each other. All this is part of strong people bonds and the caring environment at Southwest. Similarly, family situations are respected. Southwest employees point with pride to the over 1,000 married couples working for the airline. Bobby Debenport, Southwest's chief dispatcher, who met his wife 23 years ago at the airline, would not mind if one of his three daughters—the oldest just graduated from high school—came to work here. "Southwest is a great place to work," affirms Bobby.

And Chairman Herb Kelleher sums it up: "I feel that you have to be with your employees through all their difficulties, that you have to be interested in them personally. They may be disappointed in their country. Even their family might not be working out the way they wish it would. But I want them to know that Southwest will always be there for them." No wonder that people "luv" to belong to the Southwest family!

FINAL TRIBUTE TO THE CULTURE COMMITTEE: LEADERSHIP BY EXAMPLE

For those of us who are accustomed to clearly defined organizational patterns, the Southwest Culture Committee is an amazing creation. There is no hierarchy, no reporting relationship, no budget, no performance evaluations, but still—Herb Kelleher has often stated that the Culture Committee is the most important committee at Southwest Airlines.

We asked the question how Libby Sartain, Southwest's VP of people at the time, and her department might view the Culture Committee, as most of its activities overlap with the human resources area. Libby has since left the company to pursue other opportunities. Sunny Stone, Southwest's manager of culture activities since 1993, responded: "As a matter of fact, she encourages these activities and has some of them going on in her own department." There seems to be very little departmental jealousy at Southwest. No "fiefdoms" exist. "The Culture Committee helps to keep that from happening," adds Shubert, "because you have people from every department [on it], all over the system."

The Southwest Culture Committee congregates a large group of role model ambassadors, of living examples of a great company culture, who go out and strive to perpetuate that very culture, embracing their fellow workers, lifting their spirits, and leading them by their example. The results are tangible: Over the last 10 years, Southwest has more than tripled in size, while keeping its spontaneity and family spirit, without which that very expansion would not have been possible. Herb Kelleher and Colleen Barrett, among others, have provided strong leadership, but the creative spirit of the almost 300 members and alumni of the Southwest Culture Committee has been the real power behind the airline's growth. "And you want to know something," concludes Stone, "at Southwest Airlines, we have over 34,000 people who are talented at this!"

The Executive Perspective: Colleen C. Barrett— Nurturing the Southwest Spirit

"If you can show people that you not only care about them in terms of their professional life, their career, or their business life, but that you care about their personal situation, and that you will consider it when asking them to do something; if you can show them that you care about them as much from a personal as from a business perspective, people are going to kill for you!"

With this emotional assertion, Colleen Barrett, the new president and chief operating officer of Southwest Airlines and one of its legendary leaders from the early days, describes "what Southwest is all about." Former chairman and founder Herbert D. Kelleher and Colleen Barrett, affectionately called "Herb and Colleen" by their employees, helped build an exciting work environment that *FORTUNE* consistently ranked one of America's best places to work. To the daily fascination of her coworkers, Colleen embodies the very spirit of Southwest. We asked Colleen for this interview—and she rarely agrees to be interviewed—because she is the heart and soul of Southwest's Culture Committee, which she founded in 1991, inviting about 30 employees from different quarters of the company.

"The reason for forming the first Culture Committee," explains Colleen, "was very simple: Southwest was growing at a fantastic rate. Our system was expanding away from Dallas. However, to understand the history, the spirit, and the culture of Southwest, new hires needed to come to headquarters and interact with people and departments here. Part of the learning process at Southwest consists of being around people responsible for leadership issues. Unfortunately, the Wright Amendment [which does not allow direct flights from Dallas's Love Field, where Southwest is head-

quartered, to states other than those four that are contiguous to Texas] created problems requiring employees to spend an extra day coming and
going. Therefore, instead of bringing new hires to Dallas, we decided to
take the Southwest culture to them. Everybody would help to mentor. We
wanted all employees—no matter where they are—to understand Southwest's core values and why these values and Southwest's family spirit
have led to our successes and accomplishments."

The creation of the Southwest Culture Committee was an unusual and
innovative move, most critical to the company's successful expansion.
Colleen Barrett readily admits that without it, the Southwest culture
would not exist in its present form. "Instead," she says, "we would see little pockets of different cults, like the Southwest Airlines of the West, and
the Southwest Airlines of the East." Being in charge of Southwest's customers, Colleen sees her responsibility directed toward both the airline's
passengers and employees. Both are her customers. In her view, "if you
don't maintain Southwest's culture, you don't have anything special."
Colleen encourages a fun environment at the airline. She wants people to
be individualistic, to be themselves, and to feel comfortable in their work
environment. Part of Southwest's family culture is to hire and support
married couples, of which there are over 1,000 today.

We questioned the two-year limitation for staying on the Culture Committee. Was that established from the beginning? And when did the
alumni organization start? "Yes," explained Colleen, "[the limitation] was
there from the beginning. We always wanted new blood in the committee.
While the first 30 members were hand selected, we later invited new
members based on employee suggestions, and we allowed people to nom-
inate their successors. It is important to keep a good mix of job classifica-
tions and system locations, as well as different seniority levels. As to the
alumni system, initially, it was not contemplated. However, people were
crying to stay on, as it meant a lot to their own rejuvenation. That's how it
started. Alumni are asked to pledge participation in at least three culture-
supporting activities and to afterward report on what they did. In general,
that's the way we measure the success of Culture Committee activities: By
feedback from employees, by memos, personal notes, reports on operational issues—there is constant feedback."

There can be no doubt that Southwest Airlines's culture has had an
impact on people's lives and careers. It has created a spirit of compassion, of
caring, of initiative and professional pride. Leadership is at the center of
people's learning efforts, supported by the airline's University for People.
We may quote here Colleen's mandate for new Culture Committee members: "Each of you was asked to serve because you exemplify the Southwest

Spirit and Culture and we need your leadership style and skills out in the field in order to keep, nourish, and enrich that very Spirit and Culture."

Colleen Barrett and today's over 100 members of the Southwest Culture Committee will assure that the Southwest spirit stays alive for many years to come. (The interview with Colleen Barrett took place on July 14, 1999.)

CHAPTER 7

A Different Perspective: Cultures with a Passion

The two case studies on Mercedes-Benz and Southwest Airlines open another perspective on cultures: Both work environments are highly charged and marked by the excitement of participation and involvement. Relations between the people are close, and personal interactions and communications are vibrant. These are "cultures with a passion"!

At Mercedes-Benz (MBUSI), groups or teams that are working in certain isolation—the feasibility study team or the function groups are examples—contribute to a close bonding of all members. They experience the unusual excitement of participating in a fundamental change of direction for the company. They work in close proximity and keep open communications. The weekly meetings of all function groups facilitate everyone's input and underscore the fact that communications are essential to the success of the project. Finally, "team Alabama" becomes the culmination of the emotional experience, kept alive by the extraordinary efforts of all members, by long hours and hard work, and, ultimately, by the success of the M-Class vehicles.

Similarly, the close relations among its people and the family spirit embracing employees, customers, and communities alike clearly are the "passion" driving the success of Southwest Airlines. To keep this culture alive and strengthen the bonds among their people is the main thrust of the airline's Culture Committee.

There is such incredible fun of involvement and participation among the employees that the events held to support the family spirit—Hokey Days as an example—become true celebrations. When people are hugging each other, it means sincere appreciation. That's how they truly feel about each other.

Programs like "Days in the field" or "Walk a mile in my shoes" provide opportunities for interacting and getting to know each other's responsibilities. They are indispensable tools for face-to-face communications. It's part of the effort to reach out to fellow workers and to start appreciating their unique talents and contributions.

Again, let's ask the question: What different distinguishing practices, principles, and beliefs can we identify at Mercedes-Benz and Southwest Airlines?

EXCITEMENT OF INVOLVEMENT AND PARTICIPATION

Considering groups and their inner workings, there has been long-standing research on the concept of teams as an organizational design—making better use of resources and offering greater flexibility for the task at hand—or as a social system—its dynamics influencing people's behaviors and a certain role differentiation among its members. More recently, however, researchers' interest has started focusing on the psychological or emotional dimension of groups.

It has been shown that certain events—of success or adversity—reinforce the motivational energy and overall productivity of teams. Its members make unusual work efforts to "earn" their place on the team. For some of the members, the greatest reward is to have been on that particular team. It's a type of seductive enthusiasm that sets in motion a "self-fueling spiral of team success" (Hackman, 1990). Good teams get better!

As we observe the Mercedes-Benz employees participating in the project of bringing a new sport-utility vehicle to market, the excitement of contributing to a "fundamental change of direction" of the company is palpable. The developers feel that "sense of mission" that keeps them in the office trailer until late at night. The function groups are motivated by the ability to make decisions and negotiate huge supply commitments. And "team Alabama" experiences the "opportunity for personal impact and unusual responsibility."

Motivation is at a high level when people have full control and responsibility for their job. But that motivation gets stronger the more a person's "heart is in it" and the more he or she is emotionally engaged. Being able to make important decisions, to innovate, and to be creative leads the Mercedes-Benz team to work hard and fight for "their" project. But it is the exhilarating experience of being part of this change of direction for Mercedes-Benz that takes people's productivity and motivation almost beyond human limits.

We can see a similar spirit embracing everyone at Southwest. The airline's operational statistics are telling and impressive. Southwest gate and ramp agents—with the enthusiastic support of their pilots and flight attendants—handle more planes and more passengers than their competitors because they are able to turn planes around in 20 minutes. Other airlines need at least one hour for the arrival and departure process. Is it because management whips them into faster action or because planes are not supplied or cleaned well? By no means! Employees are proud of their work ethic and of the success of "their" airline. We mentioned the challenge of earning the fifth Triple Crown—being first in on-time arrival, luggage handling, and customer satisfaction—as determined by the U.S. Department of Transportation. This accomplishment clearly shows the Southwest people as the force behind the company's success, working with a passion as one big team.

BONDING WITH FELLOW EMPLOYEES

As we reviewed some aspects of motivational theory in the introduction, we mentioned Abraham Maslow and his work on needs motivation. One of the basic needs defined by Maslow in his concept of a "hierarchy of needs" is the need for affiliation. People desire to "belong," to be part of a group or team. They seek each other out for confirmation and reinforcement of their personal beliefs.

Viewed from a different angle, the close family spirit of certain groups provides satisfaction and enjoyment to its members. They are comfortable with each other, truly care for fellow team members, and go the extra step of providing personal support and counsel.

That solidarity and cohesiveness may even lead to the pitfalls of "groupthink," where members fall victim to group pressures against voicing reservations or dissenting opinions to the group's plans and convictions.

In both case studies, there is much testimony about bonding between team members. The M-Class study group spent long hours brainstorming together in their isolated office trailer. The "function groups," set up for the development effort, worked hard in close proximity over at the old crane factory. Team Alabama was involved in an extraordinary effort to set up production. Barbecue weekends and family days supported all this. "Teams still reflect the way the company used to be on a smaller level," observes team leader Joe Greene. "A lot of our teams get a chance to do things together [outside of work]."

Similarly, people at Southwest love to get together for some fun and to celebrate small and large accomplishments. During Hokey Days, they go out to show appreciation for the cleaning crews. On other occasions, they support other sectors of the company, be it reservation agents or maintenance operations. Members of the Culture Committee and, in particular, the employees on the alumni organization represent a large group of "culture ambassadors" who convey a better understanding of Southwest's history and spirit to new employees. They are role models, "setting an example for others to follow," as flight attendant Jane Compere describes it well.

The hallmark of Southwest's culture always has been to feel like family and close friends who enjoy embracing each other and lifting each other's spirits. Therefore, interaction between employees at Southwest is crucial. For that very reason, the Culture Committee was born to solve problems created by the Wright Amendment, which allowed direct flights only within Texas or to four of the neighboring states. Southwest's enormous expansion had started creating huge problems and people in California began complaining that communication was "just not as it was before."

The bonding process at these two organizations does not stop here. It includes spouses and children as an extended family. Austin Dare's remark is very telling for the situation at MBUSI: "As part of our culture, we try to integrate family members as well. They play a big role in the success of the company." At Southwest, family situations are always respected. Along these lines, it is part of Southwest's family culture to hire and support married couples. Today, there are over 1,000 couples working for the airline.

INTERACTION AND COMMUNICATION

In human groups, interaction and communication—which we may rephrase as "verbal interaction"—are important behavioral devices that shape and support the integration of a particular social system. It seems to be a spiraling process: As people escalate interaction with each other, they start developing a better understanding of each other's roles and "ways," leading to greater mutual respect. This will produce realistic but demanding expectations of work ethics and mutual support within that group.

An extension of this process of interaction is the so-called "communities of practice," where people start teaching each other certain key elements of their work and begin to form sharing and helping relationships with each other. Communities of practice are interesting new opportunities for unstructured and interactive learning at the workplace.

In these emotionally charged organizations, the awareness of other people's duties and contributions seems to be very important to provide for a high degree of mutual respect and the conviction that "we all are in this together." MBUSI introduced rotation schedules that include stations before and after your own workplace with the intent to create "customer orientation." Function groups would work in close proximity. During the feasibility phase, the office trailer environment provided similar intimacy. And we remember Thomas Harthun saying, "[In] Alabama responsibilities are broader based, extending to the whole vehicle. And the density of information is much higher than in Germany. Everybody here gets [a lot of] information on the business."

In similar ways, Southwest employees assume multiple responsibilities as part of the company's culture. Pilots may pick up trash or flight attendants help load luggage in support of each other. This even found its way into union contracts, where an additional clause, including "those duties historically performed" in job definitions, allows this type of mutual support.

Programs like "Walk a mile in my shoes" and "Days in the field" give the people and the managers of Southwest a closer look at and a better understanding of the nature of different jobs and their contributions to the organization. While "Days in the field" is mandatory for managers, the 80% rate of participation in "Walk a mile in my shoes," when it was introduced, surpassed all expectations. But this is exactly the kind of interaction and communication that forms the basis for the family spirit at Southwest.

Along similar lines, community outreach, which is extensive at Southwest, allows for interaction of employees of different areas of the company outside of work. Again, the joint experience leads people to respect their fellow workers, as they reveal fresh talents and unrelenting efforts for charitable outreach.

WHAT DID WE LEARN?

In the earlier case studies, we found three "distinguishing practices," indicative of new corporate cultures. All three—the trusting relationship between leaders and workers, true partnership based on a new role of management, and learning as a way to advance people's careers—can certainly be observed at Mercedes-Benz and Southwest Airlines as well.

Still, while the work environment is different at the companies of these last two case studies, there is the emotional stimulation of participating in an exciting venture. There is a family type close relationship among fellow employees. And there is much interaction and open communication. In summary, it is passion, the jolting emotional charge, that makes the cultures of Mercedes-Benz and Southwest Airlines so special. We have seen the measure of their success.

A FEW GOOD IDEAS TO BE ADOPTED

As we did before, we want to point out to our readers some of the initiatives at Southwest and Mercedes-Benz that caught our attention and may be worth emulating.

Forming a Culture Committee

The growth and personnel expansion that comes with business success often leads to disappointments with the inability to bond and interact like in the past. "It's just not like it was before," we heard Southwest's new and faraway California stations complain in the mid-1980s. At MBUSI, it didn't take more than four years to start longing for the "good old days."

Forming a culture committee truly is an excellent way to maintain a close "small company" environment, even as an organization grows in size and employee numbers. The Southwest example provides some indications and guidelines of what it takes to put an active committee together, including an alumni organization for employees who as lifers would like to continue to support their fellow workers.

The emphasis is on conveying a better understanding of the history and culture of the organization to new employees and to provide mentoring and bonding at the same time. Committee members and alumni alike are role models and mentors for the increasing employee population.

The result is twofold: For the organization, the committee sustains and nurtures a coherent culture and close relations among its employees. For the members and alumni of the committee, the task is stimulating and rejuvenating, in supporting a culture they are passionate about.

"Walk a Mile in My Shoes"

As we learned, this particular initiative at Southwest came about at the suggestion of the Culture Committee. Working closely with a fellow employee for a few days would help create a better understanding of the inner workings and the different responsibilities within the Southwest organization. Before, people might have imagined certain inequities when comparing their job responsibilities to those of fellow workers. The program taught them otherwise and had them appreciate fellow workers in their different roles. It led to greater respect and mutual support.

Southwest has a similar program, established much earlier, for managers. "Days in the field" required managers to work different jobs, like ramp agent or ticket agent, for a certain number of days, to stay close to the problems of the field. Along similar lines, MBUSI introduced job rotation with different stations to create "customer orientation" among their workers.

A program along these lines helps overall communications and creates a desirable openness within the organization. People see and understand what their fellow workers do and contribute. In many ways, plant and office layouts send similar signals to the employees. Bill Taylor's insistence to bring everyone—assembly, office, management—under one roof was meant to foster and bring home the concept of openness and total communications. In many organizations, separate office areas for management and other perquisites prevent this openness as well as mutual reliance and understanding from happening.

Integration of the Family

How could the family spirit at Southwest prosper, if family members were to be excluded from company events and celebrations? "Family days" at MBUSI are evidence of the importance for children to know where Dad or Mom is working and what he or she is doing. And Southwest is certainly proud of the over 1,000 married couples that work for the company today.

Integrating the family leads to pride and respect at home, which mirrors and supports the work situation. The responsible family person will turn out to be equally responsible at work. Open communications at work lead to the same openness and understanding at home. A good example of this reciprocity between home and work was an early practice at MBUSI to allow employees to take the new M-Class car home over the weekend to show it to family and friends. What a powerful way to promote both the new car and the work environment that built it!

PART III

Facing the Challenge of Change: Cultures in Transition

This may be a good opportunity to deal with the phenomenon of major incongruence between an organization's culture and external forces leading in a different direction—be it market conditions, merger situations, or executive management trying to impose divergent strategies in disregard of people's beliefs or the organization's reality.

To start off this particular subject matter, we offer the case study of Bellcore—part of the former Bell Laboratories—and the account of its CEO, Dr. George Heilmeier, which show a frequently occurring dilemma: The powerful legacy of the former Bell culture and the resulting entitlement mentality prevailing among the employees were completely out of step with the changing telecommunications market, which required flexibility, close customer relations, and innovative new technologies. Bellcore would not have succeeded without adjusting its culture to the new environment. If it had not been for Dr. Heilmeier and his skillful and tireless efforts establishing new guiding principles and leading the people through the "Team Bellcore" learning experience, the company, in the long run, would most likely have failed.

Along similar lines, the recent business history of Xerox Corporation and toy maker Mattel are examples of conflicting forces that put both companies in considerable economic jeopardy. We tried to interview employees of the two companies for this chapter but have been denied access, which is understandable but somewhat shortsighted. Talking to the people might have uncovered certain inconsistencies and helped these firms to make adjustments.

Xerox is one of America's most venerable corporations, yet after tremendous success the company ran into serious trouble involving accounting manipulation and deceit of the investment community. The way out of the crisis seems to be going back to Xerox's cultural roots and reinvigorating employee participation.

In the past, based on innovation and employee contributions, the company was able to deal well with deadly competitive pressures, technical challenges, and even product design failures. Xerox was respected for its ability to adapt and advance with technical innovations. Employee involvement and satisfaction gave the company a spot among the *100 Best Companies to Work for in America* (Levering and Moskowitz, 1993). Yet then, new executive management moved away from the organization's basic cultural tenets and put the company's future at serious risk. All this combined with a leadership deficit at the top started demotivating the very employees it depended on for success. This case study is a powerful lesson for all of us who consider a healthy organizational culture to be critical for success.

Mattel is an interesting case of misguided retrogressive management. Perhaps the greatest reason why good organizations with productive cultures lose their focus and start backing up to a more primitive organizational model is that executives who are determined to exercise their personal power and don't believe in the potential of the company's people take over. Sometimes such a manager can be successful, when dedicating his or her personal talents to a limited product area or market segment. And, indeed, Jill Barad was very successful in handling and expanding the Barbie business at Mattel. Yet when faced with a larger scope of problems and opportunities, this type of solo performance is no longer sustainable. What such "leaders" fail to recognize, often until it is too late, is that they are inheriting the legacy of an advanced culture, supported by people with all their skills, commitment, and ingenuity. Over time this is squandered, and then comes the setback. This is pretty much what happened at the famous toy maker Mattel, and the way out of it has become slow and difficult.

Another example of a failed culture that immediately comes to mind is Enron. However, we would argue that it was the very culture that permeated the Houston energy company that was responsible for part of the company's problems and led to its bankruptcy at the end of 2001. Enron had a two-faced culture. The company offered a statement of values that sounded great and certainly was an important device to attract top talent. However, when the crunch came, those values were shamelessly betrayed. People lost their pensions and their jobs evaporated, while some of the executives walked away with millions. Yet these executives denied any questionable practices and possibly convinced themselves that they had done nothing wrong. In our chapter on Enron, we examine the road to infamy as well as the self-deception, conniving, and chicanery that led to the company's collapse. Enron and dozens of similar cases have certainly shaken investor confidence and in the minds of some people have raised questions about the self-correcting ability of the whole capitalist system.

The experience of cultural conflict and maladjustment may be very frustrating and, at certain times, even traumatic for the employees. They may decide to leave, or, worse, they may stay but be discouraged and resort to a behavior of job withdrawal. We have included the example of the European Manufacturing Company (EMC) to illustrate that this particular problem, quite frequent in other parts of the world as well and affecting 25% to 35% of the workforce in some countries, damages an organization, often below the surface, in its day-to-day operations.

Job withdrawal is a paramount example of a negative or counterproductive element of culture that serves the interest of some individuals or groups of people. It is a way a person copes with boredom, the organization's failure to use their innate talents and abilities, and the lack of a trust-based motivating culture. Through job withdrawal, a person transfers and displaces his or her creativity, social cleverness, and interest from the organization to the pursuit of personal objectives while remaining employed. This is practiced in a way that enhances life on the job for the individual but at a great loss for the organization so affected. It's a payback for a defunct culture.

In summary, this section of our book offers several case studies of companies that once held great promise but had their future imperiled and in one case virtually destroyed through what can be described as cultural illness. This section demonstrates the need for careful attention to creating and maintaining a healthy organizational culture.

CHAPTER 8

Building the New Bellcore

Today, Bellcore is the Telcordia Technologies subsidiary of SAIC, but we have chosen to describe its history in a separate chapter in order not to burden the SAIC story with too many details (see chapter 14).

Bellcore—a successor company to AT&T's venerated Bell Laboratories—came into being in 1984, when the U.S. government split up the Bell System. Bellcore was to serve as a research consortium to the seven Regional Bell Operating Companies (the RBOCs). Based on the generous budget provided by the RBOCs, Bellcore flourished and pioneered many important telecommunications services, such as toll free numbers, call waiting, and caller identification.

During the early 1990s, however, the telecommunications market started to change. The advent of new technologies and movement toward deregulation led to increased rivalry among the RBOCs. Stronger competition prompted the need for cost reductions. In order to maintain technological leadership and economic viability for Bellcore, the company had to change and become more diversified and market driven. In the spring of 1991, the former chief technical officer of Texas Instruments, Dr. George Heilmeier, was hired as the new CEO of Bellcore to spearhead the change and transformation.

THE BELLCORE PREDICAMENT

A few months after Dr. Heilmeier joined Bellcore, it became clear to him that the company had to change. What he did not expect, however, was the degree of resistance that he would face in trying to introduce the changes.

Many of Bellcore's problems and shortcomings were obvious:

- *Absence of sales and marketing expertise*—Since the RBOCs defined their technical needs and assigned research priorities within a $1 billion-plus budget, there had been no need for any particular sales capability at Bellcore.
- *"Stovepipe" orientation*—The different divisions at Bellcore were structured as independent entities, responsible in their assignments to certain councils of the RBOCs. Critical information was not always shared with fellow divisions.
- *Restrictions on non-RBOC work*—Work for non-RBOC customers needed to be "sponsored" and overseen by one of the RBOCs! At times, even leading-edge work in new areas such as the Internet or data networking, proposed by Bellcore researchers, would not be supported by the RBOC research councils.
- *Absence of profit objectives*—Based on the "entitlement culture" of the old Bell System, accountability for project results and a profit mindset were completely amiss.
- *Low customer satisfaction*—At Bellcore, customer feedback was not taken seriously. Instead, there was certain arrogance toward customer comments. This situation was exacerbated by deficiencies in software quality control.

In addition, Bellcore was carrying an enormous overhead: For every five people working directly on projects, there were three people on overhead. With RBOC revenues down by 13% in 1993, all this took on a greater sense of urgency.

THE PROCESS OF CHANGE

In a joint effort with senior management, Dr. Heilmeier plunged into the change process with a memo to all employees and a brochure outlining Bellcore's vision and values, the strategies for "Taking Bellcore to the Next Level," and people's roles and responsibilities.

Sensing a lot of resistance, Dr. Heilmeier decided to take his message directly to the people, conducting town meetings with up to 100 employees at all possible Bellcore locations. There would be no prepared remarks or viewgraphs, but Dr. Heilmeier would answer all questions in an open-ended format.

The priorities for change at Bellcore were

1. commercialize Bellcore business systems and reduce costs,
2. sustain core RBOC revenues and grow non-RBOC business,
3. adopt a value and profit/loss orientation and establish personal accountability,
4. improve quality and customer satisfaction, and
5. start developing new products and services for new markets.

MARKETING AND SALES

Bellcore hired a VP of marketing and started building a marketing organization, which ultimately comprised 130 professionals. In parallel, a commercialization task force was created to oversee the whole spectrum of marketing and sales activities. In an innovative organizational approach, a "Customer Solutions" business unit was formed as a link among the research, software, and professional services groups and Bellcore's market partners. Customer Solutions would help drive the development of a new product and services portfolio, the absence of which was mentioned before. Promoting Bellcore's offerings on the World Wide Web, at trade shows, and at user meetings like the Information Officers Conference or the Bellcore Forum, non-RBOC business grew at double-digit rates, reaching a level of 20% of revenue in 1997.

DRIVE TOWARD HIGHER PROFITABILITY

Cost-reduction efforts included major downsizing efforts during the 1992–93 period. From a peak of 8,800 employees, Bellcore started re-engineering its business processes and increasing efficiencies, reducing employment by over 35% to 5,500 employees. At the same time, management was reduced by one-third.

Quality improvement efforts and better customer focus led to an unprecedented increase in customer satisfaction: From a 72% level of overall satisfaction in 1992, positive customer response reached 94% in 1997.

Thirdly, newly introduced financial systems allowed for improved profit and loss measurement. At the same time, they provided support for sales and marketing and offered new tools for decision making.

HUMAN RESOURCES AND COMPANY CULTURE

Of all the changes implemented by Dr. Heilmeier's team, the ones put in motion in the human resources area were probably the most interesting.

As to *management*, compensation plans were drastically changed from an "entitlement" approach to performance-based systems. A "Success Sharing Plan" was introduced, including customer satisfaction as an important yardstick. Also, 360-degree performance reviews were instituted.

More importantly, however, the *Team Bellcore* program was developed to facilitate a major change in the company's culture. This program stretched over three years, extending to all employees of the company. While it was only one of the levers of corporate change, it was certainly a highly visible one. Initially, groups of 20 to 30 employees would participate in a three-day learning experience, which would focus on team building, cooperation, and win-win attitudes, as well as accountability. In-house facilitators were trained to conduct the meetings. As mentioned before, it was an experiential or inside learning effort, rather than a training exercise. Preferably, intact working groups would be invited, together with their leadership, to assure leadership commitment ("shadow of the leader" was an example of the new language derived from this experience). Thirty days later, the same groups were brought in again for a follow-up day to share work experiences, to enlist mutual support, and to strengthen the sense of accountability.

As a concurrent development, a set of *guiding principles* evolved from the Team Bellcore effort, which included not only most of the elements of the Team Bellcore program but additional values like openness and trust, respect, and continuous learning. The focus on learning tried to induce people to grow and look for new trends in business. Learning was seen as a behavior-changing experience. New skills had people operate in new ways.

LESSONS AND RESULTS

The process of change in its many facets allowed Dr. Heilmeier to successfully establish a new company culture. The town meetings and his personal involvement in them were important factors, as well as the Team Bellcore initiative. Management commitment and firm dealing with resistance, especially in the management ranks, was convincing. Equally persuasive was the recognition of real contributors to the new Bellcore.

Economic success based on growth initiatives and new products and services would not be long in coming: Bellcore was able to develop and introduce the MediaVantage family of systems and other new telecommunications software built in a modular approach, useful for smaller carriers and global applications. Another example was the Internet, where Bellcore did pioneering work on Internet telephony and introduced its AdaptX system for Web page development. Last but not least and after its acquisition by SAIC in 1997, the company has become a very successful contributor to the new owner's present success.

The Executive Perspective: Dr. George Heilmeier— Leading the Change

The transformation of Bellcore from the "paternalistic entitlement culture" of the old Bell System into a competitive, commercially minded company was a difficult task by any measure. To make the new venture successful, Dr. Heilmeier certainly brought with him the experience and management principles needed in the driver's seat. However, even then it was tough. Let's get a taste of his experiences:

This process [of change] involved a lot of training: You had to train people in "what is marketing?" "how do you sell?" "what is a profit & loss statement?" "how do you manage a profit & loss statement?" "how do you account for customer satisfaction?" "what about the product line?" and "how do you find out what products and services our customers really need?" Many companies change and they change one thing. We were trying to change and build everything at the same time.

I used to wake up at 3 o'clock in the morning and couldn't go back to sleep. I stopped listening to my voice mail and reading my E-mail after 7 o'clock in the evening because, inevitably, there would be bad news. And it would keep me up and awake at night. It wasn't a pleasant time. As a matter of fact, in retrospect, it was one of the worst experiences I have ever had.

Before joining Bellcore, Dr. Heilmeier, as Texas Instrument's senior VP and chief technical officer, worked in a totally different environment: "TI was an 'in your face' type of culture. [There were] no hidden agendas on the part of anyone. When I came up here, I saw all kinds of hidden agendas. [TI was] very goal oriented, very project and success oriented. There was a lot of teamwork in the company. Texans have a very high work ethic and they are very friendly people; so teamwork came quite naturally. The so-called 'Protestant ethic' of 'work hard and you'll be successful' was very much ingrained in people there, completely different from the North-east."

No wonder Dr. Heilmeier was taken by surprise by what he saw at Bell-core and by the resistance he experienced. "I didn't think cultures such as I found at Bellcore existed anymore in American industry." And using obvious exaggeration to underscore his impressions, he went on: "The attitude around here among some of the technical people was almost one of: 'Look, you don't understand how we operate. We are smarter than our competitors and our customers. It's the job of the owners to send us money, and then we do what we want to do with that money. And when the money runs out, we tell them to send some more. When they ask us what we are doing, we essentially say 'never mind, because we are smarter than you.' That characterized the mindset of some of the people here who came out of Bell Labs and had a paternalistic entitlement view."

In the beginning, Dr. Heilmeier's management philosophy for Bellcore showed his naïveté: "I thought it was so clear that we needed to change that, as soon as we started articulating it, everybody would say 'of course, why didn't we think of that'." He expected people to rally to the cause, but, instead, there was a lot of resistance. "The way people resist change in large bureaucracies, is that they will either wait you out or wear you out." Dr. Heilmeier was not going to let that happen.

His approach, however, had to be a careful one: "I didn't want to lose key technical talent, because the knowledge worker is the true asset of a company like this. Your assets walk out the door every night and, hope-fully, they come back the next day. So, I couldn't be too heavy handed in this." Dr. Heilmeier decided to move forward on three fronts to launch the change process.

First, he started scheduling 'town meetings' all over the company: "I decided that the best way to get this message to our people directly was to hold town meetings. They were very informal, something that had never been done around here. In the hierarchy of management of the Bell Sys-tem, the president or CEO rarely talked to the troops. But I was finding so much in the way of passive resistance that I thought I had to get the mes-sage directly to our workforce. In the town meetings, . . . I tried to articu-late how our clients and the world were changing, how things were becoming more competitive, how we had to become more responsive to our customers . . . That message was not well received. Some people left, some we didn't want to see leave."

"[At the town meetings] we would entertain any question that [people] wanted to ask. [Holding two meetings a week with about 100 people attending,] I wanted all the employees to see me and hear it directly from me. [At the same time] I smoked out some of the real problems by saying 'if you have heard any rumors that I have not heard, I would like to hear them.' And people would start opening up."

Secondly, he began downsizing, something that had never been done at Bellcore. "Clearly, we had to lay off some people. The RBOCs had started downsizing, . . . they offered a package to everyone. We had to do it differently here because we would have problems with the good people leaving. We did it the old-fashioned way, based on merit . . . When I tried to institute a system of evaluating and ranking people—strong resistance from my direct reports . . . We did it anyway. And we made some people very unhappy. We took the company from roughly 8,800 people down to 5,500. And you know what? The customers didn't notice!"

However, it became increasingly apparent that change at Bellcore could not be forced top-down. Some people did not respond too well to this kind of pressure. To illustrate this, Dr. Heilmeier has a striking example: "In one of my talks, I used the metaphor of 'raising the bar'—we needed to get better—and you would have thought I used a four-letter word in church. I was shocked by the response. 'How can you say such a thing. We are already way up there. We are working so hard.' [At that point] we felt that the hard-nosed approach would not work in this environment because the good people would leave, and we could not afford that. We had to build a team and some consensus here, and so we started a program on what we called 'Team Bellcore.' After the first layoffs, which were traumatic, we needed to bring people together again. There was some cynicism at first, but then more and more people began to see that this was a good idea."

Team Bellcore, Dr. Heilmeier's third initiative in the change process, became in many ways its most important element—not sufficient in itself, but crucial because of its timing: "People began to see that, if we didn't change, we would be on a going-out-of-business curve. It became very apparent." Team Bellcore training very much focused on relationships among coworkers, teamwork, and perceptions of each other. Dr. Heilmeier freely admits that in the process he took some rough edges off himself and started listening more. His message to his direct reports characterizes his leadership qualities: "We all need to change and that includes me."

As to the lessons learned from the process of change at Bellcore, Dr. Heilmeier summarizes: "Part of being a good place to work is to feel that there is mutual respect, that you are appreciated and you are recognized for what you do. There was a latent view on my part that these were very important things, and I thought the town meetings were important, too. They were important to me personally because I learned a great deal. But I thought they were important for people [who] never had any contact with their CEO."

"The CEO's role in a corporate transformation cannot be overestimated: At all times, the CEO must 'walk the talk' and move immediately to discipline those who do not. Similarly, the [CEO's] most powerful statements are those made through actions. For example, the people whom the CEO hires and promotes become overnight role models. [On the other hand,] no single individual at any level can drive change at a major corporation without the support of others. [This reminds us of] an old Chinese saying: 'Of the great leaders, people do not say that he did this or that. They say we did it ourselves'." (The interview with Dr. G. Heilmeier took place on November 30, 1999.)

CHAPTER 9

Xerox Corporation: Violating Core Values

It's hard to believe, but on April 11, 2002, the SEC filed a complaint against Xerox in United States District Court written in unusually harsh tones and characterizing the company's culture as one of manipulation and deceit.

From at least 1997 through 2000, Xerox Corporation ("Xerox") defrauded investors. In a scheme directed and approved by its senior management, Xerox disguised its true operating performance by using undisclosed accounting maneuvers—most of which were improper—that accelerated the recognition of equipment revenue by over $3 billion and increased earnings by approximately $1.5 billion. . . . Many of these accounting actions violated the established standards of generally accepted accounting principles ("GAAP"). . . . Xerox employed a wide range of tools to enhance its revenue and earnings picture, . . . overstated its earnings by using so-called "cookie jar" reserves and interest income from tax refunds, disguised loans as asset sales, and otherwise manipulated its accounting in violation of GAAP. . . . These accounting actions were directed or approved by senior Xerox management, sometimes over protests from managers in the field who knew the actions distorted their operational results. . . . Moreover, during 1997 through 2000, senior Xerox management reaped over $5 million in performance-based compensation and over $30 million in profits from the sale of stock.

It is indeed hard to believe that this is the same company that in the 1960s became one of the icons of corporate America after the enormous commercial success of its model 914, the first automatic plain-paper office copier and the "top-selling industrial product of all time" (*Business Week*). That same company was introduced as "America's corporate success story of the 1980s" in the R. Levering and M. Moskowitz 1993 bestseller on *The 100 Best Companies to Work for in America*.

Xerox settled the SEC charges on the same day they were filed, paying a $10 million fine—one of the largest civil penalties ever levied on a corporation. However, the damage to the company's credibility and reputation with customers, shareholders, and employees may be far more significant. How did prestigious Xerox allow this to happen?

Over the following pages we'll review some of Xerox's history, the highs and the lows[1] of the venerable company. In its recent past, there was a fascinating personality, David T. Kearns,[2] who as CEO singlehandedly revived Xerox at a time when Japanese competitors such as Ricoh, Minolta, and Canon had almost driven the company from its quintessential market with smaller, cheaper, and more reliable models.

Then in 1997, after some years of steady development and market success, under Paul Allaire, Kearns's successor, Xerox hired an outsider, G. Richard Thoman,[3] as Allaire's heir apparent and change-agent for the company to succeed in the digital age. Expectations were that Thoman would revitalize Xerox in much the same manner as his mentor Louis Gerstner had turned around IBM. Thoman's 13-month tenure as CEO ended in a management fiasco, at the same time exposing the weakness and misdirection of Xerox's executive culture.

In August 2001, shortly after Thoman's departure, assistant treasurer James F. Bingham[4] made a presentation to CFO Barry Romeril and two other senior executives. Bingham stated that since 1997, the company had used improper accounting techniques to inflate revenues and maximize short-term profits. A few days later, Xerox fired Bingham, citing "disruptive and insubordinate behavior."

These different accounts will help establish certain of the elements of the Xerox culture and how it deteriorated from its high point in the early 1980s, during David Kearns's tenure. From there it will be easier to draw certain conclusions as to the factors that contributed to the disaster of April 11, 2002.

THE HIGHS AND THE LOWS

Xerox was founded in 1906 as the Haloid Company, manufacturing and selling photographic paper. As a major step toward technological innovation, in 1947 the company acquired an exclusive license to Chester Carlson's basic xerographic patents, held by the Batelle Institute. The first xerographic copier, Model A, was introduced in 1949.

From then on, Xerox started building its successful business, expanding to Canada and to Europe. Its culmination was the 1959 introduction of the 914 copier, the first automatic plain-paper office copier, which for almost 20 years remained the standard and benchmark of the copier market. In 1961, the company changed its name to Xerox Corporation and started listing its shares on the New York Stock Exchange.

Jumping ahead, in the early 1980s, Xerox had lost its dominance of the copier market to Japanese competition. Employee morale was at an all-time low. In 1982, the company had to stop production of its 3300 copier because of its total unreliability. David Kearns had just become CEO and at an employee meeting was subjected to an embarrassing encounter with Frank Enos, one of the assembly line workers, who told him: "We all knew the 3300 was a piece of junk. We could have told you. Why didn't you ask us?"

Within the next few years, David Kearns put every one of Xerox's 100,000 employees through a six-day quality-training program, starting with himself and his executive team. Xerox bounced back, regaining market share from the Japanese. And in 1989, when Xerox received the coveted Baldridge Quality Award, Frank Enos was invited to attend the ceremony.. The company's people-oriented values had been revitalized.

Paul Allaire, who succeeded Kearns in 1991, continued on the same track and Xerox went on flourishing. Employee freedom and autonomy were expanded. At the plant level, "family groups" epitomized Xerox-style teamwork. Every October on "Teamwork Day" a large number of employees congregated to be honored, with customers and suppliers looking on. Public social responsibility initiatives were supported through the Xerox Community Involvement Program, which provided seed money for worthwhile ideas involving company employees.

In 1997, Richard Thoman was hired to become Paul Allaire's successor. Thoman had spent most of his career following his mentor Louis Gerstner—from McKinsey to American Express, Nabisco, and IBM. In April 1999, he became CEO of Xerox and began a massive reorganization. His new vision for the company, to sell "solutions" rather than copy machines, borrowed heavily from the IBM-model of his mentor but was well accepted by Wall Street. Xerox shares started to rise.

However, Thoman's leadership and people skills were poor. With his aloof and high-handed management style, he alienated a lot of the old-line managers and started losing the confidence of the employees. His business strategy was poorly executed, producing disruptions and dissatisfaction among staff and customers. With just over one year in the CEO position, Thoman was booted in June 2000, but by then Xerox revenues were stagnating, earnings had crashed, and the stock had dived from its peak of $63 to below $7 per share. The company, saddled with huge debt, was on the verge of bankruptcy. Employee morale was again at a very low point, which was surprising considering Thoman's short tenure. But people were frustrated and discouraged. "He was a hopeless leader," said one former Xerox executive. "Good people didn't want to work for him."

Finally, in August 2001—after a short period of time where Paul Allaire had moved back into the CEO spot—Anne M. Mulcahy was appointed CEO of Xerox and has since come a long way in pulling the company from the brink of bankruptcy. Her career with Xerox started in 1976 in field sales and later in sales management, but in 1992 she became vice president of human resources. Subsequently, she held responsibility for global customer operations. With this well-rounded background and a positive image throughout the company, Mulcahy seems to be on the right track in executing an increasingly difficult reorganization. While it is too early to comment on Xerox's turnaround, Mulcahy's support by managers and employees indicates that people's trust and motivation is being restored.

DAVID T. KEARNS

It is amazing, but in looking over David Kearns's credentials, he is best known for his term as deputy secretary of education under President George Bush in 1991 and 1992. David Kearns had written a provocative book on education in 1988, entitled *Winning the Brain Race: A Bold Plan to Make Our Schools Competitive*, and soon followed with the blueprint of *America 2000* to reinvigorate the nation's school system.

But by then, Kearns had a reputation of being able to recognize urgent problems and their solutions. He was among the first corporate leaders to preach the value of employee involvement, within the framework of the total quality approach. Kearns had worked for IBM, advancing in the sales and marketing area of the company. In 1971, he decided to accept an offer from Xerox, with ambitions to someday run the company.

When Kearns became CEO in 1982, Xerox's share of copier installations in the United States had plummeted. Japanese competitors had inundated the market with more reliable copiers at lower prices and had slashed Xerox's dominant market share to just 13% in 1982. Employee testimony from those years bears witness to Kearns's leadership in rebuilding the company. He established a compelling vision for the Xerox people and shaped a new culture of continuous improvement. Kearns became a role model of "quality" that demonstrated his personal commitment to the troops. Senior managers, including Kearns, were required to answer customer complaints at least once a month and would interrupt any of their other activities to take the call. In Kearns's view, quality wasn't met until and unless the customer was satisfied.

The results were stunning. Xerox was able to reclaim lost market share in the United States and even started taking business away from the Japanese manufacturers on their home turf. People at Xerox were driven to action and inspired by a man of fierce perseverance managing in a profoundly democratic style.

G. RICHARD THOMAN

In certain ways, the circumstances of Thoman's arrival at Xerox resemble David Kearns's rise to the top in 1982. The company had introduced the first digital copier in 1995, but the Japanese competition was expected to gear up to bring low-priced alternatives to market. Almost simultaneously, as we now know from the SEC investigation, Xerox started employing questionable accounting techniques to compensate for the slowdown in business success.

Thoman seemed to be a perfect match for these challenges and able as change-agent to take Xerox into the digital age. His resume looked impressive with four advanced degrees, including a Ph.D. in international economics from Tufts University. The French government had awarded him the Legion of Honor for helping to build American tourism in France with the support of the American Express organization under his command. Having spent his entire business career working for Louis Gerstner, people counted on Thoman to bring his mentor's golden touch to the new job.

He did not. Thoman, in his almost three years at Xerox, remained the perpetual outsider. Says his predecessor (and eventual successor for a very short time) Paul Allaire: "The problem Rick had was [that] he did not connect well enough with people to get a good feel of what was going on in the organization and what was and wasn't possible." In many ways, Thoman was not a good fit for the Xerox culture.

Thoman liked freewheeling, intellectually charged discussion. He could be blunt in his criticism and articulated his views with clarity and urgency. But he was incapable of small talk and genial involvement with people approaching him or fellow executives. "He is not really a warm person," confirmed one of his former colleagues. Within the Xerox ranks, opposition was steadily building. Thoman and CFO Romeril didn't see eye to eye to the point where Romeril offered to retire at the end of 1999. In the end, Thoman lacked the ability to assimilate and grasp the Xerox culture and to become part of the "Xerox family." At the time of his departure, there remained just a handful of senior leaders who believed in his change agenda.

Thoman's strategy to position Xerox more firmly in digital technology was sound, but the restructuring of the company was poorly executed. Thoman changed the objectives of the sales organization before starting to retrain the people. "It was a good design, but we went too far too fast," explained Thomas Dolan, president of the Documents Solutions Group, in charge of North American sales. Dolan would have been an important ally for Thoman in his restructuring task, but they clashed among bitter disagreements. With Dolan antagonized, Thoman lost another supporter, Dolan's sister Anne Mulcahy, who had tried to bridge the growing divide between the CEO and his fellow executives. In October 2000, it was Mulcahy who had the courage to admit to a group of Wall Street analysts: "We have an unsustainable business model."

JAMES F. BINGHAM

James Bingham, assistant treasurer and a Xerox veteran of 15 years of service, had begun his own investigation of some of the accounting irregularities that started surfacing in 1999. Bingham's duties included oversight of the treasury functions in Mexico and other developing markets. While the official version of the developments blamed a small group of Mexican and other Latin American managers, acting "in collusion to circumvent our policies and practices," Bingham disagreed and saw the root of the Mexican problems at corporate headquarters.

In order to maximize short-term profits, instructions from headquarters had Mexico and other developing markets book future lease income up front at artificially low currency rates. These entries routinely included future services and supplies, a clear violation of accounting rules. "No one at Xerox believes the figures," Bingham was saying, "because they are far from economic reality."

In addition, Bingham found other improper accounting techniques, establishing certain reserves "without any basis" related to specific purchases and acquisitions and using them later to offset ordinary expenses. Another method for booking revenues and profits up front was factoring income from future rentals to banks, without disclosing it in the company's public statements.

Initially, Bingham addressed these problems in a memo to his immediate supervisor, Eunice Filter, but she objected to broader distribution of his memo. When he proceeded to send a revised version of his memo to CFO Romeril and the new president Mulcahy, Ms. Filter through an assistant ordered him to recall and "destroy" the memo. Still, on August 28, 2000, Bingham got his "day in court" and had the opportunity to meet with Romeril and two other senior executives. The outcome, a few days later, was his dismissal from the company for "disruptive and insubordinate behavior."

In a statement made to the media, spokesman Greg Tayler, Xerox's controller, explained that Bingham's allegations were taken seriously and presented to the audit committee of the board and to the company's auditors. "We took a look at the issues he raised," said Tayler. "We believe they are factually without merit."

Bingham sued Xerox for wrongful termination, claiming he was fired in retaliation for his "efforts to rectify fraudulent accounting and financial reporting practices." As a certain vindication of his efforts, Xerox created a new senior management position for corporate business ethics and compliance as of September 1, 2001.

THE IMPACT ON THE XEROX CULTURE

From all we learned over the preceding pages, there can be no question that the company's culture has been seriously compromised. Senior management at Xerox has betrayed people's trust by manipulating revenues and earnings in order to report progressively misleading financial results. As we are told in the SEC complaint of April 11, 2002, against the company, "these accounting actions were directed or approved by senior Xerox management, sometimes over protest from managers in the field who knew the actions distorted their operational results." People knew and couldn't believe what was happening, as James Bingham tells it in his suicidal August 28, 2000, presentation.

People must be more troubled by the fact substantiated by the SEC investigation that "senior management reaped over $5 million in performance-based compensation and over $30 million in profits from the sale of stock." Again, these actions—with or without intention—demonstrated total disregard for the trust and respect of the company's employees or shareholders. They clearly violated Xerox's core values of "excellence" and "responsible behavior." Leslie Goff, in the May 1998 edition of *Computerworld*, says about the Xerox culture: "In fact, the corporate culture not only encourages dissent, but also provides plenty of avenues for its expression." Mr. Romeril and his fellow senior executives must not have been aware of this particular facet of the Xerox culture.

In little over a decade, from the end of David Kearns's chairmanship in 1990 to January 2001 when Anne Mulcahy was appointed to the highest executive office at Xerox, the disparity between the company's culture and an ill-chosen executive strategy led to disaster and demoralized the employees. Admittedly, there were also market influences. But the frustrations of the employees became a crucial factor in all this. People took an "I told you so" attitude and let things slip. The inconsistency between leadership's behavior and the company's culture became a self-fulfilling prophecy.

Anne Mulcahy is working hard to rebuild the culture. In her own words, she is "fighting fiercely" to revive values and traditions. In her first year in office, as she mentioned in a speech on March 14, 2002, at the Executives' Club of Chicago, she "did six live television broadcasts for employees, held more than 40 town meetings, sent out more than 20 letters to the troops, did hundreds of roundtables, and logged about 100 thousand miles visiting employees in more than a dozen countries."

Today Xerox is a leaner company, down to 67,800 employees at the end of 2002 from over 100,000 in earlier years. Revenue in 2002 was down to $15.9 billion with a $91 million net profit, after restatement of the books for the 1997 to 2000 accounting periods. On its Web site the company prides itself as a "Great Place to Work." "The power of its people," we are told, "makes Xerox tick. Xerox's success is directly linked to the outstanding, go-the-extra-mile kind of people we have working for us." This makes us wonder why our request to interview some of these outstanding people was denied because the company was "not comfortable pursuing the opportunity."

Anne Mulcahy[5] had some words of wisdom that will help rebuild what was lost: "The way out of trouble is sometimes back to basics—the things that made you great in the first place. When things are unraveling fast, it's tempting to look for quick fixes and new answers. In our own experience at Xerox, the real answers lay in getting back to some things we had always done well, but had abandoned . . . Our culture puts a premium on quality, empowerment, results, diversity, fairness, putting the customer first, corporate responsibility. They are the reasons a lot of us came to Xerox and why we stayed."

NOTES

1. "Xerox' History: The Highs and Lows," *Business Week* online, 5 March 2001. In Frank Enos: R. Levering and M. Moskowitz, *The 100 Best Companies to Work for in America* (New York: Doubleday, 1993). On Thoman: "The Paper Jam from Hell," *FORTUNE*, 13 November 2000.

2. "The Mission: David Kearns' Crusade to Fix America's Schools," *Business Week* online, 22 March 1999.

3. "Xerox: The Downfall," *Business Week* online, 5 March 2001; "Bringing Xerox Up-to-Date," *FORTUNE*, 14 June 2000; "Xerox Jam Is Too Much for Thoman," *FORTUNE*, May 2000; "Xerox Sure Is Cheap, but That Doesn't Mean It's a Bargain," *FORTUNE*, 24 January 2000.

4. "Executive Discovers a Problem That Costs Him His Job," *Wall Street Journal* online, 9 February 2001.

5. Presentation for the Executives' Club of Chicago, 14 March 2002.

CHAPTER 10

Mattel: Losing the Focus

Mattel, the California toy maker, combines the rich cultures of the Barbie company, founded in 1945 by Elliot and Ruth Handler, and of Fisher-Price, founded in 1930 by Herman Fisher, Irving Price, and Helen Schelle. Both organizations, which merged in 1993, had similar philosophies, to support and inspire the potential of children. It is a wonderful story how Ruth Handler created the Barbie doll watching her own daughter Barbie play with some paper dolls. Ruth Handler thought the Barbie concept might help teach young girls about what they wanted to be when they grew up.

Today, Mattel has close to $5 billion of total revenue and employs over 30,000 people. Its culture is based on family values and people enjoy teaming and bonding with each other. They are proud of innovative and quality toys, created by their own ideas and efforts.

In recent years and in particular under the ill-fated leadership of Jill Barad, the company ran into financial and cultural trouble. "Mattel had lost its focus," remembers Robert A. Eckert, the company's new CEO since May 2000, in a "First Person" article in the November 2001 issue of the *Harvard Business Review.* "Several top managers had left. Morale was at an all-time low and the stock price wasn't far behind. Mattel no longer knew what it was or what it stood for."

BARBIE—THE VULNERABILITY OF SUCCESS

The Barbie doll was introduced in 1959 and became an immediate success, as it focused on typical women's careers of the 1960s. The concept was exactly how Ruth Handler had pictured it: Barbie became a model of life's opportunities for young girls as they grew up.

When Jill Barad, Mattel's later president and CEO, joined the company and in 1982 became director of marketing for the Barbie line, sales had reached a level of $200 million. Over the next 15 years, revenue increased to $1.9 billion, as the marketing concept expanded to include the greater variety of workplace options for women, both single and married, focusing on a new professionalism and including unusual careers such as astronaut, physician, rock star, or corporate executive. Barbie, as her peers in real life, was breaking cultural, ethnic, and racial boundaries. At the same time, collectors of Barbie dolls became an important target market for Mattel. Today, about one-third of total revenue comes from this particular segment of the market.

The driving force of the Barbie success, however—the expansion into new territories beyond the traditional boundaries—made the line vulnerable to changes in customer preference. All of a sudden, the American toy market began focusing on electronic gadgets and on video games. The Disney movies, *Star Wars*, and *Toy Story* brought new characters to life. Children past the age of five were no longer interested in playing with Barbie dolls. In 2001, while international sales still grew at double-digit rates, Barbie sales in the United States declined by 12%. To some degree, the events of September 11 and the slowdown in retail sales caused by them contributed to the general trend, but demand for Barbie dolls started weakening. Mattel plans to counter by stronger promotions abroad—Europe and Latin America in particular—and by developing new marketing strategies. Even at its reduced level, the revenue of about $2 billion for the line continues to be an amazing accomplishment.

THE CULTURE OF THE 1980s AND 1990s

The founders of Mattel, Ruth and Elliot Handler, continued to manage the company through the 1960s and 1970s and expanded the successful product range, which included Hot Wheels miniature die-cast vehicles, introduced in 1968, and talking toys and dolls, popular in the 1960s. However in 1975, Ruth Handler, after a brush with breast cancer, left the chairwomanship of the company. Ten years later, Mattel was at the brink of bankruptcy after the collapse of its video game business and some poor management decisions.

In 1987, John Amerman was hired from Warner Lambert's Chiclets division as chairman and CEO of the company and over the next ten years put his imprint on Mattel's culture. Amerman was calm, distinguished, and trusting and encouraged employees' input on how to turn the business around. He fostered entrepreneurial attitudes, which made the company successful again but at times led to tough competitiveness and internal politicking, as divisions and their managers fought for his attention. This was the climate when Jill Barad joined Mattel in 1981, and it fit her combative nature quite well.

Amerman's reign culminated with the acquisition of Fisher-Price in November 1993. Fisher-Price had passed through difficult times after being acquired by Quaker Oats in 1969 and spun off again in 1991. From a business viewpoint, it was a perfect fit for Mattel, as Fisher-Price provided enormous strength in the infant and preschool markets. More importantly, however, the Fisher-Price tradition was very much in line with the culture that Amerman was trying to establish at Mattel, Fisher-Price was fostering teamwork and promoting an environment that inspired employees and brought out their creative talents, focusing on the needs and the potential of children.

John Amerman was to retire soon, however, and unfortunately his heir apparent Jill Barad, who had become president and COO in 1992, was not a team player.

JILL E. BARAD—RISE AND FALL OF AN ICON

When in 1997 Barad[1] assumed the CEO position at Mattel, she had become a role model for the many women managers in the corporate arena who try to balance their professional careers with the responsibilities of raising a family. Barad had gone back to work after having her first child. She started in a new position at Mattel and aggressively pursued better opportunities, finally landing a job as product manager for the Barbie line. She helped build the business from a level of $200 million in the early 1980s to almost $2 billion at the height of her success, using a strategy of segmentation, selling dolls for countless "play patterns," such as shopping, dating, partying, or going to the beach.

The source and driver of Barad's success—her aggressiveness, her toughness, and her flamboyance—became her Achilles heel for the top job. As mentioned before, Barad was never a team player and was never afraid to advance her own interests to the detriment of her colleagues. She also had a tendency to micromanage and to get involved in details of design concepts and marketing decisions, which did not endear her to the people working for her. Early on in her CEO tenure, her lack of people skills and her inability to hold on to some good people became a problem. Barad was emotional, intense, and competitive while at the same time glamorous in high heels and tailored Chanel suits, "more Hollywood than corporate." All in all it was not the appropriate mix to nurture a culture of entrepreneurship and creative talent.

What brought Barad down in the end was an overly expensive and poorly executed acquisition of financially troubled The Learning Company, a maker of entertainment software. Barad had lost her credibility with Wall Street and the support of Mattel's Board of Directors and decided to assume responsibility for the failure of the acquisition. She resigned. However, to the chagrin of the people in the company, her departure was sweetened by a golden parachute of almost $40 million. It looked like the reward for failure was greater than the reward for succeeding.

As Barad's successor was able to observe, the damage to the Mattel culture was tangible—the infighting, the unscrupulous practices, and the absence of any team effort at the upper management level had taken a heavy toll on employee morale.

NEW MANAGEMENT—ROBERT A. ECKERT

Mattel's new CEO—an outsider like John Amerman, from Philip Morris's Kraft Foods subsidiary—wasted no time in reorganizing the company, focusing on three basic business areas for girls, boys, and preschoolers and strengthening Mattel's core brands. Potential future bestsellers include an upcoming line of "Harry Potter" toys, based on the book series about a young English boy's encounters with the supernatural. At the same time, Mattel is trying to sell its investment in The Learning Company.

More importantly, however, Robert Eckert focuses on management development and career opportunities for employees. In his message on the company Web site, Eckert points out: "We credit our success to our employees who never forget that they were once kids. Their integrity and their ownership of everything they work on makes them responsible for the results of the business and the development of their fellow employees."

"Looking back," asserts Eckert, "I realize how important the people issues were, too. I know how essential it was for everyone at Mattel to feel, hear and reach out to me in a human way . . . I am convinced that Mattel's success in pulling out of the dark days has been due to the employees' renewed commitment to the company."

WHAT DID WE LEARN?

The Mattel story is a particularly revealing example for the sensitive nature of culture—in a toy company, which allows people to be creative and develop ideas that may inspire kids and help lead them into the adult world. We remember the story of Ruth Handler, watching her daughter play and transforming that image into a very successful concept. Such an environment requires values that are taken from everyday life in our families.

Under these circumstances, the character and personality of the chief executive becomes enormously important as a role model for the organization. When interpersonal relations in an organization are positive they tend to build trust and support among the people; when they are negative they subtract from it. More importantly, when a person holds power over others and is combative, competitive, and given to internal politicking, there are consequences, whether immediately measurable or not. Contrarily, if that same person encourages employee input, fosters entrepreneurial attitudes, stresses teamwork, and promotes an environment that inspires people and brings out their creative talents—that too will have consequences, whether immediately measurable or not.

Industry history is full of brilliant loners whose cleverness and aggressiveness propels them to the top. In a command-and-control environment where employees are seen as having limited abilities and therefore need to be directed, such individuals succeed. But the consequences are that the focus is on obedience and little if any on initiative. In such an environment employees are concerned with their survival and subsistence needs and contribute on a minimal order, just to get along. When an environment of fun based on autonomy and participation is reversed to one of command and control, people's motivation evaporates, except maybe for a few winners. It is quite the opposite for the many losers who tend to leave, hold back on their contributions, distort information to suit their own purposes, and become passive when challenges arise.

There is a need for congruence of an organization's culture and the leadership principles of top management. Mattel's employees were and continue to be warm, sensitive, and caring and, in the long run, had little patience for Barad's politicking and maneuvering, advancing her own agenda and persona. Getting the corporate culture back on track is a time- and energy-consuming task. But it appears Mattel is well on its way.

NOTE

1. "The Rise of Jill Barad," *Business Week*, 25 May 1998.

CHAPTER 11

Enron Corporation: What Went Wrong?

Any new examination of failing organizational cultures would be incomplete if it did not include the Houston energy company that went bankrupt at the end of 2001. Enron had an incredible history, growing from a small, sleepy natural gas pipeline company in 1980 to a global giant with $100 billion in revenue and 21,000 employees in 2000. "Enron's performance in 2000 was a success by any measure," stated the letter to the shareholders in the company's Year 2000 Annual Report. The report points to the company's values: communications (" . . . we take time to talk with one another . . . "), respect, integrity ("We work . . . openly, honestly and sincerely . . . "), and excellence. After a successful business year 2000 and with all this in place, what went wrong?

In the pages that follow we'll try to get a better understanding of the Enron culture and to find some answers why it failed. We'll explore Enron's rise and fall, based on a timeline provided by BBC News on the company's dramatic up and down development. A segment on questionable practices at Enron, taken from different sources,[1] will highlight certain of Enron's ways of being that contributed to the company's demise. The following sections on Jeffrey Skilling, former CEO of Enron,[2] and on the lone anonymous whistle-blower[3] give two sides of the same story on the ultimate responsibility for what happened. It's a kaleidoscope of facts and information that will be of interest in reviewing different aspects of the company's culture.

As we'll have the opportunity to observe, quite different from Enron's advertised and printed culture, there was another one, widespread throughout the company, of secrecy, obfuscation, and deceit. There was much arrogance as well. Jim Alexander, former CFO of Enron Global

Power & Pipeline, which was spun off in 1994, calls it "hubris, an over-weening pride, which led people to believe they can handle increasingly exotic risk without danger."

And there was greed, evident even in the early days. This was by no means limited to the executive ranks. Everybody was trying to make money on Enron stock, which led to pressure on almost everyone to inflate the value of the shares by whatever means possible. At Enron, these practices were labeled "earnings management," techniques to accelerate earnings and revenue funds through outsourcing, disguising loans, and unlocking benefits from negative tax positions. The practices were even "sold" to customers and other corporations on a consultative basis. It was Enron's culture of deceit again, permeating the company much beyond the actions of Enron's CFO, who was blamed and dismissed over this issue.

Enron was known for spending lavishly at all levels—gifts of Waterford crystal for Secretaries' Day, office lunches at the best Houston restaurants, or leaving $100 bills on each employee's desk the day in 1998 that Enron shares passed the $50 mark. Most of Enron's employees felt they deserved the perks since joining the company often meant long workdays or extended and frequent travel. While they knew that certain of Enron's businesses were not making money, they enjoyed participating in the spending spree. Circumventing accounting controls by charging expenses to outdated cost centers was common practice. Enron's was a go-go-corporate culture and "the extravagance is what made it great to work here," as one of the employees phrased it.

Obviously, the executives took much more advantage of that culture, encouraging employees to buy company stock and to invest the full value of their 401(k) funds in Enron shares, while cashing in on their own holdings. However, almost everyone participated and joined in to "play the game." There is the story of Enron's new venture in energy trading, Enron Energy Services, set up in early 1998. In order to impress a group of visiting Wall Street analysts, the company built a fake trading floor and for days trained a number of computer technicians and secretaries from other departments in how to pose as energy traders in front of the analysts. It was fun and everyone took part. In hindsight, it's very revealing to look at how the employees saw Enron. This section of the chapter is based on testimonials taken from several series of "Enron Letters" published by the *Houston Chronicle* in early 2002. It finalizes our Enron story and allows us to reach some conclusions as to what went wrong with the company's culture.

ENRON'S RISE AND FALL

Enron was founded in 1985 with the involvement of Kenneth Lay, who—after a career in academia and government—became the company's chairman and CEO. Enron was the result of the merger of Houston

Natural Gas with Omaha-based Internorth, both of which were in the business of gas pipelines. Kenneth Lay had great plans for Enron to expand its business into the evolving market of energy trading. In 1990, Lay hired Jeffrey Skilling, an ambitious and aggressive consulting executive from McKinsey, to help implement the transformation of Enron into a major player in the market of energy futures. The increasing trend of deregulation of the energy business offered Enron a unique opportunity to provide clients with price stability while betting on the future movement of energy prices. Enron became highly successful and, by the early 1990s, was controlling up to one-quarter of the U.S. gas business.

With the success of the energy trading business assured, Skilling felt confident to expand Enron's activities into bordering business lines, beginning with a myriad of energy-related products; moving further into offering hedges against adverse price movements of other commodities; and from there to hedging against general risks from external factors like the weather. At the end of the 1990s, close to 90% of Enron's income came from its trading business.

Year 2000 became a watershed time period for the company. Enron started trading on the Internet, cannibalizing somewhat its own traditional phone trading business, and also moved into broadband networks, trading bandwidth capacity and with that participating in the booming dot-com economy. The ideas appealed to investors because Enron seemed to be firmly anchored in its old-economy energy area. However, even at Enron nobody really knew if these new trading operations were profitable. The company's main focus and concern was its ever-rising stock price. In the late 1990s, Enron started to use sophisticated and complicated accounting techniques, transferring operations with significant risks and potential liabilities to unconsolidated partnerships while posting the attained revenues, cash infusions, or gains in fair market value as Enron profits. Possible downsides were offset and guaranteed with Enron shares, a dubious procedure in case both share values and underlying operations started to recede.

For a while, however, and well into 2000, Enron was able to project the image of a highly successful company. Trouble was brewing on two fronts. One was the California energy crisis. As we'll see later, Enron was able to profit from that crisis through several clever but irresponsible schemes, which were recognized by outsiders and started tainting the company's reputation. The other was Enron's growing dependence on partnership investments and the related questionable accounting practices.

At the end of 2000, Kenneth Lay stepped down as CEO of Enron, passing his responsibilities to Jeffrey Skilling as of early February 2001. After only six months in office, Skilling resigned abruptly "for personal reasons" as of August 14, 2001. The next day, Kenneth Lay, who returned immediately as CEO, was warned by one of his senior employees about the risks and questionable accounting practices related to two of the partnerships, posing a significant threat for Enron's future viability. From that point forward, the financial scandal involving CFO Andrew Fastow, Enron's senior management, and the auditors Arthur Anderson unfolded quickly, leading to the decline of the company's stock, an SEC investigation, and the bankruptcy filing on December 2, 2001. It's an eerie contrast to the earlier statement, made in the company's Annual Report for the previous year, that "Enron's performance in 2000 was a success by any measure." However, in view of the increasing accounting irregularities relating to the partnerships, the veracity of the results and the continued viability of the company was in any case questionable.

QUESTIONABLE PRACTICES AT ENRON

As we'll see, almost all of the questionable practices at Enron were serving one single major purpose—to increase and maximize real or perceived profitability in order to increase the value of the company's shares. It was human greed; there is no other explanation for it, given the broad distribution of stock options and shares throughout the company. It lets us question how seriously management was embracing and advancing Enron's stated values, with integrity—working openly, honestly, and sincerely—being one of the company's four values. We remember another power company among the ones we studied where it was not enough to practice integrity at work. It was expected to become part of people's personal life philosophy.

The Enron *partnerships* were designed as innovative accounting entities, which Enron effectively controlled, albeit with outside investors. At times, employees were invited to participate as a bonus for their hard work and loyalty, later on also to reward them for their complicity. While certain of the earlier partnerships would help substantiate future revenues or profits from investments, in later years the intention was to shift bad assets or debt into these unconsolidated entities or even recognize a flow of funds into a partnership set up with a promise of Enron stock. "It's like robbing the bank in one year and trying to pay it back two years later," as whistleblower Sherron Watkins characterized these deals in her anonymous letter to Kenneth Lay.

Participation in these partnerships made a few company insiders very rich quickly and with almost no financial risk. Over a two-month period in early 2001, CFO Andrew Fastow turned a $25,000 investment of his family foundation into a $4.5 million windfall. Others like Enron attorney Kristina Mordaunt or treasurer Ben Glisan earned $1 million from a $6,000 investment. It's the choice of greed over integrity!

With the immense pressure to increase the value of Enron stock, the partnerships were the vehicle that allowed people to cross the line from aggressive accounting to fraudulent misrepresentation.

Another example of questionable business practices occurred during the *California energy crisis* in the summer of 2000 and the following winter. In particular in early 2001, Enron traders used a series of clever strategies to profit from the state's inability to control and monitor its own energy needs. Enron used several fraudulent schemes to manipulate the system in its favor. "Death Star," as an example, created fake congestions on the California power grid, leading to credits from the state for corresponding relief. "Ricochet" exploited California's price caps for intrastate energy. Enron would buy power, send it out-of-state on its regional grid, and bring it back in at a higher price. While some of these strategies exploited certain loopholes available to the energy providers, a criminal investigation is underway to substantiate the fraudulent nature of these transactions.

Quite common in the corporate landscape but indefensible at a company that has the value of integrity on its banner is the practice of *doing business with family members*. The *New York Times* first reported that Chairman Lay's son Mark and his sister Sharon had benefited from business relations with Enron. Mark Lay had invested in two privately held companies, which shortly thereafter were approached by Enron to establish business relations. As part of the deal, Mark Lay was hired on a three-year $1 million contract as a consultant. Sharon Lay was co-owner of the Alliance Worldwide travel agency, which retained over half of Enron's travel business and received in excess of $10 million of bookings over several years.

Lastly, Enron's *power contract with India* stands out as a bad example for poor practices and the lack of ethical concerns in dealing with a third-world country. As reported by Ted Fishman in *USA Today*, Enron got the deal to construct and run a huge power plant in the state of Maharashtra in 1991 at above-market electricity rates and government guarantees. On paper, it looked like revenues would quickly pay for the facility and afterward turn a nice profit. The reality, however, was different and it soon became clear that Enron would not be able to deliver on the contract because of economic viability questions. Enron had to close the plant and lost millions. In the following legal and political struggle, Enron used its contacts in Washington and other avenues on the local level to buy influence through political contributions, with the purpose to recover money from the local authorities or from an insurance carrier who covered the political risk of the project. Unfortunately, the dispute left a bad taste for American foreign investments with the host country and the local environment, which is left without a solution to its power needs.

JEFFREY SKILLING, FORMER CEO OF ENRON—THE CULPRIT?

In his congressional testimony in early February 2002, Jeff Skilling portrayed himself as a pillar of rectitude and responsible management. He maintained he did not know about any dubious financial practices at

Enron and was not aware of the questionable purposes of the many partnerships established during his watch. He professed faith in Enron: "I did not believe the company was in any financial peril" at the time of his abrupt resignation in August 2001.

Why would someone even think of considering him as the culprit for Enron's demise? In the attempt to pierce the Teflon-like quality of his armor, let's look at some of his statements in published interviews. Talking to *Frontline* on March 28, 2001, Skilling represented himself as very knowledgeable on the California situation. He had spent a lot of time there in 1995 and 1996, looking at the methods proposed for deregulation, and understood the marketplace. Did Enron exercise any market power during the summer of 2000 and the following winter? "No, I really don't think so," was Skilling's response, " . . . everybody was working extremely hard to get every possible electron into the Californian market." When confronted with calculations that, given supply and demand, there was no real reason for prices to go up as high as they did, Skilling reflected: "I would be shocked if there was any kind of price manipulation going on. . . . We are working to create open [and] competitive fair markets. . . . We are the good guys." With the recent disclosure of Enron's clever strategies and Skilling's intimate knowledge of the marketplace, it is hard to believe Skilling was not aware of what was going on.

Let's look at another example, Mr. Skilling's view of the partnerships, as reported by the *Houston Chronicle* in January and February 2002. Skilling put the blame for creating these entities and, in particular, the LJM partnerships, which heavily contributed to the $1.2 billion write-down on bad investments in October 2001, squarely on CFO Andrew Fastow, stating that forming these entities was his idea. "It was my understanding that the purpose of the transactions was to provide a real hedge, [locking in profits from technology investments]" explained Skilling. However, Fastow made it clear that the LJM partnerships "were formed at Enron's request in order to benefit Enron." Apparently, he had also told a board of directors meeting in West Palm Beach that Skilling would approve all the partnerships. Skilling didn't remember that remark: "I was in and out of the meeting and don't recall if I was there specifically at the time Andy made the comment" was his evasive reply. Skilling obviously had to know about the problems with the partnerships, a fact that is corroborated by former Enron treasurer Jeffrey McMahon, who in March 2000 complained to Skilling about certain conflicts of interest of his boss Fastow regarding the partnerships. McMahon was soon reassigned to a different position within Enron and recalled Fastow saying to him: "You should assume everything you say to Mr. Skilling gets [back] to me."

David Boje, who analyzed the Enron situation in an article entitled "Leadership in a Postmodern Age" that was first published in December 2000 and later revised in April 2002, talks about Skilling's theatrics and showmanship and how he made fear and deception the cornerstone of Enron's corporate culture. He recounts an episode in 1997 when Peco Energy was renegotiating its rates with Pennsylvania state regulators. Enron and Skilling saw all of a sudden a chance to enter the Pennsylvania market. The day Peco filed its plan, offering rate cuts, Skilling got up at 4.30 A.M. and by 9 A.M. had done several radio interviews. By noon, he had an airplane circling Philadelphia with a banner reading "Enron doubles Peco rate cuts." He was not to be outdone.

After Skilling's congressional testimony in February 2002, Dan Ackman in *Forbes* compared his management technique with one favored by Mafia families: "A system of plausible deniability seems a critical aspect of Enron controls: No one should know what the guy down the hall is doing; when anyone asks, refer them to the lawyers or the accountants." In his testimony, Skilling said that Enron failed because of a crisis of confidence, that it was solvent and profitable, but in the end not liquid enough. "If all was well, why did he leave?" questions Ackman and calls the details of Skilling's decision "an enduring mystery." We don't quite agree. It seems to us Skilling contributed more to Enron's nefarious culture and bears more responsibility for the company's failure than he would like to admit.

THE LONE ANONYMOUS WHISTLE-BLOWER

On August 15, 2001, one day after Jeffrey Skilling resigned as CEO of Enron, Sherron Watkins, vice president of corporate development, sent an anonymous letter to Kenneth Lay, who had taken over as CEO again. Watkins later identified herself and met with Lay for an hour to supply additional documentation.

In her letter, Watkins anticipates "a wave of accounting scandals" in the wake of Skilling's departure and with the spotlight that will now be on Enron. She points to two of the partnerships where immense gains in fair market value of the underlying investments had been booked in 1999 and 2000 and where the write-down of today's losses was avoided by committing more Enron shares. Watkins feels Wall Street scrutiny will uncover these questionable practices and continues: "My eight years of Enron work history will be worth nothing on my resume; the business world will consider the past successes as nothing but an elaborate accounting hoax."

She also makes a comment about the outgoing CEO: "Skilling is resigning now for 'personal reasons,' but I would think he wasn't having fun, looked down the road and knew this stuff was unfixable and would rather abandon ship now than resign in shame in two years."

Kenneth Lay, while he found Watkins "credible and sincere," acted in true Enron fashion of "plausible deniability": He referred the matter to Enron's law firm Vinson & Elkins for review, although they had a conflict of interest, having provided earlier opinions on some of the partnership deals. Vinson & Elkins in their limited review interviewed CFO Andrew Fastow and Arthur Anderson partner David Duncan and concluded that the concerns expressed by Watkins did not warrant further investigation by independent counsel or auditors.

"I was incredibly frustrated with Mr. Lay's actions or lack thereof," Watkins testified before the Senate Commerce Committee. "I believe that Enron had a brief window to salvage itself this past fall, and we missed that opportunity because of Mr. Lay's failure to recognize or accept that the company had manipulated its financial statements."

Watkins may not have realized it at the time she wrote the letter, but she and a handful of hard-core believers in the company were the ones who were deceived by the standard-bearers of the Enron culture. Her peers were people who believed Enron to be a company that encouraged and rewarded entrepreneurial ideas from the rank and file; that allowed workers to try their hand at new jobs; that promoted people on merit, not seniority. There was the case of Fred Philipson, as told by Susan Orenstein in the March 2002 issue of *Business 2.0*, who—from his days as financial analyst at Continental Airlines—proposed "a plan to build an online trading product based on airfreight capacity. Finally, the big break: a call from an executive to meet at the Starbucks inside the building to discuss the idea. There, to his surprise, he got not only the green light but also an overnight jump in status, complete with new office space on a different floor and an administrative assistant. 'I felt like I'd been discovered for a movie,' he says." Philipson lost funding for his project after four months and went into "redeployment," a job category for those without a current position. He was laid off in December but still today finds it difficult to believe that Enron executives have done anything wrong. In this context, we may want to look at some of the testimonials of Enron employees.

HOW THE EMPLOYEES SAW ENRON

In January and February 2002, the *Houston Chronicle* published several series of "Enron Letters," which are testimonials of employees of their impressions of and feelings toward the now bankrupt company. They provide an interesting mirror on people's perceptions of Enron.

In many instances, there was a feeling of awe and amazement on how the company operated, how matters were handled and certain benefits provided. "There were 35 aerobic classes a week," writes a trade accountant from the London office, "and all the towels and shampoo were provided free—it was awesome. It was like having your own set of servants." In another letter, a former Houston employee explains: "As part of the analyst program, I received an $8,000 'back to school' bonus when I left the company [to go to graduate school]." This tradition of lavish spending is also described by the *New York Times* in a February 26, 2002, article where we read: "Spend they did. In the fall of 1997, the 1,000 or so employees of Enron International gathered at the Del Lago Resort outside Houston for the unit's annual meeting. To open one morning session, the two top executives, Rebecca Mark and Joseph Sutton, rode into the room and onto the stage on Harley-Davidson motorcycles, engines revving as the Survivor song 'Eye of the Tiger' blared. Dressed in lather jackets and chaps, they told the pep rally that the international unit was unstoppable. . . . The capper was when one executive in charge of Enron's big power project in India rode in on a horse and another entered on an elephant."

There are other letters that express people's admiration for certain positive attributes of the Enron culture. A current employee who prefers to remain anonymous writes: "We have been trained [in] and used the most up-to-date technology and have worked in a very fast-paced environment that allowed us to develop diverse interpersonal skills." Writes another: "Enron has had such a pull for 'the best and the brightest' because they treated us as adults, didn't micro-manage and let us run [the business] to realize our full potential." Adds Kathleen Salerno, who has since left Enron: "We all believed that we were part of something special . . . Enron management really appeared to believe in and follow through with their stated visions and values. Apparently, this was all smoke and mirrors."

Much of this last sentence is a recurrent theme of many of the "Enron Letters." People feel let down and deceived by management and by some of their fellow workers. Writes Peter B.: "To me, the downfall of Enron can be summed up in one word: Greed!" Adds another anonymous employee: "Enron was flying high in those days, and the employee mentality was always 'how can I get a piece?' and many employees were only concerned with their own advancement . . . That 'me-first' mentality was rampant among Enron's upper management." Comments another letter writer: "People felt like they had to make somebody else look bad so that they could advance."

Some of the reasons for Enron's problems become apparent as well. Again, Peter B. writes: "Upper management at Enron was filled with very young, mostly early 30s and 40s men and women who were promoted faster than they could move to their new offices." Another letter of an anonymous employee is very telling: "My supervisor was 23. She came to work around 9.30 A.M. or so, checked her E-mails, surfed the Net, chatted with her friends on the phone and then went to lunch for an undetermined amount of time."

Again, many of the letters are bitter about how people's coworkers, friends, and peers have been treated, how they lost everything and now have difficulty finding new jobs because they are being stigmatized for their prior association with Enron. The letters are testimony to a close-knit relationship and culture that had great possibilities but was perverted and misdirected by management and spurious values.

THE FINAL QUESTION: WHAT WENT WRONG AT ENRON?

Following Skilling's judgment, did Enron fail because of a crisis of confidence? Was it in no financial peril, was it solvent and profitable but had a liquidity problem when "the run on the bank" began? Or as Sherron Watkins tells us, did Enron's questionable practices turn many years of successes into an accounting hoax?

After all we learned in the preceding pages, both answers don't capture the reality of what happened. Enron would have failed sooner or later because of its culture and the values that the organization and its leaders embraced. Let's take one more look at what we heard.

We were told that the Enron culture was "awesome"; people were in "awe" of the company's lavish spending and unusual benefits, the opulent extravagance and copious excesses, which the employees came to expect at meetings, celebrations, and company parties. It was, however, a pseudo-culture of appealing lies, of hype, and of hubris—a cultlike environment of deceptive magic. As a banner in the lobby proclaimed, Enron styled itself as "The world's leading company," creating intoxicating publicity around its alleged successes, which again kept people in "awe."

Enron's clear and unambiguous values—communications, respect, integrity, and excellence—were certainly displayed on office walls and discussed at some length in each of the company's Annual Reports, but they were never sincerely embraced by its executive leaders. The real and ever-present value was greed, an unhealthy focus on money and the inflated value of Enron's shares. It led to a "me-first" mentality, to a culture of self-enrichment and of promptly advertised personal financial success that contributed to the "awe."

At most of the other organizations that we studied, one important tenet of the new cultures was the focus on skills and personal mastery, leading to self-actualization and the full use of people's potential. At Enron, there was little incentive for learning or mentoring and there were few if any supportive leaders respected for their experience and expertise. People's imprudent and irresponsible confidence in the company's success in the untested markets it entered was commonplace. Leaders in upper management lacked extensive professional experience. Promotions were decided at the local Starbucks, based on whom you know rather than who you are.

In the view of our source material, Jeffrey Skilling in a sinister way embodies and stands for the Enron culture. Skilling was considered to be clever to the point of recklessness. He was portrayed to camouflage statements and facts in trendy consulto-speak. As he explained it, Enron was not simply a trading company but engaged in "substituting hardwiring with markets for the benefit of vertically integrated industries." He was considered "awesome," inspired fear, and was deceptive to an extent where he was able to deny, didn't know or believe, and wasn't directly involved. He was seen as a tough and self-confident manager but devoid of ethics, loyalty, and values. In the press, Skilling rightfully has been acknowledged as the key architect of the company's culture and, therefore, as the main culprit for its demise.

There was another contributing factor. When the press freshly noted the unraveling of the Houston firm, several prominent writers attributed Enron's woes to a social phenomenon known as "groupthink." Characteristic of groups that are highly cohesive, groupthink at Enron was founded on almost total emphasis on increasing the value of the equity, allowing people to cash in on stock options or to add to the appreciation of their pension funds. Diversity of thought was not appreciated and tolerated at Enron. People found it hard to challenge the company's actions and strategies.

Dr. Irving L. Janus, in his quintessential work on this phenomenon, defines the "illusion of invulnerability" (taking excessive risks), the "belief in the inherent morality of the group" (they are the good guys), and the "illusion of unanimity" (silence is consent) as three of the basic principles of groupthink. The critical antidotes to groupthink offered by Dr. Janus appear to have been missing in the Enron situation. He suggests that in its decision-making process a group should appoint a devil's advocate who will purposely take the opposite side to find weaknesses in the group's intentions. He also suggests openness, freely sharing ideas, feelings and information among participants in any group decision, as well as the broad use of observers.

The lessons from Enron's collapse are sobering: The company's go-go culture had a powerful and captivating influence on the employees. For most of them it was similar to a state of addiction or dependency, which lasted to the end. In August of 2001, when many questions were already raised about the company's credibility, when Jeffrey Skilling had resigned and Kenneth Lay stepped back into his former role as CEO, people gave him a standing ovation at a meeting where he announced his return.

There is one important aspect that goes beyond the perverted Enron culture and where it led its people. This failure—which may have the consequence of criminal charges for some of the Enron executives—has undermined the public trust in the integrity of institutions like boards of directors, auditors, and regulatory bodies, which were thought to guarantee credibility and accountability for millions of shareholders. This will remain the major fallout from the failure of Enron's misguided culture.

NOTES

1. "Partnership Practices May Have Been Illegal," *Houston Chronicle,* 9 February 2002; Associated Press, "Enron Partnerships Meant Big Cash for a Few Insiders" (reprinted by Montanaforum.com), 7 February 2002; "How to Be an Enron

Millionaire," Salon.com, 29 January 2002; "California Scheming," *Time*, May 2002; "Enron Forced Up California Prices," *New York Times*, 7 May 2002; "Lay's Son, Sister Profited from Dealings with Enron," *New York Times* (reprinted by HoustonChronicle.com), 1 February 2002; "Enron's Past Returns to Burn Us All . . . ," *USA Today* (reprinted by Fiforum), 30 January 2002.

2. Interview with Jeff Skilling, *PBS Frontline*, 28 March 2001; "Did No Wrong, Skilling Says," HoustonChronicle.com, 17 January 2002; "Enron's Former CEO Says He Knew of Nothing Improper or Perilous," HoustonChronicle.com, 7 February 2002; David M. Boje, "Leadership in a Postmodern Age," David M. Boje online, rev. 2 April 2002; Dan Ackman, "Enron's Man Who Didn't Know Too Much," *Forbes*, 8 February 2002.

3. "The Letter to Ken Lay," *FORTUNE* online, 16 January 2001; "Watkins Blames Lay For Failure," HoustonChronicle.com, 26 February 2002.

CHAPTER 12

Job Withdrawal at European Manufacturing Company (EMC)

While we have chosen not to identify the company, we include it to show an interesting phenomenon that is particularly widespread and common in many European countries. This European manufacturing company (EMC) has broad global manufacturing operations, reports total revenues of close to EUR 8 billion (the equivalent of about $8 billion), and employs about 33,000 people worldwide.

Until some years ago, the company was family owned and its culture was paternalistic, albeit with many participative leadership opportunities. At a certain juncture, a progressive statement of mission and vision was introduced and enthusiastically embraced by the employees. It focused on entrepreneurial attitudes and on people as a major source of success. Workers, through their motivation and creativity, would contribute to a high level of performance. Among the expressly stated prerequisites to reach common goals were open communications and an honest and constructive dialogue between management and employees.

Up to about 1990, business had been stable and profitable, developing at a steady pace. However, in the early 1990s, several negative factors came together and revenue and earnings took a dive. A promising new product introduction failed and an important joint venture did not perform as planned and produced considerable losses. Consultants were brought in to analyze staffing and other cost-saving opportunities and, in total secrecy, a plan was drawn up to implement changes and reduce personnel—difficult to do in Europe—by means of early retirement and legally possible layoffs.

When this was communicated, it came as a shock to the employees because the measures and their execution clearly went against the spirit of the recently introduced statement of mission and vision. People were disappointed and discouraged and the incidence of "job withdrawal"—almost like retiring on the job—drawing a paycheck but doing very little to earn it—increased to significant levels, estimated at more than one-third of the staff personnel.

DISEMPOWERMENT OR *INNERE KUENDIGUNG*

Both of these terms describe a form of job withdrawal of an employee leading to diminished collaboration and behavioral negation at work. It's what we call "to work by the book." People will just do as much it takes to get by. The behavior is one of avoidance. There is no participation in any longer-term endeavors such as planning or strategic thinking. The focus is on reduction of input without raising supervisory suspicion. The work attitude is one of indifference.

For lack of a better term, Mohrman (1993) has named this type of behavioral job withdrawal *disempowerment*, leading to minimalist work behaviors. In Germany and Switzerland, it has been described as *Innere Kuendigung* (internal resignation) by researchers such as Loehnert (1990), Faller (1991), Hilb (1992), and Krystek, Becherer, and Deichelmann (1995). In Germany alone, the incidence of this problem is assumed to affect at least 25% of the workforce.

Susan Albers Mohrman, a researcher with the University of Southern California, in an article entitled "A Perspective on Empowerment" considers power and empowerment—"being able to make a difference in the attainment of individual, group and organizational goals"—as one of the important resources of high-involvement organizations. If workers feel "*they* won't let them do things," disempowerment occurs. It's a conditioning process, very much like Seligman's concept of learned helplessness in which lack of control leads to depression. Employees limit themselves to minimalist behavior.

Winfried Loehnert, in his pioneering research on *Innere Kuendigung*, sees people's job withdrawal as a long-term development, caused by lack of control in the work situation and a mismatch between their expectations and/or qualifications and the requirements of the job. Low probability of success leads to reduced efforts. To compensate for frustration, people transfer their productive energies to outside interests and private hobbies. The majority of employees will resort to a reactive job withdrawal, which allows them to stay employed but with minimal effort and engagement. A certain minority of employees will draw particular motivation from actively renouncing any interest in the job, thus obtaining a renewed sense of control over their work situation.

Michael Faller, in his dissertation on *Innere Kuendigung*, confirms many of Loehnert's assumptions but provides a much broader perspective on what causes job withdrawal. There may be unfair treatment, frustration, stress, and other kinds of dissatisfaction at work. Job withdrawal becomes a defense mechanism, which protects the individual from psychosomatic consequences and, at the same time, offers the opportunity to rationalize the reasons for behavior by finding fault with his or her superiors.

Martin Hilb, in his summary of an *Innere Kuendigung* symposium held in Zurich in 1991, considers job withdrawal as a silent protest. He differentiates between active—as an act of revenge—and passive job withdrawal. In the latter, people curtail their work efforts to a point where negative consequences are still avoided.

Finally, Ulrich Krystek, D. Becherer, and K. H. Deichelmann, in their survey of *Innere Kuendigung*, focus on the importance of a trust-based and motivating culture as a crucial antidote to job withdrawal. Krystek urges management to identify with the organization's principles and values and to lead in credible, predictable, and trustworthy ways to assure the continued motivation of employees.

In summary, disempowerment or *Innere Kuendigung* is considered a self-protective behavior of employees who try to come to terms with their lack of control and participation in the workplace. People feel helpless, often angry, and react by performing their duties in a minimal way, renouncing any active involvement and initiative in company matters. While work is performed in strict adherence to official requirements, the focus of personal interest and motivation is transferred to after-work and leisure activities.

WHAT HAPPENED AT EMC?

Returning to the situation at EMC, their corporate restructuring resulted in considerable cost savings and brought earnings back to previous levels, to the point where the family owners decided to take part of the company public. Outside executive management replaced the former family members and, with it, a complete change of the culture and the overall workplace environment took place.

Today's climate is "tough," focusing on financial performance and maximizing shareholder value. Employees are measured against a "plan" and evaluated by their contribution to the company's success. The former mission and vision statement has been replaced by a wordy but rather vague affirmation of purpose, which includes a focus on entrepreneurial thinking, rendered an illusion because of tight top-down decision making. This only aggravated the problem of *Innere Kuendigung* that existed before.

It's a travesty. A corporate culture of a strict quid pro quo of performance-related compensation and rewards, of "be competent and motivated or you are out" is outwitted by a cleverly applied scheme of noninvolvement and nonmotivation. At a level of one-third of the employee population, it translates into significant productivity impairment for this company and many others in similar circumstances.

CHAPTER 13

Why Do Cultures Fail?

Successes as well as defeats and failures can cause tension in an organization. Challenges that are manageable—which stretch us a bit and sometimes a lot—can provide the pleasurable excitement that leads to high performance and to the joys of achievement. When an organization's culture is solidly founded on the fully developed talents and abilities of its people, it creates the type of stress one experiences in a rewarding exercise program. Specialists who study stress have long maintained that stress, up to a point, is healthy and called "eustress." Beyond a healthy limit it is called "distress" and can cause increasing damage to its practitioners. Xerox met and overcame enormous challenges when its culture was broad-based and involved all of its human resources. In recent history, however, its culture started failing, stress passed the healthy limit, and the company went downhill for quite some time.

Cultures that evolve often do so in piecemeal fashion—a bit here, a bit there. But without an overall guiding philosophy or a set of supportive practices, this unsettling change is fraught with danger. At one extreme, it can become vulnerable to the unpredictable fancy of a charismatic leader who, having reached a dominant position, can try to shape the organization to his or her whims. At the other extreme, the employees evolve faster than the organization. In that case, people may become demotivated and have difficulty coping with the disparity. Mattel is offered here as an example of an organization afflicted by the first condition, while the European Manufacturing Company (EMC), with its culture of apathy and diversion, is a clear case for the second one.

The worst scenario, of course, is the example of a culture that rots to the core. In the Enron case we explored how external pressures and the lack of ethics corrupt a culture such as Enron's. In the course of this chapter we explore ways to identify Enronism, avoid it, and build a strong, productive, and equitable culture—using examples from our focal cultures examined earlier in this book.

CULTURAL TENSION—EVOLUTION, REVOLUTION, OR REGRESSION?

When cultures are well matched to their environment, meet their members' needs and expectations to a reasonable extent, and are guided by an overarching rationale that supports the structure of the society in a believable fashion, tensions tend to be manageable and sometimes minimal. This has been the state of much of human history around the globe.

The hierarchical organizational structure with power exercised top-down in a world of scarcity, with the masses of people at the bottom expecting little and getting little, and with a prevailing belief system that supports the status quo, famines, wars, and plagues could come and go, often with little effect on people's culture, expectations, or behaviors. Dissent was moot or quickly dealt with and technology developed very slowly.

But as new ideas, new technologies, and new belief systems evolve and are used by some, cultural tensions develop, personal stress increases, and conflicts arise. History is replete with examples of cultures that expanded and shrank; became more democratic and then were repressed, became more inclusive and then exclusive again—yet after each shift the world would have a memory of the events and things were never again as they once were.

When we examine the history of organizational cultures, we find the same kind of ebb and flow, but after each tide the landscape in some places is never quite the same as it was. This is partly because culture is formed of many different elements and only some flow forward and back. The general educational level in democracy itself and new concepts, ideas, and technologies are cumulative powerful forces for change—and they don't stand still or waffle.

Both of the authors have witnessed what happens to an advanced organizational culture of the type we describe here when it comes under the control of someone who takes the organization backward to a more primitive culture of position power from one that emphasized the individuals' personal inner power; back to one of old-line command and control rather than one of self-management and personal responsibility; and back to one of secrecy, low trust, and privileges rather than one of openness, trust, and equality.

However, going backward to earlier mental models of organizational behavior is eventually unsustainable because of the enhancement of other societal factors not under the control of any given organization. For example, an individual's or group's efforts to restore the perks, prerogatives, and ego satisfaction of the hierarchical structure for themselves creates inevitable conflict with the desires, aspirations, and goals of the people who work for them. People who are increasingly educated, capable, and world wise have expansive goals for themselves but not necessarily at someone else's expense.

Therefore, the advanced organizational cultures we have been reporting on offer personal power and autonomy, a cooperative workforce, and the joys of personal achievement in a supportive environment instead of one of solitary ambitions and grandiose schemes. And once having tasted freedom and the opportunity and fun of cooperative achievement, they are unlikely to put up with the old stuff for very long. Many will seek a more conducive environment, withhold their potential valuable contributions, and eventually seek to reassert themselves.

The greatest danger at both ends of the spectrum is that neither fully takes into account what has been going on in the general culture that surrounds it. In "How to Avoid Enronism," James Lucas warns us of "the discovery of a new business model that can't be explained." He says that every business generation sees them, but that "any idea that can't be explained to an intelligent outsider is probably destined for disaster." Dotcoms that have flaky business plans and neither profits nor any prospects of any for long periods while spending lavishly on unearned perks should implode at no one's surprise.

Lucas also posits an interesting take on the visionaries who arrogantly claim to be able to see more clearly through the fog of the future. He asks, "what happens when we think we see what no one else sees?" He states that "arrogance is always founded on a belief in the ignorance of others" and claims that organizations that assume their superiority will usually fail, often spectacularly. We suspect that you, our reader, could name a few that have done so.

Therefore, to sail unsuccessfully between the twin perils of revolution and repression implies an evolutionary pushing of the envelope—to be more inclusive, progressive, and trusting of an organization's people, proceeding at a quickening pace that matches or reasonably exceeds that of our general culture. That is what solid leadership is all about!

THE SCATTER-SHOT APPROACH TO CULTURAL DEVELOPMENT

The first half of the twentieth century saw great growth in public education and a raising of the bar as to how much was enough to earn a decent living in what was then called *terminal education* in the United States. This standard was not an absolute by any means and varied widely from state to state. However, fourth grade was about the average for education around

1900, rising to a high school degree by midcentury. Also, by then an enormous culture shift had occurred in other aspects of American life as well.

The first two decades were considered the era of *scientific management*, where stopwatch time study, the total dumping down of work, and efforts to turn employees into robots held sway. The Hawthorne experiments in the late 1920s showed the downside of that approach, and public resistance was intensifying. Also, the increase in the professional ranks led to a growing body of research in the social, management, communications, and human resources fields, which pointed to a more cooperative style between management and employees. But because organizations change their cultures slowly and often sporadically, not much happened until the middle of the century.

The next 50 years were marked by the development of some practical and very human tools and techniques of particular value to management in dealing with a better-educated, less passive, and more aspiring workforce. However, many of these concepts and techniques were put into practice and very often offered piecemeal by trainers and consultants, preferably to management personnel through public seminars, workshops, and training courses. Some were brought in-house but still mostly offered to managers and professional personnel at the lower organizational levels.

Short courses in techniques such as win-win negotiating, active listening skills, motivating others, and, more recently, mentoring became very popular. Also, management seminars about new systems such as managing by objective, zero-base budgeting, and quality management were used to implement restructuring and organizational changes. Many of them turned out to be fads that soon faded, only to be replaced by a new panacea for corporate problems. Yet, fortunately, there are signs of significant change.

In the 1950s, the almost universal approach for training supervisors centered on the five components of a supervisory job. His job—and almost all supervisors at the time were men—was to plan, organize, direct, coordinate, and control workers and their assignments. These activities did not include much thinking and brainwork for the employee unless he or she was a respected professional. Most of those were in staff positions and their involvement limited to supporting line managers who ran the enterprise.

There were at that time some notable exceptions. Pioneering firms such as Gore, SAIC, and Johnson & Johnson were places where those repressive notions never took hold. But in the general business climate of that period, these "guides" were virtually holy writ. Times were changing, however. In the late 1960s, it was becoming apparent that much of the workforce didn't like being *directed* or *controlled*. As back pressure developed, managers and their supervisors in most firms held firm to *planning, organizing,* and *coordinating* but started compromising on the other two. At the same time they began to learn all kinds of new skills such as conflict resolution, people assessment, and meeting management abilities.

The dawn of the information age was first proclaimed in the 1950s. This happened because of the flood of new research results that were becoming available in the majority of professional fields. However, until the advent of the computer age, culture change in most organizations occurred at a reasonable pace, first when the number crunching was introduced and then when the personal computer began to appear, first at nearly every workstation and later in virtually every home.

The productivity gains resulting from the use of personal computers and the information systems that quickly followed allowed many top managers to launch a massive downsizing of their workforce. The less-publicized and concurrent reduction of middle management layers produced flatter structures, more flexible responsive systems, and quicker management decisions. At the same time, however, the investment hype of the new technology sector led to the obsolescence of old rules and traditional principles in some organizations, started outdating cultural paradigms, and permitted incredible abuses of public and employee trust.

We don't need to elaborate much on these beyond the case studies of failing cultures we have reported on in the preceding chapters. The details of new scandals of insider trading and accounting manipulations seem to appear in the media almost every day. What we do need to focus on and draw from are the experiences and principles of the advanced cultures that have shown to be reasonably resistant to such problems.

Let's start by bringing closure to some cultural factors that offer hope for and from the larger culture in which these organizations operate.

First, the piecemeal acquisition of new skills and knowledge that is practiced today and has characterized the training and education efforts of most organizations may be coming to an end. That step-by-step approach left many competency gaps among the personnel and allowed top managers and executives to avoid participation at all.

Second, the old hierarchical structures with only a few at the top wielding the power to reward and punish needs to be revised because it leaves them immune to ethical accountability or even attempts to discuss their conduct.

Third, new forms of personal and organization development are coalescing around broad areas that can in time be used to build stronger, healthier, and more ethical organizations. Three of them are worth mentioning:

- Many grade school children are being exposed to an emerging curriculum based on "character development." Early findings indicate a growth in self-assessment and a revision of their attitudes and behaviors in a constructive way. However, this will take decades to reach the workplace and we have run out of time.

- A similar comprehensive approach to building a strong culture of ethics, trust, and loyalty is available to employers featuring moral fitness exercises, mentoring, and assessment instruments for measuring personal and group development. These programs work best when started at the top and moved downward through the organization to build a new, more responsible culture.

- An increasing number of organizations are responding to the early reports in the media of groupthink being a critical factor in the Enron debacle and some other firms that followed. This realization can be a cultural antidote to the irrational exuberance that infected the workplace in those organizations when their stock prices were being manipulated upward.

These and similar programs can lead to improved and stronger cultures. Ironically, those healthy organizations we reported on here created highly productive, caring, and motivating cultures without any such broad developmental efforts. Also, the people employed by these organizations adopted the often-unusual cultural traits, found joy in their work, and became enthusiastic producers. However, when an organization has been wounded by mismanagement, betrayal, and at times downright crookedness, serious remedial approaches may be necessary.

It is also a clear fact that the general business climate, investor confidence, and public faith even in our economic institutions have been seriously impaired. It took nearly two decades for the Dow Jones industrial average to return to its 1929 level after that meltdown of the stock market, which also affected economies on a global scale. Drastic measures may be in order.

KEYS TO BUILDING A STRONG, PRODUCTIVE, AND JUST ORGANIZATIONAL CULTURE

Lucas, in the lead article of the American Management Association's new magazine *MWorld* (2002), listed several ways a company can avoid Enronism. We believe this is a reasonable set of criteria for judging how well the healthy organizations we have studied measure up. To suit the purposes of this chapter, we have chosen to limit and rearrange Lucas's sequence of points somewhat. At the same time, we have chosen to counterbalance each point with examples from the seven case study organizations.

His causes of Enronism include:

- *The "chain of command"*—Lucas considers this the perfect metaphor for most organizations. It is a culture of "think at the top and do at the bottom" rather than any sharing of power. There is virtually no upward communication or bottom-up participation.

  Counterpoise: The U.S. Coast Guard, among the organizations we studied, is the one most locked into a chain-of-command structure by law, regulation, and tradition. When the service set out to overhaul its civilian personnel appraisal system, Commandant ADM Loy was concerned about building a system that would be widely accepted by its users at every level and would "work" because of that. Therefore, the design and implementation teams were encouraged to build the information and decision-making process in a way that started at the worker level, allowing ideas and information to flow upward continuously.

- *The wrong question on openness*—Lucas qualifies as a sign of Enronism asking the question, "Is there any reason to share this with our people?" Great organizations would rather put it a different way: "Is there any real reason why we shouldn't share this with our people?" Can you imagine executives who are manipulating the accounting and "cooking the books" asking that question?

Counterpoise: All of the organizations we studied are very open to their employees in terms of providing access to cost data so that people can assess the potential gains of ideas they propose. But perhaps the best example of sharing virtually any type information is SAIC, a model corporate culture described in the next chapter. The reason here is not only that the company is employee owned and considers its people as partners in the growth of the business. SAIC thinks of itself as an organization of professionals who cannot make informed decisions without having access to the full underlying data.

- *Unfettered competition*—Lucas says, "In many organizations, we preach teamwork and cooperation but reward dog-eat-dog competition between individuals, teams and departments." He continues with the question: " Is there any voluntary cross-pollination of ideas between business units, functions and positions?"

Counterpoise: We believe our case studies convincingly demonstrate that all real motivation springs from within each of us and doesn't flow from manipulative rewards and punishments offered by the power holders. That type of presumed motivation is a delusion and the individuals so approached make their own decision, based on the assessment of what best serves them rather than the power holder. The effort and commitment expended to comply is often intended to avoid negative consequences. For real enthusiasm generated by a cooperative spirit and inner motivation, people at Southwest Airlines are the best example among the organizations we studied.

- *A narrow view of profits*—Lucas maintains "shareholder value is a summary measurement of how well we are providing 'profits' to everyone who can make a difference." His next question is what return we are giving to our employees to "invest their creativity, passion and commitment" in the organization. Enron-type companies seem to offer a bubble of little real substance.

Counterpoise: Our candidate for best example among the organizations we studied is Southwest Airlines. When all of the four major airlines downsized their operations, dismissed employees, and incurred huge losses after September 11, 2001, Southwest continued expanding, kept their workforce, and maintained their profitable situation. While the major airlines wiped out senior citizen discounts, Southwest announced they would keep them. All this doesn't happen by accident. Everyone who has flown Southwest and was able to observe the cooperation, inventiveness, and high morale of their employees can appreciate that here is an organization where people support each other and treat each other well. The result is a healthy view of "profits" and contribution to shareholder value.

- *Growth as a goal*—The "grow or die" chant has beguiled many. To quote Lucas again, "Intelligent and ethical growth is a good thing, but growth as goal leads to unrealistic expectations and desperate behaviors." In today's economy there is no shortage of classic examples for this. Lucas continues: "What will we do— what will we *have* to do—to make those relentlessly increasing expectations, like numbers that are way beyond 'stretch'?" In all too many cases, companies that practiced growth by acquisition for the gain of power and prestige it appeared to offer failed to consider the possible culture clashes that often put the business combination in danger, and they started suffering from acute organizational indigestion, leading to certain death or sometimes to becoming food for other corporate sharks.

  Counterpoise: From its inception as a basement business launched by chemist Bill Gore, W. L. Gore & Associates embraced the principle of "Making money and having fun doing so." This is quite a contrast to those who are tightly focused on "making money through growth." Adding the word "Associates" to the company name was also no accident. Gore's employee-centered expansion is based on an inner sense of unusual values. The company's growth is brought about by the entrepreneurial aspirations of its leaders. Each facility is limited to approximately 200 people. Bill Gore believed that such was the maximum number where all of the plant's employees could get to know each other. That sense of community was considered key to high employee productivity where no one would feel left out, avoiding any possibility of a culture clash.

  Gore's philosophy of growth was based on individual initiative and on people's ability to lead others. This is how we described its foundations in our earlier book *A Better Place to Work:* "The Gore company and its people represent the very ideals of a new workplace based on leadership determined by followership, on fairness towards each other, on freedom to take risks, on self-generated commitments, and on consultation with colleagues." The method of growth is critical and rests on a particular form of leadership: Any employee who has a "viable" new product idea, the expertise to adequately bring the idea to market, and can attract enough followers is allowed to remain as its leader. This entrepreneurial approach is not an easy one, but it has made Gore successful for over 40 years. Though privately held and owned by its associates, the success has propelled Gore to a level of revenues and income comparable to a *FORTUNE* 500 corporation.

None of the foregoing guarantees that any of these organizations will not suffer setbacks, but it does indicate that it is possible to create a culture that inoculates the organization against the dangers of Enronism and the shenanigans that have become common and much publicized since the Enron debacle.

PART IV

A Model Corporate Culture

In today's work environment, if you were asked to develop a blueprint of a model corporate culture, you would most certainly insist upon the following criteria:

- Having your personal autonomy at work and the freedom to make all job-related decisions.
- Getting the opportunity to develop your potential and talents, leading to personal growth and higher self-esteem.
- Being able to share your daily routines and experiences with coworkers, valuing each other's unique abilities and forging close bonds with each other.
- Espousing the organization's principles and values that are to be consistent with your own.

The case study that follows, of Science Applications International Corporation (SAIC), provides a surprising match for such a blueprint, and we have chosen to offer it as a model of the new corporate cultures we are describing. SAIC, in spite of employing over 40,000 people, is not a well-known company, maybe because of its close involvement with national security. SAIC history and operations provide an exciting kaleidoscope of features and qualities that come together as a true model of a truly inclusive and participative culture.

CHAPTER 14

Science Applications International Corporation (SAIC): Entrepreneurial Spirit and Employee Ownership

INTRODUCTION

In February 2001, when SAIC marked its 32nd anniversary, the company had many reasons to celebrate. Since its founding in 1969, SAIC had experienced unprecedented success. Revenues had grown without interruption from $243,000 in Fiscal Year (FY) 1970 to $6.1 billion in FY 2002. The work environment continued to be excitingly different, to the benefit of an increasing number of SAIC employees, from the initial 22 to today's over 40,000.

SAIC's culture is unique, worth being emulated by other companies. Not the least important of these traits is the fact that, since inception, SAIC has been employee owned. SAIC's founder, Dr. J. Robert Beyster, felt at the time that "those who contribute to the company should own it, and ownership should be commensurate with that contribution and performance as much as feasible." Today, 33% of SAIC stock is owned directly by employees, 3% by elected officers and directors (including Dr. Beyster's share of less than 1.5%), 19% by former employees and outsiders, and 45% by various SAIC retirement plans.

As we know from extensive research sponsored by the National Center for Employee Ownership (NCEO), employee ownership will not automatically lead to increases in work motivation and productivity. Ownership has to go hand in hand with appropriate management philosophies. SAIC seems to have found the right formula to stimulate entrepreneurial spirit and participation among its employees. Our observations during several roundtable discussions with SAIC employees and managers from different areas of the company have been a vivid testimony to this philosophy. Similarly, we interviewed Telcordia managers to assess the impact of this important acquisition. It was an unusual experience to witness enthusiasm as well as serious involvement of the employee-owners at different levels of the organization.

Looking at the sheer size of the SAIC operation, managing its future expansion is to be a significant challenge that will stretch people's abilities. Along the path of its history, SAIC has developed ideas and tools to accomplish that, using the concept of "active participation" and creating mechanisms to allow for dialogue and communications, to make sure that the employees' input is received. With this in place, the SAIC story represents an exciting model for a present-day workplace.

"WHAT'S SAIC?"

Larry Kull, former president and COO of SAIC, recalled from the early days of the company: "The first question people would ask when you walked into their office, was 'What's SAIC? I've never heard of that'." Obviously, at a business level of $6.1 billion, that has changed, although even today SAIC is far from being a household name. In part, the explanation for this is that SAIC, since its inception, has spent very little on advertising its corporate identity. Also, the very nature of much of the SAIC business, supporting and cooperating with the federal government on issues of national security, tends to limit extensive publicity.

Nonetheless, SAIC is involved in many well-publicized projects. Let's sample some of the past and current SAIC activities:

- *http://www.netsol.com*—Network Solutions was a subsidiary of SAIC until it was sold to VeriSign in June of 2000. Network Solutions has become a pioneering force for the Internet as the global registrar of the .com, .net, .org, and .edu Web addresses.

- *Composite Health Care System (CHCS)*—Being awarded a billion-dollar contract for the implementation of CHCS for the Department of Defense was a major milestone for SAIC. At the time, the contract was the largest in the company's history and put SAIC on the map as a major systems integrator. In 1996, the General Accounting Office (GAO) reported on SAIC's progress: "As the backbone of Defense's medical operations, CHCS will provide personnel with almost instant access to patient information, from medical history to current treatment and vital statistics." The new system integrated thousands of technical specifications and accommodated users ranging from large facilities such as Walter Reed Army Hospital to small clinics in rural areas.

- *Three Mile Island*—When disaster struck at the nuclear power plant in Pennsylvania, government officials immediately contacted SAIC for help and assistance, bringing the SAIC mobile radiochemistry laboratory to the site for testing and stabilization efforts. SAIC response teams routinely perform different kinds of environmental services.

- *1–800–555–1212*—Bellcore—now SAIC's Telcordia Technologies subsidiary— pioneered many well-known telecommunications services, such as toll free numbers, call waiting and caller identification.

- *America's Cup*—In February of 1987, Dennis Conner won the cup back for the United States, which, at the same time, represented a technology victory for SAIC. The company was a major support contractor for the America's Cup team.

Welcome to SAIC and its universe of captivating businesses, which provide many opportunities and intellectual challenges to their talented employees! We may imagine the nature and the culture of the business organization that supports these activities. As a matter of fact, they have been an excellent selling point for recruiting new talent.

Before we move on, however, to describe the company, its history, and its culture in more detail, we would like to focus for a moment on certain concepts for a modern work environment that are validated by the SAIC culture.

CONCEPTS FOR A MODERN WORKPLACE

We have mentioned before how, during the last decade, both the technology revolution and the competitive global market have changed the work ecology. The nature of work in today's economic environment requires less structure and more flexibility. Downsizing and restructuring have eliminated traditional job security.

Today's modern workplace seems to be guided by a new unwritten contract between employers and employees, a voluntary tacit agreement that fulfills the altered expectations of both sides for their mutual relationship. The nature of work may have changed, but in today's economy, motivated people in control of their destiny are more than ever the most important source of competitive advantage. Here is what we consider the new priorities of management and labor. In many ways, SAIC helps to establish their validity.

We see as employers' priorities:

- *Profitability*—Management focuses on "shareholder value" by controlling costs, maximizing productivity, and tying overall compensation to performance. Organizational structures are flattened and middle management is thinned out. The goal is to keep operations profitable under pressure from global competition.

- *Quality*—The quality movement had its origins both in cost considerations and in the increased requirements of the technology era. In today's environment, management is looking for more education and higher skill levels.

- *Flexibility*—Following the ups and downs of demand, management is keen on maintaining a flexible workforce, with no guarantees of tenure. This will allow for frequent adjustments of the production base to changing market conditions.

On the other hand, employees' priorities seem to be:

- *Ownership*—As we interpret this term, it includes real share ownership as well as job control, being in charge, and making important decisions. Replacing the former loyalty bonds, this becomes the main source of employee motivation. It requires totally open communications throughout the workplace, with management's role changing to one of coordination, being available as a resource of experience and support.

- *Personal growth*—In the absence of job guarantees and tenure, people look for learning opportunities, being able to acquire diverse and marketable skills that make them more flexible, and help finding a new assignment in case of termination. In our earlier research, we found learning to be an important driver of work motivation.

- *"Fun"*—For lack of a better term, "fun" comprises all elements of job satisfaction. Work must be rewarding and intellectually challenging, along with the ability to team up with friends and feel appreciated and recognized by peers and management. It includes fairness of compensation and benefits, the more so as job guarantees are no longer available.

As we review the SAIC history and culture, it is interesting to observe how priorities have sometimes shifted from one side to the other to adjust to changing business realities.

SAIC HISTORY (I)—THE FIRST DECADE

Founded by Dr. J. Robert Beyster in February of 1969, SAIC from its beginnings developed along unconventional lines. Dr. Beyster, with degrees in engineering and physics from the University of Michigan, had joined General Atomics in 1957 to head their linear accelerator facility. The acquisition of General Atomics by Gulf Oil totally changed its research priorities. This prompted Dr. Beyster to leave and to open his own firm, based on two research contracts from Los Alamos and Brookhaven National Laboratories.

Explains Dr. Beyster about his plans at the time: "Rather than having a grand design, we started with some contracts and a few people with ideas, and growth started to snowball." Revenues evolved from $243,000 in the first year, to $1.2 million in FY 1971, and to $3.35 million in FY 1972, illustrating the explosive growth pattern. By the end of the first decade, SAIC had passed the $100 million mark.

Since its inception, the most unconventional feature of SAIC was employee ownership. Dr. Beyster had made the fundamental decision to share ownership with the people who came to work for him. Later he explained: "I imagine people now regard me as 'out of my mind' for diluting my ownership position from 100% to 10% within the first year. For me, it was simply the right thing to do, to share ownership of the company with those who make it successful."

A typical example of SAIC's success in developing new business was the opening of the Washington, D.C., office in 1970. Dr. Beyster had been able to attract Bill Layson and some of his associates to start this important location. The agreement was to develop $1 million worth of new revenue within the next 18 months, doubling the company's present revenue, and in turn to distribute a sizeable stock award to make Layson and his staff employee-owners. The new office reached the goal within the agreed-upon time frame, with all the people who contributed to the success sharing the reward.

While in the beginning SAIC had to fight for survival, the next priority was to establish credibility with important customers. Early on, SAIC became involved in matters of national security, including policy review, scientific investigations, and simulation studies for various agencies of the Department of Defense. Even now, in FY 2002, government work, including national security, accounted for about 58% of total SAIC business, which explains some of the low profile and restraint toward image advertising that persists at SAIC today. It has also led to a particular focus on ethical standards, explained in more detail in Exhibit 14.1.

One of the important success factors was to establish offices close to customer locations and staff them with qualified people. Offices for the company's Space & Missile Systems Group opened in Chicago, Tucson, and Huntsville, Alabama, in 1971. SAIC surprised the defense industry by winning a multiyear contract for independent software verification and validation for the U.S. Army anti-ballistic missile program, to be handled by the Huntsville office. In Virginia, an SAIC subsidiary won an important National Institutes of Health contract for planning research on heart disease and cancer. The areas of energy research and environmental assessment became an important focus after the energy crisis of 1973. More than 20 universities participated in a program to do baseline characterization of the Southern California outer continental shelf region in 1975, a program coordinated by SAIC.

These few examples may help to illustrate the diversity of SAIC activities. During that same time period, the number of professionals and employees grew from 22 people in a small seaside office in La Jolla to 1,200 people at 45 locations at the end of FY 1976. Concluding the first decade, SAIC employment stood at 3,600 people, with 1,360 or 37% being direct shareholders, while most of the others owned stock through retirement plans. An amazing feat!

Before we move on in our review of SAIC history, it may be useful to assess the SAIC culture as it had developed during this first decade, with particular attention to employee ownership.

Exhibit 14.1.
The SAIC Employee Ethics Committee

> SAIC is rightfully proud of its ethics . . . which as employee-owners is
> more than just a slogan or a required annual briefing for most of us.
> James P. Reams, vice president, SAIC

As many of SAIC's employee activities, the Employee Ethics Committee
was created in 1984 at the suggestion of Dr. Beyster. Given the high share
of government work in the company's overall business, Dr. Beyster
insisted early on in establishing core values and principles in order to
maintain high ethical standards of business conduct. "As employee-
owners of SAIC, we must all share a common focus on ethical leadership,"
he says. "Our conduct must not only look right, it must be right. We cannot cut corners on ethics nor allow others to do so."

The Employee Ethics Committee has 25 members who are nominated
by the different group leaders and then appointed by Dr. Beyster. Each of
the more important business groups has one representative and that
includes some foreign members. The spectrum of people ranges from staff
employees to senior managers. While members are appointed for the long
term, there is obviously certain turnover due to business constraints.

For many years, Bill Layson, the successful founder of the Washington,
D.C., office and longtime SAIC employee-owner, headed the Employee
Ethics Committee. Richard T. Shearer, who joined SAIC in 1996 after a suc-
cessful navy career, succeeded him in 1999.

The Employee Ethics Committee meets face-to-face on a quarterly basis
during SAIC Meetings Week and, in addition, keeps close contact through
monthly teleconferences. Many years ago, SAIC issued guidelines on
"Standards of Business Ethics and Conduct" and it is up to the committee
to monitor the SAIC ethics program. Once every two years, each and
every SAIC employee is required to attend a one-hour ethics training session to get updates on his or her individual responsibilities.

More importantly, however, the Employee Ethics Committee serves as a
point of contact for employees who have ethical concerns. On average, the
committee is approached about 500 times a year, with about 15% of the
issues requiring some form of closer investigation. In recent history, mis-
use of Internet access has been the most frequent problem from an ethical
viewpoint.

The ethics initiative has served SAIC well, as Dr. Beyster confirms: "We
believe there is strong linkage between ethics and quality at SAIC, which
is reflected in our Ethics Motto: 'Ethics and Quality: Good
Values . . . Good Business'."

SAIC Culture and Employee Ownership

Reflecting upon the business history of the first decade, certain early characteristics of SAIC's evolving culture stand out:

- *Entrepreneurial spirit*—As we can witness over and over again, people join SAIC to build new business in areas of their interest and to capture the opportunity for success. People value their independence and the ability to make decisions. They are able to create and develop their own niche. The breadth of opportunities is unusual: The sky is the limit for go-getters! Junior employees may get an early chance "to carry the flag." Within a rather flat hierarchy, senior managers generally leave day-to-day decisions to their people.

- *Intellectual challenge*—In hiring talented and qualified people, SAIC provides a dynamic, exciting, and challenging work environment. People can be creative and may enjoy the professional strength and diversity of background of their peers. At the same time, this contributes to competitive tensions. Success may depend on peer recognition and appreciation of one's personal skills. This may be tough: SAIC is no "caring and feeding" organization!

- *Employee ownership*—At SAIC, employee ownership represents not only the opportunity to acquire shares as part of compensation or retirement programs, it is an overarching management philosophy. In Dr. Beyster's view, employee ownership was intended to place the broad interests of all employees as a driving force for the newly founded company, rather than being guided by narrow financial goals of outside shareholders. Employee-owners were meant to help set the company's direction and to take important responsibilities for growing SAIC's business.

  In the early days of SAIC, there were ample opportunities to purchase stock or receive stock options as reward for bringing in new contracts and profitable business. Programs were refined to motivate outstanding performance as well as to assure widespread participation in company ownership, which continues to be the hallmark of SAIC's employee ownership system. As owners, people are expected to "actively participate in addressing important corporate issues and have a strong voice in the company's decision-making process."

  Over time, SAIC has devised several different stock purchase programs, starting with an opportunity for "First Time Buyers," providing two stock options for every share purchased up to $1,000. Stock bonuses are distributed as merit awards, while "contingent options" are offered as an incentive to reach certain goals based on agreed-upon objectives. "Future Leaders" receive deferred stock bonuses as an incentive to stay with the company and reap the rewards of their successful initiatives. Along similar lines, certain "New Stars"—promising new hires with less than three years with SAIC—receive stock options. Additional incentives for the purchase of SAIC stock are offered as part of the retirement plans or through an employee stock purchase plan, which gives employees a 10% discount on stock purchases.

  SAIC's stock price has grown at a phenomenal rate, during the past five years alone at an annualized rate of return of 38%. Clearly, employee-owners have reaped huge rewards, ultimately resulting from their contributions to the company's success. Today, to benefit from the financial rewards of the employee ownership programs requires staying with SAIC for at least four to six years, due to vesting schedules on stock options and certain stock bonus awards. However, as Jim Reams, an SAIC vice president, puts it: "If all you are looking for is to draw a salary and pay back student loans, you are at the wrong place!" Employee ownership is a long-term approach that depends on educating new hires about its exciting possibilities. In 1998, SAIC founded a working group to look after these aspects and the need for ownership communications.

- *Interaction*—Early on, SAIC introduced a practice of quarterly meetings on different issues, which were soon bundled into a "Meetings Week" event. Initially, the board of directors, management council, and certain committees on incentives, company stock, and other topics would meet. Later on, it became an opportunity for many other committees and management groups to meet and evolved into an exciting event that congregated most of the senior levels of the company. Participation became the key to Meetings Week and in this way provided broad interaction and communication to all involved.

In summary, the SAIC culture of the first decade of company history solidly supported management priorities of financial growth and close customer relationships. Professional excellence ensured the quality of products and services. For SAIC employees, there was ownership in the broadest sense, with the simultaneous opportunity to acquire shares and to be in charge. Work was "fun" and SAIC employees formed a close-knit fraternity because the size of the company allowed for close contacts and for personal recognition of management and even of Dr. Beyster. SAIC was well ahead of its times!

Technical Environment Committee

Toward the end of the first decade, a particular problem developed: SAIC was growing and started getting large contracts for software integration work that required many "helping hands," people hired specifically to perform the multiple tasks related to these contracts. These employees became part of a somewhat different culture, devoid of the attributes of entrepreneurship and intellectual challenge that so much characterized the SAIC culture at the time. At the same time, new levels of management were created and prestigious outside members joined the SAIC Board of Directors. Employees began to question whether senior management would be able to maintain close contact with the technical staff. They began looking for ways to share their ideas regarding the work environment with senior management.

In order to address this problem and upon personal involvement of Dr. Beyster, the Technical Environment Committee (TEC) was formed as a conduit of information among the Board of Directors, senior management, and the employees. It developed into a unique tool to impact the SAIC work environment. From its inception in 1982, the TEC offered an exciting opportunity for employee participation. Dr. Beyster called the TEC the "conscience of SAIC" and the "watchdog of employee ownership," facilitating communications in all directions and allowing the TEC to brainstorm with management on a broad spectrum of issues intended to build a better work environment. Every single aspect of this environment can be reviewed and discussed with top management. The TEC reports directly to Dr. Beyster, who openly stated: "No aspect of the corporation's business is out of bounds to the TEC."

As of today, the TEC has 40 members and is organized within a regional framework to ensure participation of a reasonable cross section of the employee population. Membership in the TEC is reserved to nonmanagement staff employees. The chairperson of the TEC, who rotates every three years, continues to have direct access to Dr. Beyster. The TEC chair is routinely invited to attend senior management and board of directors meetings and report back to the employees on issues of general interest. The initial focus of the TEC was on supporting a sound and productive work environment and fostering high standards of professional excellence. Today, the issues to be addressed have been expanded to include questions relating to employee benefits, training and development, and employee assimilation and retention as well as questions of motivation and employee morale.

The creation of the TEC was a very timely and well thought out measure to restore the basic principles of "ownership" to all SAIC employees. The support of top management has made the TEC initiative valuable and effective and has strengthened the concept of ownership by establishing direct employee participation. More details on the functioning of the TEC are provided in Exhibit 14.2.

SAIC HISTORY (II)—EARLY 1980s TO MID-1990s

There could be no question about success. Given the attributes of the SAIC culture of the early 1980s and with the efforts of top management to solidly establish participatory ownership and to make SAIC a "fun" place to work, the company was poised to take off. And take off it did!

As mentioned before, SAIC revenues reached the $100 million mark at the end of the first decade. Revenues passed $500 million in FY 1986, $1 billion in FY 1990, and $1.5 billion in FY 1993. In the same time span, employment reached 6,400, 11,400, and 14,900 people, respectively. The overall growth of SAIC exceeded all expectations. It would lead too far and go beyond the framework of this study to go into the details of this successful development. A few examples of specific areas may suffice here.

Environmental assessment had become an important expertise at SAIC. In 1979, when disaster struck at the Three Mile Island nuclear power facility

"What's on the TEC agenda? What are your major goals and objectives?
How do you contact and reach SAIC's employees?" Those were some of
the questions we posed to Julie Kahn, past chair of the company's unique
Technical Environment Committee (TEC). Julie Kahn gave us a surprising
answer: "I think the most important thing to say about the TEC's agenda
is that it is derived directly from feedback that we get from employees. It's
that feedback that actually sets our priorities for the year—literally."

During its 20-year history, the TEC has developed many ways to reach
its audience. There is *TEC-Talk*, the committee's newsletter distributed by
E-mail to all employees. The company's internal communications Web site
called ISSAIC sponsors a special section on TEC matters. Each of the committee's 40 members, who come from about 30 different SAIC locations,
organizes quarterly briefings for his or her colleagues at that site. And
there are other opportunities to contact fellow employees during the quarterly Meetings Week gathering or at other occasions. The employees'
response to all of these efforts is about 1,200 E-mails per year with questions, suggestions, or complaints. Not bad considering the dispersed and
multifaceted structure of the company!

TEC members maintain their job with the division they belong to but
are given 100 labor hours per year for TEC activities. As the TEC expects
its members to be active contributors, they will typically volunteer
another 100 hours of their own time for the committee. They will participate in at least one of the four TEC subcommittees, which handle issues of
employee ownership, human resources, environment, and communications. The chairs of the subcommittees together with the TEC chair form
the Operating Council, the planning and managing body of the TEC.
Operating Council members are given 300 labor hours per year, while the
TEC chair may dedicate between 50% and 75% of his or her time to TEC
matters. Again, all Operating Council members will volunteer sizeable
amounts of personal time for the committee.

The agenda of the TEC's quarterly meetings—which are open to the
employees and to one of which we were graciously invited—typically
deals with employee concerns such as professional development,
employee morale, motivational questions, and employee retention. The
TEC maintains a close collaborative relationship with the human resources
department and its executives take part in the meetings by telephone
hookup, discussing questions such as incentives or internal mobility. "One
of the things I try to emphasize as chair," explains Julie Kahn, "is that we

Exhibit 14.2.
(Continued)

don't just go in with our hands out, asking for more in the way of benefits, but that we also bring potential solutions to the table and offer to help."

In recent TEC history, the environment subcommittee has come to the forefront because it tries to tackle questions of career development, training, and telecommuting, so crucial to today's work environment. "If you can instill in your employees the sense that the company is willing to invest in them and therefore values them," remarked Julie Kahn, "I think that can do a lot for your retention."

As to career development, the TEC has been able to create an online tool kit and navigational aid, which lists all available resources for training. Simultaneously, a chat forum has opened at the new Web site called "Career Development Navigator" for employees to explore the company's career development tools and resources and how to use them, as well as to raise related questions and suggestions. "It's important for people to know where they are and where they can go in their careers," comments Julie Kahn. "It's a tall order for a little committee like the TEC to address, but we made some good progress."

The efforts of the TEC are indeed "a tall order." When the TEC was founded, the company had about 4,000 employees. Today, this number has not only increased to about 43,000 worldwide but the organization is much more complex due to a universe of subsidiaries and subcultures with diverse human resource structures and environmental features. There is a growing trend—wholeheartedly supported by the TEC—to create satellite committees in order to accommodate the expansion and diversity of SAIC. Such committees already exist at Telcordia, at the United Kingdom subsidiaries, and at Intesa in Venezuela. During her time as chair Julie Kahn has promoted ideas to establish the TEC as a mentoring partner for these new committees, trying to avoid segregation and helping to assimilate new employee groups. Along these lines, an Environment Committee Council has been created as a unifying force for these committees.

The TEC and its efforts and activities are an important part of employee ownership at SAIC. Julie Kahn vividly remembers a meeting in 1998 when Dr. Beyster, chairman of SAIC, in addressing the participants stated that "employee participation is vital to Employee Ownership at SAIC. Without it Employee Ownership is a 'sham'," meaning that it would be hollow and worthless. There can be no doubt that after 20 years of fruitful service to the employees, the TEC is an institution and tradition of participatory employee ownership to be continued.

in Pennsylvania, SAIC engineers played a key role in responding to the accident. Two years later, the company helped assess and monitor the massive chemical contamination of the Love Canal area in upstate New York.

In the national security sector, new missile technology studies for the Department of Defense included the Trident and MX projects and the B-1 bomber. They culminated in a major award for systems engineering of President Reagan's Strategic Defense Initiative, giving testimony to the company's national reputation.

Even before the terrorist bombing of PanAm Flight 103 over Lockerbie, Scotland, SAIC had started working on a nonintrusive explosives detection system. At the urgent request of the FAA, this development effort was accelerated, leading to its successful conclusion in 1988.

And last but not least, when skipper Dennis Conner won back the America's Cup in February of 1987, it was a technology victory for SAIC as well. As a major support contractor, the company helped make important changes in yacht design methods, resulting in a technically superior boat.

Along with the growth in revenue and people, SAIC opened new facilities in Campus Point/San Diego, where its corporate headquarters moved in 1988. Concurrently, the McLean, Virginia, facility, first opened at the end of the first decade, doubled in space during 1989. Not surprisingly, the size of the company's operations required more structured management. In 1988, Larry Kull was named president and COO to support Dr. Beyster in the day-to-day management of SAIC. At some later time, a group of executive vice presidents was appointed as part of an official executive committee.

These changes notwithstanding, the company's corporate structure remained flat and "entrepreneurism" continued to be SAIC's hallmark. However, the difficulties described before and related to numerous large contracts, in particular in the software and systems integration area, continued. Due to the different makeup and management organization of these contracts, they presented different challenges in terms of motivating and integrating new employees into the SAIC culture. At the same time, the company was experiencing a rising problem of employee turnover, common for the information technology (IT) employment market. Therefore, more emphasis on "recruitment, retention, and motivation of talented people" was added as a formal corporate objective.

We should stop here again to assess certain changes to the SAIC culture that occurred toward the end of this period, leading to the development of statements of mission and values and to a renewed focus on employee ownership at SAIC.

SAIC Culture of the 1990s: Need for New Ideas?

Let us for a moment get back to the concepts outlined earlier and look at the unwritten contract between SAIC management and the company's employees. In light of the formidable business success described in this chapter, all of the company's priorities seem to have been fulfilled: SAIC revenue and profits increased beyond expectations over the 15-year period. Quality was held high with the introduction of new quality assurance and program management procedures. And the company's organization was streamlined and adjusted to the needs of the business, introducing a different management structure.

As to the employee priorities, we began to sense a dilution of the previously strong culture that so much supported and propelled the SAIC success. The *entrepreneurial spirit* that characterized the SAIC workplace and evolved into a driver of revenue growth continued to be alive and well. However, the independence of certain sectors of the company started leading to internal competition. Independent "fiefdoms" emerged here and there, and "stovepipes" were erected, sometimes hampering synergy and cross communication. People felt the need for an overarching vision for SAIC to inspire its employees and lead them into the future.

With an abundance of exciting and demanding assignments, work continued to be *intellectually challenging*. More and more, however, the large contracts generally required few technical leaders and a sizeable staff—"all others," as they saw themselves. In some cases, the reward systems did not consider qualities like timely performance and teamwork at the same level of importance as technical and management expertise, leading to certain discontent. At times, development possibilities and a career path for staff employees were felt missing. Similarly, new hires were often discouraged by the lack of growth opportunities and learning emphasis at SAIC.

Most importantly, *ownership* remained the company's overarching philosophy. As we pointed out before, ownership was not limited to acquiring SAIC stock as a promising investment but meant that the common interests of all employees were to become a driving force for the company. Here, maybe, management overestimated certain aspects of the employee ownership structure that were thought to be intrinsic and apparent. For many new employees, owning SAIC stock was not important enough—at least not in their first few years with SAIC—to motivate hard work and strong performance. On the other hand, the broader participatory meaning of ownership was not made clear so that it would be more highly valued by these people. Undoubtedly, this contributed to the increasing turnover problem among the employees.

In the 1990s, recruiting for professionals in IT had turned into a tough business: Increasing demand made it hard to find good people and paying finder's fees became common practice. The consequences for SAIC were unexpected: Instead of being a most attractive enterprise to be joined by large numbers of young professionals, SAIC, on occasion, had to compete aggressively with other IT firms to fill open positions.

Again, top management moved quickly to counter these adverse trends. *Statements of mission and of values* were drafted to define a set of general directions and the company's strong culture for the benefit of all SAIC employees. The mission statement included teamwork and cooperation as important priorities. Rewards from the employee ownership system were to drive outstanding performance. The SAIC work environment was to encourage professional growth and entrepreneurial freedom. The statement of values went on to explain that "widespread employee participation is a fundamental part of SAIC's employee ownership system." Employees should "have a strong voice in . . . decision-making processes."

In order to involve large numbers of employees in the final wording of the two statements, the drafts were widely circulated and discussed in focus groups. The outcome of these discussions gave evidence for some of the problems mentioned above. In any event, defining the SAIC mission and explaining the company's values to all employees was an important first step in creating proper and essential conditions for future success.

A second initiative—forming the *Employee Ownership Working Group (EOWG)*—focused more deeply on the issue of ownership. It was felt that "active employee participation is a critical element of successful employee-owned companies." At SAIC, however, "employee ownership provides a powerful incentive and rewards system, but it is often poorly understood." Apparently, little was done to give new employees good information on the meaning of ownership as the founding philosophy of SAIC. This would not only include the financial aspects and mechanisms of stock acquisition but, more importantly, the role of an employee-owner and avenues for participation. Among SAIC employees, perception about ownership seemed to depend on their tenure with the company, on having had the opportunity to buy or be awarded stock, and on their general sense of empowerment.

The EOWG was established as a permanent committee in early 1998 with the mission "to communicate, educate, and promote SAIC's employee ownership to all employees." Initial actions included the creation of a curriculum to explain the meaning and importance of ownership. A network of trainers was developed by recruiting volunteers from the technical and administrative staff. While it may take more time to sense the impact of these initiatives on the SAIC culture, the EOWG has started serving as a focal point for employee ownership communications and educational initiatives.

Before we proceed, we need to review the impact of a major acquisition, the 1997 merger with Bellcore, on SAIC. Bellcore—which in March 1999 adopted the new name of Telcordia Technologies—had emerged as one of the successor organizations to Bell Labs, to become the research arm of the "Baby Bells." SAIC acquired Bellcore toward the end of 1997, with the promise to keep it as a subsidiary. Since then, SAIC has forged a closer relationship between the two organizations, exploring business synergies and streamlining operational practices. In view of the size of Bellcore with about $1 billion in revenue and 5,400 employees, the combination of the two companies required special efforts and thoughtful initiatives to make the merger successful.

TELCORDIA—INNOVATIVE TELECOMMUNICATIONS

In many respects, the acquisition of the former Bellcore worked to the benefit of SAIC. Bellcore's core competency in telecommunications, its recent transformation from a research consortium at the service of the Regional Bell Operating Companies (RBOCs) into a successful commercially minded and customer-driven company, and its newly established culture have proven to be a major asset to SAIC.

In order not to burden the SAIC story with too many details of Bellcore's history, we have chosen to describe the latter in a separate chapter (see chapter 8), together with a revealing interview of Bellcore's former CEO Dr. George Heilmeier. However, it may be interesting to summarize here a few developments at Bellcore (now SAIC's Telcordia subsidiary) that may have an important effect on the SAIC culture.

From the moment Dr. Heilmeier joined Bellcore, he worked hard to forge a commercial mindset and create a profit orientation among the Bellcore people. He understood the soft issues and welded his people into "Team Bellcore," mandating three days of management training for everyone as a "culture transforming experience." A set of eight guiding principles, shown in Exhibit 14.3, was introduced and reinforced in the Team Bellcore training sessions. Recognizing the importance of communications, Dr. Heilmeier insisted on a common desktop environment for all Bellcore employees, providing the right tool for leadership messages. Company leaders were held accountable for informing their people and were measured against the recently introduced guiding principles.

Another Bell legacy, learning and continued education, was given high priority by Dr. Heilmeier. Shunning very detailed job descriptions, Bellcore would often select aspiring managers on the basis of their attractive technical and personal background. After their initial assignment was completed, new hires were expected to "roll," to be flexible and leverage their knowledge moving into their next job. "Continued learning and a commitment to professional growth, that was management's training philosophy," added Gwen Taylor, Bellcore's now-retired vice president of human resources, who benefited from her own professional training opportunities.

The new Bellcore that emerged from the process of change became uniquely customer focused, welded together in its strategic direction, and, at the same time, very flexible. People embraced a team spirit; followed a clear mission and a set of guiding principles; relied on "ownership" to

Exhibit 14.3.
Bellcore Guiding Principles

Teamwork

- Support One BELLCORE

Accountability

- What More Can I Do?
- No Victim Behaviors

Openness & Trust

- Clear Hidden Agendas
- Give It to Get It

Respect

- Treat Others the Way They Want to Be Treated
- Look for the Strengths

Commitment to Change

- Expand the Comfort Zone
- Flexibility & Innovation

Winning

- Focus on Customer Value

Coaching & Feedback

- Give and Request Appreciative/Constructive Feedback

Continuous Learning

- Use Every Opportunity to Grow Personally and Professionally

---

control their destiny, on professional excellence, and on continuous learning; and last but not least were supported by internal communications second to none.

This was the situation when, in late 1996, SAIC appeared on the horizon as a potential buyer of Bellcore. An initial employee meeting with Dr. Beyster, explaining SAIC's intentions and its management philosophy, was followed by a year of "due diligence," with intense communications and face-to-face meetings between SAIC and Bellcore leaders. SAIC was little known at the time, but expectations among Bellcore employees were high. Comments like "finally we are going to break free from the old culture" or "this will allow us to realize our own potential" characterize the high psychological acceptance level at Bellcore. There were anxieties as well: SAIC's heavy government orientation and its extensive involvement with defense-related matters raised questions because of the changing world order. Bellcore's ability to continue its successful expansion into telecommunications under new management and the continuity of business plans and corporate identity carried uncertainties for the future, aside from the obvious questions of compensation levels and benefit plans. In a hot job market, the Bellcore workforce seemed to be vulnerable and in danger of becoming heavily recruited by other Bell companies and high technology firms.

Fortunately and as a testimony to the strong culture established by Dr. Heilmeier, the heavy drain on personnel during 1997, due to the uncertainties of the acquisition, could be stopped quickly. In 1998, turnover at the new Telcordia was down to the single digits. The company's business continued on the upward path and SAIC's strong client base with federal, state, and local governments created profitable synergies. The financial success has allowed Telcordia to remain quite independent. As for the future, management in both companies has concluded that integration of the two partners needs to be anchored in certain business realities. The international arena is an example where integration has gone forward, using the strength of the more successful company in each market. In theory, the two cultures might blend, relying on the strengths of each partner, but business realities and people may chart a different course. To that extent, Telcordia sees the need of strong people players who can leverage each partner's strengths and abilities.

There is an additional very encouraging factor in the SAIC/Telcordia combination: To date, over 60% of Telcordia employees have become direct shareholders of SAIC, while all of the employees have invested in SAIC stock through their 401(k) plans. Positive influences came together: Ownership communications were well handled, the stock market was booming, and compensation and 401(k) programs provided monetary availability. Nevertheless, the participation rate is fortunate and a good omen for the joint journey of SAIC and Telcordia. It may be good judgment, however, to use some of the strengths of the Telcordia culture to foster the integration of both organizations and to heighten the attractiveness of the "SAIC ways." This brings us to the final section, looking at some perspectives and conclusions for the future.

LESSONS FOR A MODERN WORKPLACE

Over the past more than 30 years, SAIC has been extraordinarily successful. The company's culture has been unique, challenging, and the driver of its success. Let us try to summarize some of the model features of this culture and work environment for the benefit of the reader who may be interested in following the SAIC example. At the same time, we'll highlight possible adjustments that may be considered for the future.

First, there is people's *entrepreneurial spirit*—the ability to create one's own market niche and to capture successful opportunities. This is SAIC's earliest and foremost success factor, a driving force from the times of the company's inception to this day.

It is strengthened by *ownership*, both real stock ownership and a participatory environment that sustains motivation and people's productivity. As we have witnessed over the years of SAIC history, ownership has served the company well in driving its business. With the increase in the size of SAIC's operations, new mechanisms for share ownership have been developed to maintain ample opportunity to acquire stock. At certain times, however, the participatory aspect of ownership has not received equal attention. Communications about the meaning of ownership at SAIC were not always sufficient. Often, new hires did not realize that they had to take charge and shape the work environment to their own needs and to the common interests of fellow employees. As expressed by the Telcordia guiding principles, "what more can I do" and "give it to get it" need strengthening.

With the creation of the EOWG, SAIC has taken an important step to promote ownership in an all-encompassing sense. Communications are being improved. Educational programs are put into place to broaden the understanding of the many aspects of ownership. In addition, there is another possible consideration: In the past, the TEC has been an excellent mechanism to bring employee concerns to management's attention as well as to receive input from employees on new ideas and initiatives. Since its inception, the TEC has offered exciting opportunities of employee participation. However, the TEC's task seems to be more and more difficult to perform due to its limited membership. In view of SAIC's increasing employment it may be good strategy to allow for a larger number of people to participate in the TEC.

As our second point, we would like to focus on *personal growth*. Within a new concept of a modern workplace, offering only limited job guarantees and prospects for tenure, the opportunity to acquire marketable skills becomes extremely important. While professional excellence has been a constant hallmark of SAIC, support for broader skill acquisition and consideration for employees' career paths have been a guiding principle at Telcordia. This personal growth mindset is of particular importance to new hires within a high technology environment where people look for new expertise and added flexibility. Telcordia's low turnover figures seem to confirm the validity of this point.

Certain initiatives are underway to make use of Telcordia's expertise to expand educational efforts for all of SAIC. This will serve the dual purpose of creating much-needed opportunities for learning and personal development at SAIC and, at the same time, of helping to assimilate Telcordia by adopting a proven cultural element, and, with that, abate ever present anxieties due to the merger.

Finally, throughout this case study, we have come to appreciate many features that make SAIC and Telcordia *fun* places to work. There is entrepreneurial independence and there is the ability to make decisions and to create one's own niche. SAIC's organizational structures are flat and a bottom-up approach is preferred.

However, in certain areas of SAIC, interaction and communication may not be at an optimum level. It may be worthwhile to consider pursuing Dr. Heilmeier's Team Bellcore approach to enhance an "SAIC spirit" that people can embrace. There are so many individual and divisional accomplishments that will make all SAIC employees proud of "their" company. At the same time, ISSAIC, which is SAIC's internal Web site, is available to all employees to provide ample information about what SAIC is about and what it does.

From SAIC's corporate viewpoint, this will accomplish the important goal of making the Telcordia acquisition successful by combining both partners' proven strengths. It will allow SAIC to proceed on its path of growth and profitability, based on a work environment geared toward attracting and retaining talented people.

For our readers, the lessons from this study are clear: Today's workplace must support entrepreneurial spirit, employee ownership, personal growth, and job satisfaction or "fun" for the employees. This will accomplish management's priorities of maximizing shareholder value, increasing skill levels, and maintaining workplace flexibility. SAIC, in combination with Telcordia, has all the ingredients to successfully accomplish this modern workplace.

The Executive Perspective:
Dr. John H. Warner Jr.—
SAIC: Will the Legend Continue?

For many executives in corporate America, SAIC's history has turned into a model to be emulated and a lesson to be learned. After over 30 years of uninterrupted growth, will the legend continue? We had the opportunity to interview Dr. John H. Warner Jr., corporate executive vice president and director at SAIC, on the following questions and concerns:

- How will SAIC manage future growth?
- How does SAIC assert the management responsibilities of its employee-owners?
- How can the SAIC spirit be maintained in the growing corporation?
- How important are training and personal growth within SAIC's business philosophy?

As corporate executive vice president, Dr. Warner is a member of a small group of SAIC senior managers who integrate the company's executive committee. He is in charge of Systems Integration, a major business and expertise at SAIC. Dr. Warner joined SAIC in 1973, when the company had about 300 employees, after completing his doctorate in nuclear engineering and a short stint at TRW. His reflection on those early days: "Fundamental in those days—and it continues today—was the importance placed on [hiring] technical talent. There was a very heavy R & D flavor to the corporation. And, essentially, 100% of SAIC's business was with the federal government. At that time, the federal government could award contracts without competition, if the awarding entity could justify it with getting national expertise in a particular field. In these early days, SAIC hired scientists with a national reputation in certain R & D areas who could acquire and also perform on specific business. They had a great degree of autonomy and independence in those days; they were their own entrepreneurs. This clearly and early on established the entrepreneurial nature of the corporation."

Dr. Warner has a good point here: Without that entrepreneurial spirit among the SAIC people, the company would not have achieved the level of success that it has and would not be a model for us in terms of its unique culture. However, today the company has reached a different level of complexity.

HOW WILL SAIC MANAGE FUTURE GROWTH?

Dr. Warner points to the chart shown as Exhibit 14.4, which visualizes the SAIC Group at the end of FY 2001. "That chart shows an incredibly dramatic change in the corporation in a very short period of time. Our atti-

Exhibit 14.4.
The World of SAIC

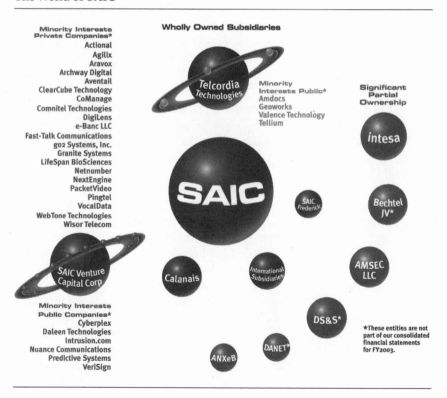

tude and philosophy was that we would do nothing short of 100% employee ownership. As we were growing, we had situations where, for business reasons, we could see the benefit to the corporation and to the employee-owners to deviate [from that concept]. The most significant example was Network Solutions. It meant a huge change in culture to take a division of SAIC and sell part of it to the public. There were other fairly substantial changes, as we entered into joint-venture relationships with other corporations, where we became partial owners. Examples are Rolls Royce, Amsec LLC, and Intesa, down in Venezuela—we changed our philosophy and culture significantly by entering into those relationships. In addition, we are now investing in equity relationships with both public and private firms, where we'll own far less than 50%. Here we see it to our benefit to have an equity investment and a strategic alliance for a particular technology or a market that is critical to grow a particular business. [In summary], what I am saying is that we have become flexible."

There is, indeed, dramatic change and a new flexibility in the way SAIC manages growth and adapts to different circumstances. But how does the new situation translate into maintaining unified values and a central vision for SAIC? How does management talent prosper in this environment?

"We place a high degree of responsibility on the individual sector and group managers, on down into the divisions," explains Dr. Warner. "[These are] decentralized organizations, where we communicate the principles of the corporation through our credo, our management meetings, our committee structure, our ethics briefings—all kinds of different ways to attempt to communicate with the employees. With time, we are placing a greater reliance on knowledge management. We are moving more information through ISSAIC, our internal Internet—we use ISSAIC and other techniques to move knowledge in a very decentralized organization. On ISSAIC, a wealth of information can be pulled up. We have set up what we call 'communities of interest,' where individuals can join and network with other people in the corporation."

Dr. Warner talks about the example of the quarterly Meetings Week sessions, where literally thousands of senior employees and managers meet and interact. Meetings Week features briefings on new business developments, new technologies, important contracts—an impressive agenda on what goes on in the company. At the same time, it serves as a forum for meetings and interaction of the more than 100 committees that handle all kinds of different aspects of the corporation. The executive committee and board of directors meet concurrently, providing unique opportunities to all participants to get involved in decision processes. "There is just a multitude of ways in which information is collected," adds Dr. Warner. "A lot of things come from different places and that's the way in which we operate."

SAIC's way to manage growth seems to have served the company well, as it announced record earnings for FY 2001, the 32nd year in a row. But then, one of the pillars of SAIC's success continues to be employee owner-ship and participatory management.

HOW DOES SAIC ASSERT THE MANAGEMENT RESPONSIBILITIES OF ITS EMPLOYEE-OWNERS?

"When new employees look at employee ownership," explains Dr. Warner, "they initially have a tendency to simply see the financial aspects. It takes some time to bridge from financial ownership to the broader responsibilities of an employee-owner of the corporation. That's more dif-ficult to convey to people as they join SAIC. It's something we'll have to work on, and one reason we have an Employee Ownership Working Group is to focus on that kind of communication."

There is the TEC as well, in our eyes an interesting and unique tool to foster and support employee participation. "[The TEC]," continues Dr. Warner "is a very useful means to solicit and obtain ideas from across the corporation; and when we have different new policies or changes that affect the employees, we use the TEC and its electronic network to get feedback prior to implementation. It is one way to promote internal com-munications. It's a very important one, but there are many other impor-tant committees, where employees are very much involved in the corporation."

HOW CAN THE SAIC SPIRIT BE MAINTAINED IN THE GROWING CORPORATION?

Dr. Warner strongly believes that the old SAIC spirit is alive and well, particularly among the smaller divisions. It will take time and dedicated efforts to infuse it into a larger acquisition or maintain it within a larger group. As to integrating 400 different businesses, "You don't," he says. "You don't need to. All you need [to provide] is a sense of employee own-ership, the basics of our credo, and where we are going as a corporation. Take the example of an organization of about 2,000 people that does work in life cycle engineering and maintenance of navy ships. It's so different from everything else we do. While you want those 2,000 people to be part of SAIC, that's communicated on a different level. They have their own mechanism to encourage teamwork and facilitate teaming with other organizations. Because of the diversity of our businesses, we have to be flexible and allow different business models to exist within the corpora-tion."

It's good policy for SAIC to have that flexibility to enhance and nurture the diversity of its business and organizational environment. That diver-sity is also apparent in the area of training and personal growth, important for employee recruitment and retention.

HOW IMPORTANT ARE TRAINING AND PERSONAL GROWTH WITHIN SAIC'S BUSINESS PHILOSOPHY?

"There is no simple single solution [for our training activities]," explains Dr. Warner. "Whatever we do in the training area must be supported by the financial situation that is affordable. So to do training, you have to generate the discretionary resources to pay for it. [But] we do have training and we have moved out in the direction of trying to utilize more computer-based training, for example, that is self-paced and targeted by the individual to increase skills in a particular area."

"What we try to do is to model our training offerings as a function of the business that an organization is involved in. Telcordia has the most extensive program by nature of its business. You are with a software product environment, as contrasted with the bulk of the rest of the corporation, which is more focused on services, on systems integration. It would be absolutely impossible to take that training culture and move it to SAIC, unless we wanted to drive the rest of the company out of business. It's got to be supportable."

Dr. Warner fully recognizes the importance of learning and continuous improvement for SAIC: "Constant improvement and what we can offer in the training area, through our corporate university, is part of our mission. Offering training to our employees to improve their capabilities to support our customers and to facilitate ways to improve their own career paths is important. However, at SAIC, we place more emphasis on the individuals to acquire that [knowledge] themselves."

To conclude the interview, Dr. Warner comments again on the concern about continued growth for SAIC. The company had its historic beginnings in government work and later diversified into the commercial market. SAIC has never forced any separation of the two areas but rather promoted their interchange, which seemed to benefit both government and commercial customers. He continues: "What we do with time is to add other vertical markets to the corporation and other horizontal capabilities that go across verticals and allow us to get into different verticals. I see that we can grow in telecommunications, energy, environment, financial services, health care, criminal justice—we can grow within these different vertical markets and can add new vertical markets, as a function of time. We have a major thrust going into E-business and into next-generation information networks. We are in a very good position to exploit the whole combination of telecom and IT merging together."

What exciting prospects for growth and what tremendous expertise to take advantage of those prospects! It is indeed amazing to observe that the SAIC culture of the first decade has, as Dr. Warner puts it, "established characteristics that continue even today." (The interview with Dr. Warner took place on May 18, 2000.)

CHAPTER 15

Summing It Up: The Essence of New Corporate Cultures

Cultures tended to take time to develop—centuries in the past—and were largely built on ideas that a group of people had in common—an affinity for certain attitudes, values, and standards of behavior that gradually developed into an unconscious guide for life itself. In the introduction, we saw how organizational cultures very slowly moved from the traditional stages—authoritative, custodial, and managerial/supervisory—to today's evolving models of participative leadership, collegial, self-management, and, most advanced, of a *community of leaders*. These new cultures are more "organic" in nature—simple, basic, and close to human values. They appeal to people because they fulfill their dreams and aspirations. With this being the case, people can join instantly and help the cultures grow and become stronger. Our case studies document some of the efforts and the reactions of the individuals who have chosen to participate. People have started to awake to the fact that certain organizations feed their spirit and mind as well as serving their physical and security needs.

How do these new culture models operate? What are the central tenets and the basic foundations upon which they are built? How is it that they are more dynamic and inclusive and encourage people at all levels of the organizations to reach extraordinary levels of motivation and achievement?

THE CENTRAL TENETS OF NEW CORPORATE CULTURES

We stated before that these new models were more organic in nature—simple and close to human values. In truth, people in our times of post–September 11 realities—but even before those ghastly events—look for a definite meaning to their lives, with work being an important part of it. Expectations are for consistency of the personal and professional domains, including beliefs and values. People so engaged feel responsible and mature. They have friends and family; they are integrated in their communities and schools; they are parents and bring up their children in a responsible way, being good examples and role models. At the same time, people want to make a difference in life and, with an acute sense of their careers, strive to reach their potential and a level of self-actualization.

These basic precepts lead to several considerations that impact today's organizational cultures. First, the desire to make full use of one's personal potential implies autonomy at work and having the freedom and the opportunity to be an equal partner at one's job, to share the authority and make all of the job-related decisions. This translates into a new concept of "ownership," to include the broad interests of all employees, that is driving today's new corporate cultures. We call it a "community of leaders" that takes people's commitment and motivation to levels not experienced before. The result is almost unlimited productivity and work effort, making a huge difference in providing the competitive edge in today's increasingly global economy.

Concurrently, we see changes in the traditional structure of corporate authority. Gone is rank and privilege, the unfortunate and unproductive chain of command that so often disguises the personal insecurity and lack of experience of managers and supervisors. Instead, today's leaders teach, mentor, and listen while serving as an experienced resource to their group. They earn people's respect for their experience, wisdom, and expertise. And, most importantly, it's not beyond them to follow their people's suggestions.

The second consideration has to do with the "community" aspect of the new cultures, which leads to considerable mutual respect. People value each other's individuality, appreciate and recognize each other's unique talents, and enjoy sharing their daily routines and experiences. It has been proven that teams draw considerable emotional stimulation from their fellowship and the personal bonds they develop with each other. In times of personal trauma and difficulty, teams reach out and support their members. It's fun to be part of the family and to enjoy the camaraderie of a close-knit group.

There is a third issue to be considered: The greater challenge of making all job-related decisions and the recognition of one's unique talents by peers and fellow workers is highly stimulating to our personal learning and development efforts. One's work experience leads to improved skills and greater personal mastery. Higher competence helps increase self-esteem. As Abraham Maslow demonstrated in his "Hierarchy of Needs," the level of self-actualization represents the highest and most stimulating driver of personal motivation. We know from personal experience that positive learning experiences are highly motivational.

Now that we identified some of the central tenets of today's new corporate cultures, let's review how the organizations that we visited and studied put these tenets to work in their job environment.

HOW WERE THESE IDEAS IMPLEMENTED IN THE CASE STUDY EXAMPLES?

TDIndustries, the EARS process at the Coast Guard, and AES Corporation mirror some of those dreams and aspirations. Their cultures—all of fairly recent origin—focus on people and on human relationships. They are based on partnership and participation. People are in charge of their jobs. Leaders and managers have chosen—a difficult endeavor—to step back from making job-related decisions for others. Their new role is being a resource to their people—giving advice and being a mentor. At the same time, people have opportunities for personal growth and advancement, based on learning new skills or being exposed to new challenges. Most importantly, however, people find that their personal values and the ones of the organization they work for are consistent.

Mercedes-Benz and Southwest Airlines offer the view of somewhat different cultures. There is the emotional stimulation of participating in an exciting venture. We see close bonding among fellow employees with great synergy developing from frequent productive interactions and open communications. In short, people's passion in their everyday work makes these two cultures special and highly successful.

Finally, we arrive at SAIC, a still-youthful organization with an extraordinary culture that has been the foundation of over 30 years of uninterrupted business success. SAIC is a large company with more than 40,000 employees and has been able to frequently adapt its culture to changing circumstances of the business and certain demands of its people. This gives our findings and conclusions more weight and relevance. We'll focus on some of the elements of the SAIC culture, which set it apart, because they have continued to support the company's growth and success over recent years. They stand out as model traits of new corporate cultures!

ENTREPRENEURIAL SPIRIT OF EMPLOYEE OWNERS

From its early days, SAIC was very R & D oriented. The company attracted talented and experienced researchers and gave them the autonomy and independence to secure and manage certain businesses. People were able to create their own market niche and capture successful opportunities. Early on, this established the entrepreneurial nature of SAIC, which has remained in force to this day. With a relatively flat organizational structure in place, senior managers leave day-to-day decisions with the frontline people who have a chance to "carry the flag."

At the same time, SAIC's founder, Dr. J. Robert Beyster, introduced employee ownership, following his belief that "those who contribute to the company should own it." Employee ownership would have been a powerful financial incentive by itself, but Dr. Beyster's management philosophy went far beyond. He expected employee-owners to "actively participate in addressing important corporate issues and have a strong voice in the company's decision-making process." This broad concept of ownership went far to strengthen people's entrepreneurial spirit. They started to share financial ownership and to be in charge as well!

At certain occasions, internal problems would begin to stifle people's entrepreneurial spirit. Sometimes, internal competition and a "stovepipe" orientation would hamper teamwork and cooperation. At other times, employee turnover would increase dramatically, signaling that people did not care about the broader ownership opportunities. SAIC senior leadership and, in particular, Dr. Beyster have taken these problems seriously and acted to counter them. SAIC introduced statements of mission and values to establish and encourage internal team building and the honest and fair treatment of fellow employees. These statements were widely discussed with groups of employees to make it a true participatory effort. As a very practical tool, SAIC also created "communities of interest," internal Web-based working groups where people could join and network with others, wherever their expertise and interests lay.

To promote the broader employee ownership responsibilities, SAIC created an Employee Ownership Working Group (EOWG), staffed by a cross section of employees, with a mandate to "market" and explain the participatory aspects of this powerful incentive. A visible result of this initiative is that direct employee ownership of SAIC stock stands at 33%. In addition, SAIC retirement plans own 45%, former employees and outsiders 19%, and elected officers and directors 3%.

As we heard from Dr. John H. Warner Jr. a member of SAIC's Executive Committee, whom we interviewed about major challenges to the company's future, the SAIC spirit is alive and well and will continue to propel future success. Because of the significance of this particular element of a motivational culture, we would like to point to another example of "entrepreneurial spirit"—very similar to SAIC, but starting 10 years earlier.

ENTREPRENEURIAL SPIRIT AT W. L. GORE & ASSOCIATES

The unique Gore culture has been described many times. In Exhibit 15.1, we briefly describe the history of the company, but, otherwise, we would like to limit ourselves to the aspect of entrepreneurship at Gore,

Exhibit 15.1.
W. L. Gore & Associates—A Short History

"Making money and having fun doing so"—the business objective stated by the late W. L. (Bill) Gore—has been widely quoted, and the story of W. L. Gore & Associates and its phenomenal success has been told many times in the business press. Let's therefore limit our account of the company's history to some highlights.

W. L. Gore & Associates was founded in 1958 when Bill Gore left DuPont, after 17 years as an R & D chemist, to pursue electronic applications of PTFE, commonly known as Teflon. The first successful innovation—a method of insulating electronic wires with PTFE—was patented by son Bob Gore, who originated the idea. In the late 1960s, another discovery led to the development of GORE-TEX (expanded PTFE, the rough, sticky fabric that seals a variety of daily-use products). This brought about a family of new products and diversified Gore's business into many different markets. Today W. L. Gore & Associates employs about 6,000 people at 45 locations around the world. The company's success stems from innovative research and proprietary technologies with a broad spectrum of applications.

W. L. Gore & Associates is a privately held company that is majority owned by its associates as they join the Associate Stock Ownership Plan (ASOP). While Gore does not publish much financial information, its sales have grown to more than $1.2 billion, which would make it comparable to a *FORTUNE* 500 company.

More surprising, however, is the degree to which the company's unique corporate structure has contributed to its financial success. Bill Gore was not only a smart businessman and entrepreneur but also a philosopher who put forth his original ideas about how to structure an organization. In a summary of the basic tenets of the "Objective of the Enterprise," Bill Gore describes the enjoyment of work as an integral part of success as an organization:

Fun includes the pleasure of working with friends on teams, the enjoyment of parties and celebrations, but also the knowledge and conviction that what we are doing is important and of high value to people throughout the world.

In the middle of the twentieth century these ideas were quite radical, but they have endured.

Bill Gore's ideas covered many different organizational concepts—we talked already about the general principles established for all associates. Gore plants were built in clusters and each individual plant was limited to about 200 associates—both measures aimed at making direct communications between associates easier. There are no titles at Gore—everybody is

Exhibit 15.1.
(Continued)

---

an associate. With the exception of the Board of Directors there are no executive committees guiding the company's operations. And while many short- and long-term goals may form a mosaic of objectives for the company, Gore does not have formalized strategic or financial plans. Business objectives are redefined quickly and inevitably as market changes impact the business.

In line with government regulations, ASOP members receive regular updates on the performance and financial status of the corporation. They are invited to attend the annual shareholders' meeting and are entitled to the Annual Report distributed to all shareholders.

Bill Gore passed away in 1986, but his legacy is very much alive, making W. L. Gore & Associates a unique model for today's workplace structures. "The complexity of enterprise in the scientific-industrial environment of today makes the task of maximizing human freedom and potential a challenging one," Bill Gore once said. No question that he succeeded.

---

which in certain attributes differs from SAIC. Gore's founder, the late W. L. (Bill) Gore, came from DuPont's R & D environment and felt strongly about individual freedom and creativity that he often saw restrained by authoritarian structures. At Gore—not unlike the SAIC culture—employees or "associates," as they call themselves, may dedicate their unique talents to certain projects, try to become leaders in them, take risks, and commit resources, striving to make these projects successful.

There are, however, two major differences between the concepts of entrepreneurship at SAIC and Gore. First, the creation and follow-through of a new project at Gore is entirely up to its leader. As a matter of fact, leadership at Gore is determined by attracting followers, and over half of the Gore associates consider themselves leaders in some area. Leadership is entirely based on individual initiative by promoting new product or business ideas and recruiting followers to support them. If needed, there is help from experienced fellow associates. Each associate has a "sponsor" from among the senior leadership who follows and evaluates the associate's progress and is available as a mentor (but is not their boss!).

The second difference is the approval process. At Gore, there is no formal hierarchy to make decisions on any project. The project's leader makes decisions after consultation with his sponsor and other leaders. Again, the senior leadership of Gore plays an important role in giving input into major projects that may impact the financial and strategic stability of the company. Gore calls projects of this nature as potentially being "below the waterline." In addition, Gore has established certain general principles that may serve as guideposts to the associates. There is a need for fairness with each other and the ability to commit to certain objectives, however, with the requirement to consult with others on the more critical ones.

In spite of these differences in their culture, there are clear similarities between SAIC and Gore in that

- entrepreneurial attitudes are seen as the driver of the company's culture—personal initiative "leads" to creating a new nucleus of activity within the overall business
- people are encouraged to participate, become leaders, "carry the flag," and contribute freely to the company's success
- a few overriding principles are to be observed as guidance, an important one being cooperation and consultation on major projects

PRINCIPLES AND VALUES TO KEEP PEOPLE ON TRACK

Why do we need principles and values in our work environment? Do they guarantee the success of a business? Probably, the answer is no. However, a set of guiding values is considered essential to the long-term success of organizations because the value focus appeals to people. Why, then, do we not simply use human values? We would choose them for the same reasons we rely on our beliefs and values in our personal life. We live and work in a community of people of diverse origins, talents, and orientations. Everyone likes to enjoy the "fun"—as AES Corporation very appropriately calls the sensation of being entrepreneurial—of making decisions, of creating new concepts, and of being successful. But those decisions, solutions, and successes must not be reached at the expense of the person next to us or of our fellow workers. To the contrary, sometimes the fun gets multiplied if it involves a group of people or a team of fellow employees. It reminds us how it is fun to watch our children learn from their experiences and enjoy progress toward adulthood.

What top four values would you consider for your organization? They would probably include fairness, integrity, respect, and mutual help and support among your primary choices. Social responsibility might also be an important priority. These values are the essence of human relationships and a culture based on these human ideals will appeal to people. That's why we consider this kind of culture "organic"—it's natural! There is total consistency of personal and work life.

There is another consideration. We have found that *a small set of values* helps focus the organization. AES has four principles: fairness, integrity, fun, and social responsibility. Gore has four as well: fairness, freedom to innovate, ability to commit, and the concept of the "waterline" and the need for consultation. SAIC has six values: Some of them are based on human ideals, such as ethical behavior and professional integrity, entrepreneurial spirit, and people excellence and team effort. Others try to set goals for the organization, such as a drive for quality and customer satisfaction, the focus on technical growth and market diversification, or the motivation by employee ownership that includes a call for participation.

In order to be real guideposts for the organization, principles and values should be kept simple. New employees need the opportunity to understand and question them. Frequent discussion and occasional revision with the employees involved will help to keep them updated and to be a constant reminder of the basic tenets of the organization's culture.

INTERACTION TO FOSTER DIALOGUE AND MUTUAL RESPECT

The free flow of information is another important element of motivating cultures. People at Mercedes-Benz and Southwest Airlines are not only informed about the progress of their respective businesses but they are aware of their fellow workers' contributions and responsibilities. Programs of job rotation and cross training or Southwest's "Walk a mile in my shoes" accomplish a better understanding of the broader context of the business and the interrelationship of its operations. It's a powerful example to have someone from the executive office help the aircraft cleaning crew to put down new carpeting in the sticky heat of a summer night.

At SAIC, extensive two-way communications and real dialogue have been taken to a different level. SAIC has created a broad spectrum of standing and ad hoc committees and forums—they number close to 100 at this time—that give the SAIC people many opportunities to participate in the process of decision making and strategy formation and to have their input and ideas heard and considered. The most important of these forums are the quarterly Meetings Week reunion, the Employee Ethics Committee, the Technical Environment Committee (TEC), and the EOWG, as well as certain technology committees like the Executive Science and Technology Council, the Software Management Forum, and the Systems Engineering Forum.

The lesson here is to provide opportunities for strong individuals in the corporation to step forward and present their viewpoints. At SAIC, the quarterly Meetings Week session is an interesting example where literally thousands of senior employees and managers interact in face-to-face meetings. This provides a quarterly update and exchange on the most recent developments in SAIC's business. Many of SAIC's committees meet at the same time, which makes it easy for everyone who wants to be involved and participate to contribute his or her ideas to the issues in discussion.

We have seen similar practices at some of the other companies we have visited. AES invites frontline workers on a rotating basis to its quarterly corporate management meetings. In addition, ad hoc working groups and volunteer assignments at other plants provide opportunities for interaction and involvement. At Southwest Airlines, the process of interaction is institutionalized with the creation of the culture committee and the parallel alumni organization. Those who want to "step out" and be leaders should be able to do so without the filter of a formalized hierarchy screening their ideas and initiatives.

A LEARNING ECOLOGY LEADS TO PERSONAL GROWTH

A learning ecology is to everyone's benefit: Most people are interested in acquiring new skills because they increase their level of knowledge, competence, and experience. This may be helpful one day when they cannot be sure if their job is safe and their employment will continue. Organizations need employees that are well trained in several trades because of the flexibility it offers. And last but not least, let's remember Csikszentmihalyi's "flow": The growth of self arising from the ability to handle ever-increasing challenges will lead to lasting intrinsic motivation.

Learning in the work environment can take different forms. We have seen vocational training at TDIndustries, ethics training at SAIC, or a broad learning initiative like Team Bellcore. All of those were mandated and formalized. It may also be the employee's choice. The Coast Guard is focused on individual development plans (IDPs), while at Southwest Airlines, the training offerings are channeled through its corporate university. It's up to the people to assess their particular interests and talents. At SAIC, learning is mostly computer based and self-paced. At Gore, the sponsor assumes certain responsibilities for the development of an employee. Similarly, cross training at another workstation at Mercedes-Benz or the possibility of requesting training in a different trade as part of a career move at AES will provide learning experiences of a different sort.

Whatever the particular shape or form that learning opportunities have taken at our seven case study companies, there can be little doubt that the opportunity for personal growth will be a healthy motivational experience. Acquiring new skills translates into the ability to meet ever-more-difficult problems. People will choose their level of challenge and develop their personal orientation. This learning disposition leads to everyone's personal mastery and builds self-esteem.

WHAT IS THE ESSENCE OF NEW CORPORATE CULTURES?

Visiting the organizations that we have described and speaking to many of their people has painted a multicolored and multifaceted picture of new corporate cultures. It has been a rewarding and revealing experience. Each of the organizations is different, has its particular history and the very special nature of its operations, and still we find many similarities in their cultures. The essence is people and human relationships.

We have seen the people of TDIndustries with their vision of true partnership and the practice of servant leadership. The EARS process seems to be ushering in a new era of employee participation at the Coast Guard and at other government agencies. AES people enjoy the fun of making decisions and follow consistent values in both their personal and work life worlds. Team Alabama and all of Mercedes-Benz have been inspired by the excitement of building the M-Class. Southwest Airlines's family spirit, supported by its Culture Committee, embraces employees, customers, and communities, driving the airline's success. Team Bellcore is part of a change process that has people transforming its culture and preparing for a successful merger. Finally, SAIC's people and their outstanding entrepreneurial attitudes have built the foundation for unusual business success.

To summarize, then, which are the distinguishing principles that characterize the cultures of these organizations?

DISTINGUISHING PRINCIPLES OF NEW CULTURES

- People's *ownership and entrepreneurial spirit* drives them to create their own challenge, take responsibilities, and become leaders, contributing to an expanding and successful business.

- Easy to understand *values* are guideposts, in part based on simple human ideals and in part on setting goals for the organization.

- People have many opportunities for *interaction* to foster dialogue and facilitate leadership initiatives or to provide understanding of the business and respect toward fellow workers' contributions and responsibilities.

- Different forms of learning opportunities support people's desire for their own *personal growth*.

All of these features have made an immense impact on people's motivation and productivity. Close to 100,000 people in these organizations give a lot of credence to our findings. Their message is powerful: Their workplaces are driven by unique and motivating cultures.

CHAPTER 16

Conclusion: Poised to Motivate— The Power of One

Choose a job you love, and you will never have to work a day in your life.

—Confucius

How can you (our reader) renew, enhance, and enrich the organizational culture you and your associates currently experience, to help it become more inclusive, adaptable, and effective?

Your influence in your organization may be anywhere from great to little, but you can make a difference. Cultures, no matter how strong, long lived, or persistent they are, can be amended by appealing ideas that seep in around the edges, by people who model new and more effective behaviors, and by those who choose to share new and more effective notions about what makes people productive.

When we show Exhibit 16.1, which demonstrates work team interchange in self-managed teams (in the middle of the diagram), at training seminars, someone in every group asks: "But who's in charge?" The answer is: Anyone can be, depending on the task at hand and/or on the best solution for that situation.

Leadership passes from one team member to another depending on who has the expertise needed at the moment. If the group is brainstorming there may be someone volunteering to serve as recorder to capture the ideas.

If this model of shared responsibility or the absence of a single decision maker bothers you, remember that the American founding fathers trusted no one to be boss in our government. The president of the United States is

Exhibit 16.1.
The Evolution of Organizational Structures

The Industrial Age Organization Chart

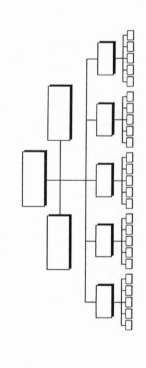

4 to 22 Additional Layers Depending On Organization Size And Structure

From This →

SOME NEWER MODELS OF ORGANIZATIONS

DIAGRAM OF THE HUMAN BRAIN
– THE ORGANIZATION CHART OF THE FUTURE –

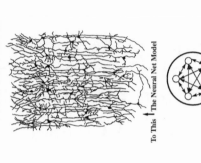

To This | The Neural Net Model

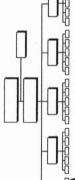

To This | Self Managed Teams

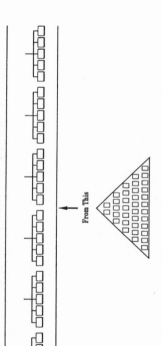

From This | The Downsized Delayered Bierarchy

a temporary employee who can't even establish his (and eventually her) own department's budget. He or she has to ask the House of Representatives for the money needed.

The examples of successful cultures we have studied in this book contain some powerful lessons about increasing democracy in the workplace. But beware when we talk of workplace democracy: We are not talking about making decisions by a majority of votes. We need to abandon such analogies before we can appreciate the remarkable opportunities we can experience every working day.

These examples clearly demonstrate that:

- when people are treated as responsible adults at work, they will respond as such and take ownership of their jobs
- virtually everyone possesses more depth and breadth of potential than even he or she recognizes
- people have an innate yearning for freedom and autonomy; once their fears are assuaged, they start growing and become creative entrepreneurs
- people enjoy learning and using new ideas; they enjoy expanding their array of talents and abilities and, given the opportunity, strive toward self-actualization
- being able to make a difference in life is a very satisfying and rewarding experience

Overall we need to recognize that people driven by their own values, goals, and accomplishments have more fun and are much more satisfied in their jobs. Their work motivation lasts longer than when they are cajoled or manipulated by someone else's rewards or threats.

External and internal forces are constantly modifying our working culture. What can you do to help shape that movement in constructively motivating ways? Some thoughts may help:

- Structure in an organization tends to solidify and seriously hamper organizational adaptability. Therefore, movement toward greater structure should be resisted and a loosening of such frameworks encouraged.
- Similarly, rules, standard operating procedures, and restrictive regulations should be examined to see if they are truly imperative—they tend to cost substantial money and time and impede goal achievement.
- Set your sights on a culture of participation, contribution, and sharing of ideas. Encourage less control and more individual initiative. Increased employee involvement in resolving issues leads to a win-win environment.
- Assume there are great pools of untapped talent in your workforce and then search them out. Rely less on staff experts and more on those who are directly involved with the product or service. Staff experts should share their expertise.
- Ego means "a sense of self," which we all need until we go overboard with it.

- Build your own leadership skills and those of others. Mentor well anyone you can. At the same time, be a follower and supporter if that best advances a worthwhile project.

You may add to this list from your own experience and thoughts. The foregoing may not have the appeal of a great management crusade (or fad), but it will probably be more easily accepted by your associates, put to practical use sooner, and in time have greater benefits for the organization.

Remember in the beginning there were only 12 apostles—imagine how fast they could have spread the word with E-mail, cell phones, and faxes.

A special note on how organizational structures grow and decrease flexibility may be helpful. A common bureaucratic response to any serious crisis, mistake, or exception to the rule is to write another rule, policy, or procedure so as to tighten control. Soon people can't move or produce. However, the organizational culture elements, which we derived from our interviews and studies, are listed and elaborated on in the following sections. These factors can provide leverage for individuals who want to help create a better place to work.

GROUP MEMBERSHIP

The most cruel and unnatural punishment we can afflict on another person is to isolate them from all human contact. Including another person in a group where she or he is a fully participating member can be a thing of great joy. In fact Abraham Maslow, the great authority on motivation, ranks meeting our social needs just behind the two most powerful motivators—meeting our survival and security needs.

We all have deep and often complex needs for group membership, peer acceptance, friendship, a sense of belonging, and particularly participation and contribution as a fully functioning member of the group. You can help by:

- welcoming each new person into the group and helping to make them feel welcome and involved
- sharing important information on what the group is doing and how it operates
- listening carefully to each person's concerns
- encouraging everyone's participation
- doing everything you can to build a sense of an inclusive work family

If you are at or near the top of your organization, you can greatly affect your culture quickly and broadly. If you are at the operating level you may have to rely on "missionary work" for a while until you can develop some synergy.

DEVELOPING A SENSE OF OWNERSHIP

Ownership is an odd word in many respects. It ranges in meaning from the legal right to the possession of a thing to a transitory allegiance to someone, an ideal, a community, a job, a task, or whatever a person chooses to claim. It can include a sense of loyalty, a defensive possessive posture, a boast, or something for which one would risk death.

Here we define a sense of ownership as a feeling of participation, of responsibility for something, or a dedication to something such as a job, whether or not the person holding such feelings owns stock in the corporation. Most organizations that are able to garner such unpurchased fealty, concern, and dedication consider it a powerful, though an unmeasured, intangible asset. As with Southwest Airlines, as an example, a sense of ownership can constructively impact on-time departures, the quality of onboard services, and ultimately the financial bottom line.

How do you develop that kind of commitment? Fun through achievement—personal and group—is the direct answer. When a person begins to feel a high level of success in his or her work individually, as a work group member, and as a contributor, affection for what he or she is doing starts to show. Personal pride, enjoyment (fun), and involvement begin to develop, similar to watching our children grow and develop under our tutelage. This affection/possession increases when the person (or the group) attains greater autonomy as to his or her (or their) operation.

To enable this to happen, management needs to get out of the way and focus more on ensuring that the employees get opportunities for personal growth as well as resources and freedom to maintain the autonomy needed to keep productivity at high levels. Employees will do it quite naturally as they learn that they will not be second-guessed by someone else and come to see experts and managers as their helpers.

ENTREPRENEURIAL SPIRIT

Deep in their heart, nearly everyone wants to be free, to create, to build something new. If you doubt that, consider the popularity of retirement, the creativity people devote to their hobbies, or how they strive to generate, preserve, and protect their children when their families are new. Sure, some consider the risks of launching a new business too great. Others have their self-esteem and self-confidence so beaten down that they think trying to build a creative career is beyond them. And still others have had their social skills so impaired that working with others in a cooperative enterprise just doesn't feel comfortable or possible.

Yet, in the organizations we studied there exists an environment and even mechanisms for encouraging employees' entrepreneurial spirit so that it manifests itself with remarkable frequency. The entrepreneurial spirit in an organization is critical to its adaptability, as is the employees' sensitivity to changes in the marketplace and their shared awareness of emerging opportunities, technologies, and market needs.

What is needed to foster this spirit? We give some examples:

- a free flow of financial data that enables a work team to assess their impact (or lack of it) on the organization's bottom line
- an environment that truly and freely considers entrepreneurial initiatives and generally supports them
- providing and encouraging employees' mobility throughout the organization
- nurturing the concept within the organization that it seeks out new ideas and initiatives
- building on little challenges at first and creating team support for such initiatives

SOCIAL RESPONSIBILITY

Social responsibility is not charity. It is broader than ethical conduct and it can even go beyond morality. Social responsibility is a wholeness of concern for humanity today and tomorrow—ad infinitum. It involves doing what we can to make the world about us an ongoing better place to live in all its attributes.

This is also no pipe dream, no grand global vision, and no plan for building a heaven on earth. Yet the organizations we studied are all demonstrating the art of taking responsibility for doing what they can to make our social ecology better for the people that work there and for their families, and for spreading their influence as far as they can.

The Coast Guard encourages employees to get involved in specific programs such as the local "Stay in School Programs" by mentoring at-risk teens and by volunteering as tutors in after-school programs in churches, schools, and community centers.

Southwest Airlines's outreach and relief efforts rank high on their list of community service goals. Within their "Hearts in Action" program, for example, employees are encouraged to dedicate three hours to a volunteer effort of their choice in a given month.

Other examples have been included in the chapters on the individual organizations. In the broadest sense, social responsibility hinges on a willingness to look beyond self-interest and self-concerns so as to be fair and supportive whenever and wherever we can be. And this is not just supporting a disaster relief project but an ongoing concern for others that creates opportunities in our mind and our deeds for everyone.

Whether the issue is third world sweatshops and the sports clothing equipment they produce or air pollution that an SUV is producing, each of us can choose our battlefield and make our decisions for the better. Also, we each need to take the long view on renewable resources, environmental pollution, and human investment in education and training for our coworkers.

Ask yourselves what you can do, or not do, to help our world and the people in it be a better place for all of us. Our children and grandchildren will reap the benefits or losses from our choices for untold decades to come.

INTERACTION BETWEEN PEERS

To paraphrase the words of President John F. Kennedy's Inaugural Address: Ask not what your company can do for you; ask what we can do for each other in our company. Bonding, sharing one's expertise with coworkers, giving and accepting recognition between peers, honestly believing that each other's personal growth and mutually having fun are as important to give as to receive—these characterize the heart of the cultures in the organizations studied. Some organizations are farther along that path than others, but searching for the common good in the culture opens up great possibilities for synergy, cooperation, and exceptional inner-driven motivation.

It may seem strange that the common virtues people often exhibit when they are faced with a natural disaster or similar catastrophe can become a daily way of life in some organizations without the crisis. Yet Baron Alexis de Tocqueville, reporting his observations on American society when our republic was very young, noted in his book *Democracy in America* that we were a nation of volunteer-helpers and that our frontier society focused on cooperation. Perhaps globalization is helping to lead us back to a culture of caring for each other and perhaps beyond borders and boundaries.

It may be difficult to appreciate such a change when we watch the daily news, but the countermovement seen in these advanced organizations may well be a harbinger of our future. Each of us must ask what we can do to help build a caring, sharing, and helping organization where we work. We must become culture-leaders who work on transforming the work environment into one that we and our coworkers will look forward to coming to every day to have fun and enjoy the consistency of our personal and company values.

One important final question remains. In what kind of organizational culture do you—and possibly your children and grandchildren—want to work? Do you accept that the traditional order of things is to be motivated (or manipulated?) by others and by external means, or would you rather be your own person, motivated by your own inner values and choices?

The answer should be unequivocal: You prefer to have the freedom to follow your own dreams and aspirations, you want to be creative and use your talents, and you would like to have the opportunity to live out your personal values. And one day, when you are retired, you will look back at your job and say, "That really was fun" and possibly wish you could be back at your former workplace.

Bibliography

Collins, J. R., and J. I. Porras. *Built to Last: Successful Habits of Visionary Companies.* New York: Harper & Row, 1994.

Csikszentmihalyi, M. *Flow: The Psychology of Optimal Experience.* New York: Harper & Row, 1990.

Faller, M. *Innere Kuendigung.* Munich: Rainer Hampp Verlag, 1991.

Greenleaf, R. *The Servant as Leader.* Self-published essay, 1970.

Haasen, A., and G. F. Shea. *A Better Place to Work.* New York: American Management Association, 1997.

Hackman, J. R. *Groups That Work (and Those That Don't).* San Francisco: Jossey-Bass, 1990.

Herzberg, F., B. Mausner, and B. Snyderman. *The Motivation to Work.* New York: John Wiley, 1959.

Hilb, M. *Innere Kuendigung.* Zurich: Verlag Industrielle Organization, 1992.

Janus, I. L. *Victims of Groupthink.* Boston: Houghton Mifflin, 1982.

Kotter, J. P., and J. L. Heskett. *Corporate Culture and Performance.* New York: Free Press, 1992.

Krystek, U., D. Becherer, and K. H. Deichelmann. *Innere Kuendigung.* Munich: Rainer Hampp Verlag, 1995.

Levering, R., and M. Moskowitz. *The 100 Best Companies to Work for in America.* New York: Doubleday, 1993.

Loehnert, W. *Innere Kuendigung.* Frankfurt: Peter Lang Verlag, 1990.

Lucas, J. R. "How to Avoid Enronism." *MWorld* 1 (spring 2002).

———. *The Passionate Organization.* New York: Amacom, 1999.

Maslow, A. *Motivation and Personality.* New York: Harper & Row, 1954.

Mohrman, S. *A Perspective on Empowerment.* Essay published by CEO/USC, 1993.

Peters, T., and R. Waterman Jr. *In Search of Excellence.* New York: Harper & Row, 1982.

Schein, E. H. *The Corporate Culture Survival Guide.* San Francisco: Jossey-Bass, 1999.

———. *Organizational Culture and Leadership.* 2d ed. San Francisco: Jossey-Bass, 1997.

Seligman, M. *Helplessness.* San Francisco: Freeman, 1975.

Index

About the Authors

ADOLF HAASEN is Managing Partner of A & R Associates, a human resources consulting firm based in Hartsdale, New York. Before founding A & R Associates, Haasen gained extensive international management experience as an executive for the German-based global pharmaceutical Merck.

GORDON F. SHEA is President of Prime Systems Company, a training and human resources firm based in Beltsville, Maryland. He has over 30 years of experience as a practicing supervisor, manager, and executive in government and private industry.